Interdisciplinary
Approaches
to
Human Communication

[Interdisciplinary Approaches to Human Communication]

Edited by
RICHARD W. BUDD
and
BRENT D. RUBEN

HAYDEN BOOK COMPANY, INC.
Rochelle Park, New Jersey

To Bev and Jann

ISBN 0-8104-5125-5
Library of Congress Catalog Card Number 78-68573

Portions of this work originally appeared in *Approaches to Human Communication*, edited by Richard W. Budd and Brent D. Ruben, published in 1972.

Printed in the United States of America

3	4	5	6	7	8	9	PRINTING
82	83	84	85	86	87		YEAR

Preface

It has almost become a cliché to say that there are so many people who have contributed to a book that it is impossible to acknowledge them all in any meaningful way. Still, that is very often the case. For us, there is a special debt of gratitude to the authors of the chapters in *Approaches to Human Communication*. Not only did they make significant contributions to that volume, but also, perhaps more than they realize, to our thinking as well. We are equally grateful to colleagues and to many of our students with whom we wrestled (and yet do) about the underlying assumptions of the field of communication reflected in our earlier book. We are hopeful that this both new and revisited work will continue to provide us with that sort of intellectual exercise. And finally, we are appreciative of the many persons whose editorial assistance have made *Interdisciplinary Approaches to Human Communication* a reality. In that domain, we owe special thanks to Bob Boynton at Hayden who, one might say, found this book.

RICHARD W. BUDD
BRENT D. RUBEN

New Brunswick, New Jersey

Acknowledgments

Grateful acknowledgment is made for permission to use the following material:

Chapter 2: Especially revised and updated for inclusion in the first edition of this book, an earlier version appeared in *Communication: Concepts and Perspectives,* edited by Lee Thayer, © 1967 by Spartan Books.

Chapter 6: Copyright © 1969 by José M.R. Delgado. Reprinted from *Physical Control of the Mind: Toward a Psychocivilized Society* by José M.R. Delgado by permission of Harper & Row, Publishers, Inc. Originally published as Chapter 5, "Extracerebral Elements of the Mind: When and How the Mind Is Formed"; and Chapter 7, "Sensory Dependence of the Adult Mind."

Chapter 7: Copyright © 1969 by Prentice-Hall. Reprinted from *Symbolic Interactionism: Perspective and Method* by Herbert Blumer, by permission of Prentice-Hall, Inc. Originally titled "The Methodological Position of Symbolic Interactionism."

Chapter 8: Selected material from Chapter 1 in *The Sacred Canopy* by Peter L. Berger. Copyright © 1967 by Peter L. Berger. Reprinted by permission of Doubleday & Company, Inc.

Contents

Introduction

We published *Approaches to Human Communication* in 1972 in response to an emerging trend in communication study that placed little premium on the development of a comprehensive framework for the discipline. We were, at that time, searching for a text sufficiently broad to serve as an introduction to a new program in human communication. The extensive review of the literature that accompanied that search revealed two things: First, the book we visualized for our purposes did not exist; second, and of greater intellectual significance, we noted the emergence of an increasingly fragmented and uncoordinated pattern of study and research that was functioning to seriously delimit generic definitions and/or explanations of the human communication phenomenon.

The nature of this dilemma has been well documented elsewhere [2, 9, 11] and needs only to be summarized here. Perhaps the most global statement regarding the development and growth of academic disciplines is offered by Kuhn. [6] He believes that fields of study follow a rather fixed and recurring cycle of paradigm emergence, acceptance, challenge, rejection, and replacement. The implication is that, during most periods, most of the scholars working in a particular discipline share and support a common paradigm, as well as a common understanding of the phenomena they are studying within that framework. But part of that cycle involves advancing new paradigms to challenge inadequacies noted in the currently accepted one. Should one of these new, challenging paradigms (which initially is accepted and advocated by only a few) gain popularity and ultimately replace its predecessor, the cycle begins anew.

In related research, Price [8] indicates that growth within scientific communities—in terms of both people and publications—doubles within

1

a 10- to 15-year time period. And Crane,[4] commenting on the processes by which this growth comes about, suggests that it occurs by a kind of "contagion effect" that runs through both the formal and informal structure of a community of scholars, thus creating an exponential growth in both the number of publications and the number of new authors entering a field. Such growth, argues Price, leads naturally to specialization and subgrouping within a discipline.

These elements fairly well characterize the trend in communication study that we identified in the early 1970s, a trend that now, of course, has become a full-blown movement. In the last 5 to 6 years, there have been dramatic increases in both the output and number of outlets for communication-related research. We have, for example, witnessed the founding of a number of new academic journals and publications devoted to the study of communication; we have watched several established speech, rhetoric, and journalism journals include more and more articles on communication; and we have seen several publications change their names to reflect that new focus.

But, ironically, neither the increased volume nor the apparent growing popularity of communication research has brought us any closer to a comprehensive framework for the discipline. In point of fact, the specialization and segmentation, which either brought on or accompanied the field's rapid growth, has seriously retarded the efforts toward synthesis. Interestingly enough, we were perhaps closer to being able to develop a broader and more general view of communication at the beginning of our disciplinary history than we are likely to now. This is in part why works by Lasswell,[7] Schramm,[10] Berlo,[1] and Klapper,[5] all written nearly 20 years ago, remain so popular. They represent, in a very real sense, the last significant efforts by communication scholars in the field to forge any comprehensive theory or synthesis of communication.

Just where one would place our discipline in Kuhn's cycle at this time is certainly debatable. One might argue that our field is in the midst of a potentially successful challenge to what has been a traditionally accepted paradigm, although the advocates of this point of view might differ widely on what constitutes both the traditional and the emerging paradigms. Or, one might argue with equal persuasiveness that there has not yet emerged from the field of communication any framework of the sort described by Kuhn. Our own tendency has been to lean toward the latter supposition as the best explanation of the current state of our relatively young field. There are, it seems to us, conditions existing in the discipline that readily support such an assumption. Included among them are the lack of a widely agreed upon taxonomy of communication, a general fad-like fascination with a variety of communication variables that, to date, lie in unrelated disarray in the pages of communication journals, and the rise of research design and methodology to paradigm-like status in the discipline.

The first of these issues, the lack of a generally accepted taxonomy of communication, has long been a concern of communication-anthropologist Alfred G. Smith.[11] Smith believes that one of the basic shortcomings of the discipline is its failure to develop any sort of cohesive and integrated taxonomy: [11, p. 79]

> Unless our view of communication is somehow systematic, our work in communication will be chaotic. Individual studies, courses, and operations can be adequate without a comprehensive framework; but the output of the whole field will be an unholy mess. Unless we view communication through some sturdy principles that are profound and sweeping, flexible and yet well ordered, the field will be just a grab bag of odds and ends. Work assignments will be at cross-purposes. Investments of resources will be *non compos*. A slapdash notion of the field can cripple our thinking about communication.

That the field lacks an overarching framework of the sort suggested by Smith is reflected in a preoccupation with research on a seemingly endless procession of concepts and processes related to human interaction. A cursory survey of research findings, published in communication journals during the past 6 years, reveals a conglomeration of concepts, such as self-disclosure, communication apprehension, empathy, persuasion, communication competence, attitudes and attitude formation, turn-taking, fear arousal, cognitive dissonance, source credibility, diffusion, violence and aggression, self-esteem, homophily-heterophily, dogmatism, meaning, coorientation, deception, selective exposure/perception, nonverbal, small groups, etc.

To a large extent, this sort of concept-hopping has been the consequence of the field's widespread embracing of quantitative methodology as the dominant vehicle for studying human communication phenomena. In many respects, quantitative methodology has functioned very much as a paradigm for the discipline, over the past 15 or so years. It is almost as if communication scholars, unable to develop a conceptual framework for the field, have substituted a methodological paradigm in its stead. As a consequence, the discipline finds itself in the midst of a rather constraining tautology. While output of and outlets for communication scholarship have grown rather substantially, the range of what is considered acceptable fare for those outlets has narrowed considerably, based almost solely on methodological considerations. The net effect has been an increasing number of published works covering a more narrowly defined range of communication behaviors—principally those that lend themselves to study by the research techniques developed within the field's governing methodological paradigm. And while what has been researched has been handled with greater statistical precision and often in considerably greater microscopic detail than ever before, our powers to generalize and relate such findings to the empirical world have been considerably limited. In effect, we may have generated a good number of answers for which we have not yet found the questions. While it is patently clear that scientific research comprises a necessary and integral part of any behavioral science, and can contribute significantly to the growth and rigor of a discipline, that alone will not suffice to meet the obligations of an academic discipline.

REKINDLING A CONCEPT

Reflecting upon such considerations, the task of revising this text presented us with many alternatives and opportunities, as well as pitfalls. In the *Preface* of the first edition of this book we wrote:

> The broader the perspective one brings to bear in his thinking about the process of communication, the more adequate his conception is likely to be. Having completed this volume, the reader will have the basics and the background necessary to begin a meaningful study of human communication and the requisite variety to build his own integrated understanding of "how communication works."

Fundamentally, our goal for this second edition remains the same: We view the materials presented here as essential ingredients for the development of a comprehensive theory of human communication.

Readers familiar with our first edition, *Approaches to Human Communication,* will notice some major changes in the way we have chosen to pursue that goal. First, we have substantially reduced the number of "approaches" from twenty-four to eight, giving preference to those pieces that we believe best serve the development of a generic framework for communication. Among those eight, two are new to this volume—Lee Thayer's "Communication: *Sine Qua Non* of the Behavioral Sciences" and Peter Berger's "Sociology of Knowledge."

Why such a drastic reduction? As we reviewed our original manuscript, it became evident to us that the first edition cut far too wide a swath. And while we would, without hesitation, reaffirm our declaration that communication is supradisciplinary in its nature, we also acknowledge that, in attempting to demonstrate this notion in our earlier work, we inadvertently made our own contribution to the fragmentation of the field that we complained of earlier in this Introduction. Many of the pieces in the first edition were, for our purposes, too microscopic. Those we have retained, or added for this revision, are both less specific and more generic. This, of course, uncovers one of the potential pitfalls referred to above. Viewed in isolation, this revised volume is open to the criticism that it urges the development of a conceptual framework while failing to provide the appropriate base on which such a framework might be built. Quite obviously, we do not want this book to be used in the absence of other supporting materials; we simply have opted not to make the volume all things to all readers.

In the same vein, at least one reviewer criticized the first edition of this book because we did not weave a unifying framework around the twenty-four chapters. We deliberately chose not to provide such a context. For reasons we perhaps understand more fully now than we did then, we believed that such integration and synthesis should be the reader's job. In the intervening period, there have been a number of communication books published that reflect a singular view of human interaction, but there continues to be, in our view, a lack of generic statements regarding the process and a diminishing availability of contrasting views stressing cross-disciplinary understandings of the phenomenon. So it is that this revised edition, *Interdisciplinary Approaches to Human Communication*, also will not provide such an integration or overview; to do so would most certainly defeat the underlying purpose of the book.

Lastly, one might argue that the mere selection of the pieces included in this edition inevitably suggests an editorial point of view. Obviously, that's an accurate observation. While we have quite vigorously and in some detail pursued such a point of view elsewhere,[3] we have left it here to be found only through inference, in the belief that the reader of these articles might come to any one of several understandings of human communication. At any rate, it is our intent that this volume, used in conjunction with many others currently available to communication scholars, will provide the stimulus necessary to move the discipline toward a new (or perhaps yet to be established) synthesis of human communication.

NOTES AND REFERENCES

1. Berlo, D. K., *The Process of Communication*. New York: Holt, Rinehart and Winston, 1960.
2. Budd, R. W., "Perspectives on a Discipline: Review and Commentary," in *Communication Yearbook I*, ed. by B. D. Ruben. New Brunswick, N.J.: Transaction Books, 1977.
3. Budd, R. W. and B. D. Ruben, eds., *Beyond Media: New Approaches to Mass Communication*. Rochelle Park, N.J.: Hayden Book Co., 1979.
4. Crane, D., *Invisible Colleges: Diffusion of Knowledge in Scientific Communities*. Chicago: University of Chicago Press, 1970.
5. Klapper, J. T., *The Effects of Mass Communication*. Glencoe: The Free Press, 1960.

6. Kuhn, T. S., *The Structure of Scientific Revolutions,* 2nd ed. Chicago: University of Chicago Press, 1970.

7. Lasswell, H. D., "The Structure and Function of Communication in Society," in *The Communication of Ideas,* ed. by Lyman Bryson. Institute for Religious and Social Studies, 1948.

8. Price, D. J., *Little Science, Big Science.* New York: Columbia University Press, 1963.

9. Ruben, B. D., "Overview," in *Communication Yearbook I,* ed. by B. D. Ruben. New Brunswick, N.J.: Transaction Books, 1977.

10. Schramm, W., ed., *The Process and Effects of Mass Communication.* Urbana: University of Illinois Press, 1955.

11. Smith, A. G., "Taxonomy of Communication: Review and Commentary," in *Communication Yearbook I,* ed. by B. D. Ruben. New Brunswick, N.J.: Transaction Books, 1977.

1

Communication:

Sine Qua Non of the Behavioral Sciences

LEE THAYER

I T IS extremely difficult to talk sense about communication. There are a number of reasons why this is so, and some awareness of the reasons for that difficulty is an important preliminary for anyone who is seriously interested in the subject. That is where this paper must begin.

SOME FUNDAMENTAL DIFFICULTIES

It would be impossible to indicate an order of importance of the several difficulties to be faced in trying to talk sense about communication. What for one reader may stand as a serious obstacle may be of little consequence for another. Hence, I make no claim that the sequence in which these difficulties are presented in any way represents the order of their importance. Since it is *conceptual* difficulties we are faced with, the pertinence of any one of them for each reader can be determined only by the individual reader.

Familiarity, Popularity

One difficulty of major import is the fact that the phenomenon of communication is a familiar one to most of us. And the term communication is a very popular one these days. From an individual point of view, the

---

* First presented as two lectures before the Air Force Office of Scientific Research 13th Science Seminar, Albuquerque, New Mexico, June 13–14, 1968.

more familiar a phenomenon, the more difficult it is to develop a sound, empirical understanding of it. From an aggregate point of view, the more talked about a phenomenon is, the more difficult it becomes to develop scientifically sound conceptualizations of it. It is even more difficult to come to grips with a phenomenon so vital to our behavior.(3, p. 11; 6; 9, pp. 86-87)

Lack of a Discipline

A second difficulty is the fact that there exists no single scientific discipline having an exclusive interest in communication or a systematic body of knowledge. There are loose "professional" associations of persons having some part-interest in communication, of course, as well as academic programs built on some special orientation; and there is undoubtedly an "invisible college" of scholars whose scientific interests and pursuits, with respect to communication, do overlap to some degree. But there is nothing like the disciplinary foundations one sees in physics, for example.

Closely related is the fact that the phenomena of communication are so basic to the life and behavioral sciences that they transcend most of the arbitrary disciplinary boundaries that do exist. Each discipline thus appropriates some part-aspect of the total process of communication as a matter of proprietary concern, the consequence being a discontinuous and fractionated hodgepodge of terms and approaches that doesn't add up to much more than any of the pieces. Not only is there no single core of knowledge to draw on, but also there is often no way to relate the part-aspects to one another. Each discipline is destined to study its own myopias. Because the phenomena of communication are so basic as to have *some* relevance for all scientific disciplines, and because each of the often diverse points of view brought to bear is self-legitimizing, no comprehending body of knowledge is likely to emerge in the near future. It is like a piece of farmland which belongs to everyone for his or her own whimsical uses; it is likely never to be properly cultivated or systematically productive.

Approachable Both Operationally and Scientifically

A third difficulty is the fact that communication can be approached either as an operational or as a scientific phenomenon, or both. That is, communication is not only something that can be studied, it is something most of us *do*. While it would seem odd to try to talk about someone "physic-ing" or "psychology-ing," it is easy to talk about "communicating."

This is an especially potent difficulty, for there is no necessary relationship between our scientific knowledges and the uses to which those knowledges are put. What the physicist learns from his inquiries into the nature of things is not likely to alter, significantly, his own social behavior—likewise, the traditional psychologist. The difficulty arises from the pervasive ambiguity that surrounds most of the writing and the talk that goes on about communication: Is it in the spirit of scientific inquiry or operational usefulness? Is the purpose to develop a reliable theory of the phenomenon, or to figure out how to "communicate" better in some way?

The fundamental issue, as Donald MacKay has often urged,[15, pp. 164-65] is whether or not there is a need for a *theory* of communication as distinct from a body of practical know-how. It would require too much space to address that issue here. But an awareness and an appreciation of this basic difficulty seems to me indispensable to an adequate posture for coming to conceptual grips with the phenomena of communication.

Scientism and the Mystique of Technology

A fourth difficulty lies in the incompatibility of our seemingly inexhaustible faith in scientism on the one hand,[7; 10, p. 20] and on the other the nature of the phenomenon itself. The power of the scientific approach is hardly to be doubted, but the cult of *scientism* is remarkably barren. The increasing efforts being made to "scientize" communication will likely reveal little more about the phenomenon than the limits of its scientizability.

Closely related is the fact that we suffer a deeply embedded cultural belief in technology as the answer to our problems. The illusion is that, no matter what the nature of our problems, we have only to await or urge on the development of some new technology and those problems will be solved. Yet the human and "organizational" communication problems we have today are not basically different from those Confucius pondered more than 20 centuries ago. A fantastic array of technology has evolved, but tacitly assuming these technologies to be an adequate substitute for a sound and comprehensive understanding of the phenomenon, has led not to the solution of our so-called "communication problems" but to an intensification of them.

In short, the inclination to assume that communication *is* whatever is easily and handily scientizable about it, and the inclination to assume that technological progress is equivalent to understanding, are basic difficulties standing in the way of talking sense about communication.

Basic Reconceptualization

Finally, it is exceedingly more difficult to reconceptualize something as basic and as ubiquitous as communication, and to come to terms with the implications of that basic reconceptualization, than it is to accumulate new knowledges. The ways in which we traditionally and conventionally conceive of communication—those being inadequate and untenable—stand as obstacles to more adequate and more potent ways of conceiving of communication.* But the lifeblood of science has always been infused by its basic reconceptualizations, not its "research." What is needed now to provide this sort of impetus for conceptual progress in the study of communication is a basic reconceptualization of the underlying phenomena.

That is what I would like to try to do in this paper: Suggest some ways of reconceptualizing the phenomena of communication which offer a means of organizing a wide range of facts and ideas from a wide range of disciplines of the life and behavioral sciences having some part-interest in communication—cybernetics, information theory, psychology, systems theory, sociology and anthropology, cognitive studies, and so on.

The reason for this long digression is that this is a task to be faced only when the kinds of difficulties described above are in full and meaningful view.

OBJECTIVES

For these same reasons, it would not be especially profitable to survey here the "state-of-the-art" of human communication theory—or research. The conceptual/theoretical foundations are neither sound enough, nor broadly based enough. Most of the "research" that has been produced to date is therefore of questionable value. Thus, my objectives here are directed not to the scientific *accomplishments* of this patchwork "field" but to the pressing scientific *need, viz.:*

1. To stimulate some thought about why, and in what ways, communication and its related phenomena are the *sine qua non* of the behavioral sciences
2. To present a basic conceptual framework for approaching those phenomena empirically and systematically

---

* Those preconceptions, our traditional concepts of communication, are often insidious. "Communication is the 'transfer of meaning'" has an appealing ring to it. But since none of our receptors is capable of receiving "meaning," the notion of "transfer" is a flagrantly untenable one. The typical formula, $A \to B = X$ (A "communicates" something to B with X result), is similarly misleading. What one person says to another is no more the product of the utterer than it is of the receiver; in fact, it is in practice difficult, if not impossible, to parcel out their separate contributions to the overall consequence. It is quite observable that the process is neither linear nor algebraic. Why we continue to cling to those faulty orientations is perhaps partly explained by the difficulties outlined at the beginning of this paper.

3. To provide a way of generating some of the far-ranging implications of this conceptual foundation

SOME BASIC CONCEPTS

At the outset, some basic propositions and distinctions need to be introduced.

Communication

First, it will be useful, if not necessary, to conceive of communication as one of the two basic life processes—one, of course, being the ingestión and processing of energy, the other being the acquisition and processing of information, or *communication.* Just as the crucial component of physical metabolism is the conversion of raw environmental processes into energy forms consumable or processable by a particular living system, the crucial component of the communication process is the conversion of raw event-*data* into forms of *information* consumable or processable by that living system.

Communication is not, therefore, a uniquely human phenomenon. We have been greatly disadvantaged by the assumption that communication is something peculiarly human, when, in fact, the process is as basic and indispensable to living systems as is their physical metabolism.

Communication and Intercommunication

One immediate advantage is that a distinction must be made between communication and *intercommunication.** The distinction can most clearly be made in terms of the separate functions each subserves.

The primitive functions of *communication* for all complex living systems are those of (1) "mapping" into itself relationships between itself and some temporary or recurrent aspects of its environment (adaptation),** or (2) confirming those relationships, or the resulting orientations, to the ends of the stability or the direction of growth or movement of that living system.

---

* There is a mysterious but widely held belief that when one talks about communication he ought to use totally familiar language. Yet conceptual progress in the study of communication has been greatly impeded by the lack of a special set of terms . Perhaps more than any other field, the study of communication sorely needs inventive constructs and special-purpose terms, like *intercommunication.*

** There are many terms for this process, which Bohm has referred to as "invarianting."

The primitive functions of intercommunication—the intentional and mutual production and consumption of event-data—are therefore those of (1) mutual adaptation and/or manipulation (or control), which in turn results in (2) the building and/or confirming of aggregate structures such as family units, communities, societies, etc., and, at the human level, of institutions, cultures, ideologies, etc.

Although an understanding of communication at the human level is hardly possible without a conception of intercommunication, it is necessary to keep in mind that communication and intercommunication are different processes subserving different (though often related) ends. The technologies employed in specifically *human* communication and intercommunication may differ, but the primitive functions subserved are similar throughout the phylogenetic scale.

The Communicational Environment

What *is* uniquely characteristic of human communication and intercommunication is the fact that the technological sophistication of human intercommunication has made possible the emergence and evolution of a purely communicational environment or reality—i.e., an environment or reality comprised of anything that can be and is talked about. Whatever can be and is talked about comprises a reality in the sense that it must be adapted to and dealt with in much the same way as that reality which is subject only to sensory validation. In other words, man's position on the phylogenetic scale has made possible the emergence and evolution of a communicational environment which has as much or more significance for man than does the physical environment for the "lower" animals. All of those conditions which function as determinants of man's thought and hence his behavior, but which are not directly verifiable by his own sensorium, are aspects of his communicational environment. Thus, most of what we term man's values, beliefs, ideologies, aesthetic standards, etc., are ultimately products of human intercommunication. Taken together, anything and everything which man can and does talk about comprises his communicational reality. Whatever one or more men can and do talk about, but which is not amenable to direct sensory contact by them, has no reality beyond what can be and is said about it. The significance of his communicational environment to modern man makes it the major aspect of his ecology. [13; 16]

Teleological vs. Telesitic Behavior

At the level of man, it is necessary to make a distinction between what might be termed his "teleological" contrasted with his "telesitic" behavior. We can do so easily by taking a brief look backward along the phylogenetic scale.

At some vague point along that scale, self-reflexivity emerges as a biological possibility. What this emergent characteristic enables man to do is conceive of himself *in relation to* those aspects of his environment which he must or would encounter behaviorally.

All living systems, from the simplest to the most complex, exhibit what has been viewed as "purposive" behavior in the teleological sense; [4] that is, given that every healthy living system is continuously and unavoidably in the process of becoming what it is, the behavior it manifests can be viewed as having purposiveness about it.*

Man's complex biological architecture and sophisticated intercommunication technologies make possible an exceptional degree of self-reflexivity; he is capable of behaving other than teleologically. Because he can conceive of very intricate and future-projected relationships between himself (as he conceives of himself) and his environments (including other people and his expectations of *their* conceptions of those relationships), man also exhibits *telesitic* behavior—that is, covert or overt behavior undertaken as rational or "intelligent" means to self-determined ends. Living systems and organized aggregates of living systems (such as human organizations) are, through the behavior of their members, both self-organizing and evolutionary. But, overlaying the teleological behavior which occurs in the service of those ends, both man and, to a greatly limited degree, some of his domesticated animals and the "infrahuman" primates evidence "entrepreneurial" behavior consistent with self-images or self-contrived ends or states. This capacity carries with it the possibility of failure to bring about intended states-of-affairs—a possibility having considerable import for the condition of man and for the evolution of his particular institutions and ideologies.[8; 14, pp. 358-59; 18]

Teleological behavior is that which a complex living system *can* or *must* engage in to its own end; telesitic behavior is that which man, for example, *would* engage in to some further end.

Of relevance here too, is the fact that all emergent capacities, such as man's capacity for self-reflexivity and for the invention of communication and intercommunication technologies, are incipient incapacities. Because man's intercommunication abilities can be deployed "consciously," that is consistent with his own self-images and intended states, they may disadvantage as well as advantage him. In and of themselves, man's capacities for communication and intercommunication are amoral. There is no more absolute good or right implicit in man's sophisticated intercom-

---

* Implying different degrees of "intelligence," of course. An interesting example cited by E. Laszlo (in a recent issue of *Main Currents*) is that of the cat and the amoeba. The amoeba evidences no anticipation (or "intelligence") in following a target such as a puddle of water with the appropriate salinity. It exhibits no ability to extrapolate the track of the source. But a cat will run to where he anticipates the mouse will be rather than where it is.

munication abilities than in the apparent muteness of butterflies. The sole criterion lies in the consequences of the ways in which those capacities are deployed.

Hence the crucial importance, in the study of *human* communication and intercommunication, of distinguishing between teleological and telesitic behavior.

Levels of Analysis

As one of the two basic life processes, the phenomenon of communication and its concomitants have pervasive implications for all of man's behavior. Whatever it is a man does, *qua* man, can be carried out only in and through communication and intercommunication. It is for this reason inconceivable that man and his behavior and his artifacts and his institutions can ever be adequately and accurately described apart from a full description of the underlying processes of communication and intercommunication, the *sine qua non* of the behavioral sciences. Yet the very pervasiveness and ubiquitousness of those processes and their concomitants make it necessary to approach them from the point of view of one or more "levels" of analysis.

The decisions one makes about which levels of analysis to use to guide his inquiries are at once both arbitrary and critical.* I have found it most useful, however, to approach communication and intercommunication phenomena from the standpoint of these broad levels of analysis:

1. The intrapersonal (the point of focus being one individual, and the dynamics of communication as such)
2. The interpersonal (the point of focus being a two or more person interactive system and its properties—the process of intercommunication and its concomitants)
3. The multi-person human enterprise level (the point of focus being the internal structure and functioning of multi-person human enterprises)
4. The enterprise-environment level (the point of focus being upon the interface between human organizations and their environments)
5. The technological level of analysis (the focus being upon the efficacy of those technologies—both hardware and software—which have evolved in the service of man's communication and intercommunication endeavors)

---

* The linguist or psycholinguist might employ the more familiar levels of the *syntactical,* the *semantic,* and the *pragmatic.* But few psycholinguists conceive of language as a technology of intercommunication. Thus, these categories, being anchored in language, are limiting. The biologist would probably prefer the categories of *metabolic, epigenetic,* and *genetic.* But, again, these seem to me limiting for the purposes of comprehensive approach to communication.

For purposes of conceptual and empirical inquiry, each successive level of analysis overlays and subsumes the preceding level. Any way of comprehending intercommunication, for example, must be consistent with the way in which communication is comprehended, and so on. A systematic conceptual framework requires this sort of interlevel articulation, a requirement often overlooked.

It can be seen in Figure 1.1 that the technological level of analysis transcends and overlays each of the other levels, as well as having an area of inquiry or discourse of its own. What this crude schematic is intended to imply is that the phenomena of interest at each level of analysis *can* be studied either apart from the technologies that are employed, or in terms of those technologies; and that the technologies of communication and intercommunication *can* be studied apart from the technologies that are employed, or in terms of those technologies; and that the technologies of communication and intercommunication *can* be studied apart from their uses at the various levels of analysis, or in terms of those levels or even outside of them. In short, this scheme is a matter of conceptual convenience and has no necessary theoretical significance. Nor is it intended to be in any sense isomorphic.

It is further no more than a matter of expository convenience to organize the balance of this paper around those levels of analysis. However, the additional space given over to the discussion of the first two levels of analysis is intended to reflect their more fundamental significance.

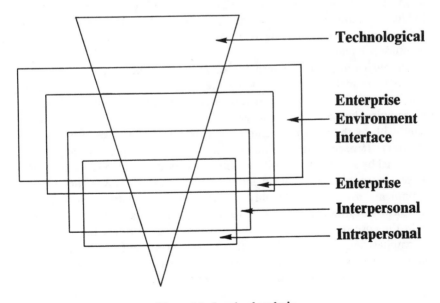

Figure 1.1 Levels of analysis

THE INTRAPERSONAL LEVEL: COMMUNICATION

I have previously suggested that it is conceptually useful, if not necessary, to conceive of the communication process as being compounded of all of those subprocesses by which a living system acquires and converts ongoing event-*data* into *information* for processing or "consumption" to some end. From that base, a comprehensive frame of reference for the study of human communication can be derived.

1. It is therefore consistent to define *communication* as all of those processes associated with the acquisition and conversion of raw event-data into consumable or processable information, culminating in an instance of taking-something-into-account. We can thus look to a given individual's take-into-account-abilities * and take-into-account-susceptibilities as the codetermining factor (along with the event-data) in the process of communication. Whatever other factors we may wish to include under the heading of "communication," the process does not occur in the absence of acquirable event-data which are at least potentially take-into-account-able by a given individual.

2. As indicated before, the ends or functions subserved by the process of communication are those of (a) enabling the individual to establish or maintain adaptive state-relationships with his two environments (the physical and the communicational) through the mapping-into himself concepts of himself, vis-à-vis those aspects of his environments with which he must have, or would have, transactions; and (b) enabling the individual to acquire and process or "consume" information about himself and his environments, having relevance or utility for some present, past, or future behavior.

Although often indistinguishable empirically, conceptually distinguishing the two functions in this way has the advantage of emphasizing, in the first instance, the process of reality-attenuation or "invarianting," which all complex living systems engage in via the process of being-communicated-with by their environments (to the extent of their take-into-account-abilities). It permits us additionally to see, for example, the applicability of Ashby's "law of requisite variety," a very general translation for the present purpose being that an individual can reliably "invariant" his environments psychologically only as his own complexity approaches the complexity of those environments with which he transacts.[1] .

In the case of the second of the two functions, it offers the advantage of emphasizing the strategic intelligence-gathering and evaluation which culminates in some "intelligent" behavior. That is, it suggests the basic dynamic of human behavior as arising out of the continuous monitoring

---

* This term should be, I believe, attributed to Donald MacKay.

of apparent states-of-affairs relative to his intended states-of-affairs (teleological or telesitic) vis-à-vis those environments.

3. This reformulation also necessitates our making clear the distinction implied between event-data and information. All event-data, potentially acquirable by an individual, are neutral and "given," devoid in and of themselves of any significance or meaning. Event-data therefore *are;* information is always *information-about* something going on. Event-data and information are of different qualitative orders. The human sensorium is so evolved and structured as to be receptive to certain ranges of certain kinds of event-data. But the functional ingredient of human perception, thought, memory, etc., is *information-about*. Taking-something-into-account involves the acquisition of certain patterns or sequences of event-data and the simultaneous conversion of that raw material into functionally processable and "consumable" information. In the same way that there is an important qualitative difference between the steer-on-the-hoof and the energy that is ultimately used by the human body subsequent to the ingestion and digestion of a steak, there is a critical qualitative difference between the event-data of one's environment (including verbal event-data) and the information-about it which he derives from it (i.e., creates out of it).

Second, man and his environments are inextricably interdependent or codeterminate. This is inescapable by virtue of the fact that all of man's "intelligent" behavior with respect to himself vis-à-vis his environments is necessarily mediated by his conceptions of those environments, which in turn are his and his fellows' creations. Thus, it is ultimately impossible to know whether those environments are orderly or chaotic. [2] So we have no way of knowing whether the process of converting raw event-data into processable *information-about* adds organization or reduces it; it would be impossible to say, for example, whether, in the process of being-communicated-with by his environments, an individual only imperfectly recreates what in its "natural" state is informationally perfect, or whether the individual's contribution to the process adds qualities of structure or organization and thus an order of "information" not intrinsic to the event-data.* What is observable and demonstrable is the development and exercise of *conventions* for acquiring and converting event-data. For purposes of communication, these may be personal and idiosyncratic, of course. It is only at the level of intercommunication that similar conventions of taking-into-account arise.

---

* It is not the "Information Theory" issue I would raise here (i.e., the matter of uncertainty reduction). It is the issue of whether, communicationally, man filters out uncertainty or adds whatever uncertainty there is.

As "properly" socialized humans, we have similar take-into-account-abilities only to the extent that we are similarly skilled in the application of conventions for the acquisition and conversion of event-data. In the process of evolving workable models of what *is* in our environments, of what *matters,* and of *what to expect* as a consequence of the manner in which we relate aspects of our environments, an illusion of isomorphism is created. The validity of that illusion is not empirically testable. Given the dynamic complexity of the human environment, the number of ways of attentuating workable realities of it may be infinite. There is no way of determining the limits of the variety of conventions which would enable us to be communicated with by our environments.

4. A fourth factor deserving of at least brief mention here is the fact that communication processes, thus conceived, may be either *morphostatic* or *morphogenetic* in character. That is, individuals (like other open systems) are informed * and altered by their environments to the extent that their communication experiences add to or alter their take-into-account-abilities, in which case the process is morphogenetic. Or, individuals inform their environments to the extent that they impose upon them prior conceptions, for purposes of stability or confirmation—in which case the nature of the transaction is morphostatic. If morphostatic, attenuated states are reinforced or maintained. If morphogenetic, those attenuated states are altered or elaborated.

While one can exercise only those take-into-account-abilities he has in order to make sense of his environments, the possibilities for the elaboration or evolution of new take-into-account-abilities are initially omnipresent.

5. Those interactive systems comprised of an individual's "workable realities," those aspects of his environment with which he would interact, and his behavior in those environments, therefore vary from relatively closed to relatively open. A relatively closed communication system is one in which once-adequate comprehensions of some aspect of the environment are not altered (remain morphostatic) either (1) because no changes occur in the environment or in the individual who would impinge upon the adequacy of the particular take-into-account-abilities involved, or (2) because the anticipated instability of changing one's comprehensions of that environment exceed his tolerance limits, and he clings to now-inadequate conceptions in spite of their inadequacy.[11; 12]

It should further be of keen interest to those concerned with human communication that it is only when an individual's self-defined ends are both completable and fully determinate that his communication systems can be completely described; the extent to which they are not fully de-

---

* A term for which I am indebted to Harley Shands.

scribable is the extent to which his communication systems are open. The fact that people talk to themselves about their telesitic ends is, in most cases, sufficient to insure dimensions of indeterminate self-organization.

6. It is thus unavoidable that an individual's specifically human competence and efficacy depends ultimately upon the communication experiences he has had and is capable of having—and, as will be evident in the next section, upon his strategic intercommunication-abilities.

Some Implications

It is only in the implications of these basic concepts that their power and usefulness can be evaluated. The question must be: What are the implications of this way of conceiving of the process of communication for the way I look at X (any observable behavior, social phenomenon, etc.)?

It should be obvious that the great range of implications thus derivable defies any exhaustive listing—here or elsewhere. Yet it may be desirable to suggest one or two examples which might incite the thinking-through of a great many more implications of particular interest to the individual reader.

One of the most significant implications is that individuals behave *not* on the basis of the ultimate realities of their environments, but on the basis *only* of the way they conceive of those realities. The determinants of behavior are not to be found in the event-data of the environments in which individuals exist, but in the interdependence of those environments with the ways they are taken into account—i.e., with the information-about those environments (and the beliefs, ideas, etc. about them) which they have available to process. And any workable reality is useful for certain purposes (e.g., the earth is "flat" enough for purposes of walking upon it).

Individual orientations to one's environments are comprised of hypotheses with respect to what is likely to happen if. . . . The test is not whether those hypotheses are "true," but whether they are the most expeditious given the conditions, the objectives, or missions, etc. The issue is not one of subjectivity versus objectivity, as some have argued, but the fact that the ways in which we conceive of our worlds (and hence behave in them) often depend more upon our take-into-account-abilities—i.e., upon our communicate-abilities—than upon the "objective" realities of the environment (which are indeterminable, of course).*

---

* The notion of "objective reality" is a purely abstract construct, of course. However, the issue I want to raise is not the philosophic issue of how one's conceptions of the world compare with "objective reality," but simply that one bases his behavior not upon "objective reality" but upon his personal conceptions of "it."

A second major complex of implications stems from the proposition that most individual behavior can be conceived of as the behaver's solution to a problem. But many commentators (and researchers) on human problem-solving and decision-making neglect the most critical aspects of the process—those of apprehending and identifying (naming) the problem which is to be dealt with.

There are two basic empirical errors made in conventional approaches to problem solving:

1. There is nothing "problematical" about event-data; event-data are meaningless in and of themselves. It is only in translation as information-about (human processing) that event-data (conditions, circumstances, etc.) are apprehended as problematical or not.
2. The conditions identified as problematical are typically presumed to be eliminated by the proper (or adequate) solution. Yet it is empirically unavoidable that the solution to a problem (at least one which culminates in some action-in-the-environment) doesn't eliminate existing states-of-affairs, but consequents in the creation of new or altered states-of-affairs. Thus, the criterion should not be sought in the excellence of the solution as such, but in the desirability of the altered state-of-affairs relative to the previous (before solution) state-of-affairs.

What is unavoidable, if we are to take what we know about communication seriously, is that (1) problems exist only in people; (2) problems exist only in the form they are conceived of; (3) the problem dealt with is the one named or identified (not the "objective" conditions of concern); and (4) given that one can "get into contact" with his environment *only* via his *own* take-into-account-abilities, the solutions (or potential solutions) one has for problems generally determine the problems he "sees" or identifies.

It is in this way that the implications of these basic concepts can be drawn out.

Associated Technologies

The technologies that have evolved in the service of communication include all of those tools and techniques developed to enhance or facilitate the acquisition of event-data (e.g., the telescope, spectacles, ear horn) and its conversion and consumption (e.g., conceptual schemata, conventions of reality-attenuation, personal "maps," etc.).

Languages, as such, are not necessary to communication. They are, however, crucial to the development of complex social organizations via intercommunication—and hence are part of the technology of intercommunication. [17, Chs. 6, 17]

THE INTERPERSONAL LEVEL: INTERCOMMUNICATION

To avoid the mentalistic pitfalls of much of the literature on intercommunication, it is important to keep in mind these basic points:

1. The way in which intercommunication is comprehended must be consistent with the basic phenomena of communication. The interpersonal level of analysis overlays and is *in addition to,* not in lieu of, the intrapersonal level of analysis.

2. There are but two ways of affecting and being affected by the environment—physically (coercively) and communicationally. Empirically, there are no alternatives. The vague mysticism that surrounds many popular conceptions of intercommunication—e.g., as the "transfer of meaning"—has greatly impeded progress toward a scientific understanding of the processes involved.

What I hope to provide here is a brief reformulation of the concept of intercommunication which is fully consistent with the empirical knowledge we do have of the underlying phenomena of communication.

3. What is characteristic of intercommunication (as contrasted with the individual process of communication) is the attempt by one or more individuals to influence, direct, control, or focus the communication experiences of one or more others. One person presents himself as an aspect of another's environment and produces cultural artifacts in the conventional forms of messages to be taken-into-account by that other in a way intended by (or acceptable to) the first.

4. The ends or functions subserved by intercommunication, then, are those of (a) mutual adaptation, via the creation and perpetuation of shared communicational environments, and (b) mutual control and manipulation, consequenting in the emergence and evolution of institutions, social organizations (of all types), cultures, ideologies, etc.

It is intercommunication which makes possible the emergence of higher-order systems, both social and communicational. Intercommunication is therefore both the means and the ends of creating, altering, maintaining, and exploiting the communicational environment, and of the social structures, ideologies, etc. embedded in it.

5. The process of communication is basic to all living systems. But what is required for successfully engaging in the sophisticated kinds of intercommunication we are all familiar with are (a) a language, (b) a minimal set of rules for the conduct of the participants of the encounter, (c) a relationship, mutually conceived of, and (d) a minimal degree of mutuality of complementarity with respect to intercommunicative intentions and their anticipated consequences.

To the extent that the process of intercommunication is "successful," we "map" each other into each other, and simultaneously "map" each other's adaptive mappings into each other. This produces an illusion of reality about those aspects of our environments which exist only in and through our intercommunication about them. But such similar or harmonious orientations, perceptions, beliefs, etc. are better conceived of as *intersubjectivities,* however, not as "reality," by tacit agreement. With respect to communicational realities, "right" and "wrong," "true" and "false" can have only normative relevance.

6. Two or more people in continuous or recurrent intercommunication comprise a second-order communication system. Such systems have properties of their own, which are not necessarily the properties of any of the individuals involved. These emergent properties function as system determinants. For example, the dynamic nature of a communicative relationship, once formed and always in evolution,* is a significant determinant of the behavior of the persons involved when they are in intercommunication.

All higher-order living systems may also be thought of as compound enterprises. Each individual involved is himself an enterprise to the extent he exercises his telesitic potentials, and the *raison d'etre* of any human organization identifies it, as well, as a collective enterprise. The conceptual difficulties this presents for comprehending higher-order systems from intercommunication up, are perhaps obvious: Not only are there individual communication systems subserving each individual, and interpersonal systems linking pairs intercommunicatively, and so on, but the collective enterprise achieves health and viability only to the extent that *its* communication system is efficacious.

7. Every intercommunicative relationship is an organization. Under scrutiny, it reveals the same conditions of "organization-ness" that any larger social structure does. That concept should perhaps be introduced here.

Anything that is organized is organized only to the extent that its parts are subordinated to the whole. In effect, this means that at least task-relevant freedoms (variances) must be either abdicated by the components (à la humans) or designed out of them or denied them (à la complex biological organisms, machines, or humans to an extent via socialization and institutionalization). To be organized, the components must mutually control one another in some fashion—either by design (as in a digital computer) or by tacit accommodation (as in human social structures of all sorts). Interpersonal relationships, however, as well

---

* Relationships (i.e., intercommunication systems) are "purposive" too, in the teleological sense, even if not in the telesitic sense. To the extent the impetus of the evolutionary (teleological) thrust of such higher-order systems is not sourced in the one or the other person involved, or "managed" by them, it becomes a system determinant by default.

as other organizational relationships, may be either *symbiotic* or *synergistic*.

Since intercommunication is the almost exclusive human means of mutual control and manipulation, it is through intercommunication that we "get organized"—whether that organization is parent-child, boss-subordinate, teacher-student, clerk-customer, husband-wife, friend-friend, or other relationship. Every continuing relationship (organization) requires the abdication or deprivation of certain degrees of freedom on the part of the members of that relationship. Intercommunicatively, it is the indeterminacy of the other's reaction which must be minimized. This is accomplished by mutually invarianting each other. Thus the ultimate trade-off in all intercommunication is between control and indeterminacy, an unavoidable trade-off of pervasive importance for all social (intercommunicative) behavior.

Some Implications

Again, the implications of these reformulations go to the depth and breadth of man's many and varied social activities and endeavors, and hence defy even representative specification here. But two examples may be suggestive.

Intercommunication is the means via which communicational environments are created and maintained. All of our institutions, ideologies, beliefs, values, theories, etc. are created in and perpetuated through intercommunication. This communicational environment—these "realities"—are, in effect, the major portion of our human ecology. As such, they essentially determine the human condition: the kind of people we are going to have, our "human nature," human viability and efficacy—in short, the potentials and limits within which all other forces must operate.

Humans are informed within their communicational ecologies, and, in turn, perpetuate them. The widespread belief of not so many years ago, that the best cure for many of man's ills was bloodletting, is no more farfetched than many beliefs held today—about human communication, for example! Because we intercommunicate and inform or institutionalize one another, we are indeed carelessly fiddling with our own destinies as humans, in the most vital ways. Urbanization and pollution do affect man's condition, but in pitifully minor ways by comparison to the potency of what we have done and continue to do to each other through the byproducts (cultures, beliefs, etc.) of our intercommunication.

We *are* the communication experiences we have had, and we *can be* what our communicational ecologies permit or force us to be. It is almost unbelievable that we continue to treat communication in a most superficial manner!

A second suggestive implication is revealed in the criterion we usually hold as the epitome of "good" communication: "effectiveness." An insidious and widespread assumption is the offhand belief that communication is in and of itself "good," and that, if some of it is good, more of it would be better. Closely related is a similarly widespread assumption that the solution to most of the world's problems—from marital to international—is simply "better" communication.*

That assumption is extremely misguided and erroneous. There is nothing intrinsically good or bad about the process of communication—and particularly not about the practices of intercommunication. If a person satisfactorily achieves his communicative intentions, vis-à-vis another person, we say he has "communicated" effectively. But this overlooks the compounding of enterprises when two or more people are involved. What is "effective" from one person's point of view may be detrimental to the other person(s) involved—as when schizophrenic mothers produce schizophrenic daughters via intercommunication or when the commander's order, faithfully obeyed, leads to the death of all hands on board or when the "I love you," "I love you too" exchange leads to hate or the degradation of one or both persons.

The much-hallowed notion of "effectiveness" is a completely inadequate one, when a second- or higher-order system is involved. What is "effective" communication from one person's point of view in no way guarantees that the consequences will be efficacious for those higher-order systems of which that person is but one (of two or more) components.

Associated Technologies

In addition to those technologies pertinent to the intrapersonal level of analysis, the technologies involved at the interpersonal level include all of those tools and techniques by which the cultural artifacts we call "messages" are produced and disseminated, stored, and/or retrieved, etc., whether individual or "mass."

Languages (or other such codes) are thus a part of the technology of intercommunication, as are the techniques of speech and writing (and other aural or oral display). All of the media (hardware), via which codified data are transported, etc., are pertinent to this level, as are the forms and conventions by which those codified data are to be interpreted and comprehended (software).

---

* ". . . an important cornerstone of American folklore holds that communication can be counted on to spread emotional warmth, that any interpersonal or intergroup problem is really a lack-of-communication problem, that conflicts, domestic and international, will disappear when people get to know one another and 'reason together'. . . . The amount of communication among components, however, appears to have little impact in either setting or changing a system's emotional tone." (5; 9, p. 59)

THE MULTI-PERSON HUMAN ENTERPRISE LEVEL

Human organizations exist in various forms—ranging from prolonged conversations to marriages to clans to communities to corporations to the "American society." What is organized about all of them—i.e., their "organization-ness"—is very much the same in all instances.

The one distinction I want to emphasize, however, is between "essentially" *evolved* organizations, like friendships or a society, and "essentially" *contrived* organizations, like a corporation or a civic group. "Essentially" because neither type is purely evolved or purely contrived. The difference is a matter of degree. A corporation is (at least at the outset) more contrived than evolved, and the larger society (at least as it matures) is more evolved than contrived.

The distinction is a useful one. The communication system(s) subserving an "evolved" human organization, evolves with that organization; it is inductively formed (i.e., as needed and as a consequence of the intercommunication that occurs). But the communication system(s) of a contrived human organization is partially contrived along with the goals and the structure of that enterprise; it is deductively formed (i.e., rationally, to fit the ends, the structures, and the functions of the components of that enterprise, their task-relationships, etc.). There are a great many implications to this distinction.

1. Multi-person human enterprises can be viewed as third-order systems, compounded of individual enterprises, interpersonal enterprises of various complexities, and the rationalized ends and means of the enterprise itself. Thus there are, at least, three orders of communication systems involved, and it is their integration or paralleling that continues to challenge information system designers and manangers alike.

2. *In addition to* all of the factors of concern at the communication and intercommunication levels of analysis, what is appropriately of concern at this level of analysis is the design of enterprise communication systems for the purposes of generating, disseminating, storing, processing and displaying, and acquiring event-data pertinent to the performance of each subtask within the enterprise. The difficulty, of course, is that the enterprise must be "open" if it is to be adaptive and viable, yet it must be "closed" in order to be organized, predictable, and efficient.

Only tasks that are completable and determinate have information requirements that can be defined (rationally specified in advance). To the extent that tasks cannot or should not be closed in this sense, the information requirements for that task cannot be completely rationalized. Thus, the design of enterprise communication systems must be both rationalized and "exigencized"—a condition that is logically unapproachable by the management and information "sciences." Stability and efficiency—which are quite approachable via cybernetics—are not the only criteria of enterprise viability, and, in fact, may be pathologic symptoms.

3. The efficacy of the design (or evolution) of an enterprise's communication systems is, in part, determined by the efficacy of the structure of the enterprise itself. Many so-called organizational "communication problems" are not at their source communication problems, but organization design problems. Otherwise efficacious communication systems can compensate to a limited extent for poor enterprise design (or for human incompetencies in that enterprise), but that offsetting measure should be seen as compensation, not as elimination of the underlying fault.

4. If we think of the internal workings of an enterprise only in terms of its efficiency, control, or "organization-ness," then what we would attempt, ideally, to do would be to design or constrain out of every member his cognizance of everything but what is necessary to the performance of his task. Then we would attempt to equip him with just those take-into-account-abilities which would enable him to apprehend and interpret problematicalness in precisely the desired way. Finally, we would organize his task-related intercommunication systems in such a way that his inputs and outputs were perfectly regulated and controlled. This is precisely what we do when we build an airplane or a computer. The difficulty is, however, that while data transmission and acquisition may be highly rationalized, *communication* and *intercommunication* are not, and largely cannot be; people are relatively open systems, and, to the extent they are open, their communication systems are open. It is human enterprising which energizes and organizes human enterprises and which contributes whatever adaptive and telesitic viability they may have. Thus, if enterprises are to evolve in an evolving environment consistent with their rationalized ends, then their communication systems must be "exigencized" as well as rationalized.

Implications

If we recognize that it is the automatistic and nonconscious nature of an individual's behavior which makes possible higher degrees of competence of skill, what are the implications for the design and management of enterprises? The fact that the good pianist practices until he is not conscious of being communicated-with by the music on the page is the condition which increases his potential proficiency. If any of us consciously had to make all of the actions necessary to driving a car, we would have great difficulty.

What is the significance of this for the design of enterprise communication systems? It seems possible that attention has been concentrated upon communication issues and problems which are ultimately picayune, while ignoring other communication issues and design opportunities which might significantly alter the structure and the viability of human enterprises. I refer to the advantages of *non*communication or of *non*cognizance at successively higher levels in the enterprise. Similarly, the assumptions that information is the same thing as communication and that more information in decision-making is somehow better than less have led us down exceedingly unfruitful—and even disadvantageous—paths.

Associated Technologies

Most of the technologies applied at the enterprise level of analysis are simply extensions of those available at the interpersonal level. However, a brief statement about the application of computers and "information systems" would be very much in order.

Confucius was concerned about much the same sorts of "organizational communication problems" that we read about today. Given that our current conceptions of the communication process are not much advanced over those held in Confucius' time (and in many respects less so), it is little wonder that the history of our concern with such matters is largely a history of our search for a technological panacea of one kind or another. The present-day faith in computerization and "information systems" as the solutions to our enterprise ills is a continuation of that historical search for panaceas.

An "information system" cannot compensate for the incompetencies of the members of an enterprise (particularly not its leaders) or for the inefficacy of the design of an enterprise. And, in many cases, the appliquéing of computers and information systems onto ongoing enterprises has led to an intensification of underlying structural and human incompetencies. There is, of course, great potential in these technologies, both in their hardware and their software aspects. But this potential will never be realized apart from some fundamental progress in the comprehension of the phenomena of communication and intercommunication and their concomitants.

Related to the pitfalls of the technological mystique is the assumptive confusion between "information" and communication. What "information" systems and computers handle are data—not information. This is not "just" a semantic matter; the stuff the mind works with (i.e., that which is processable by humans) is not of the same order as the stuff which is carried along in coded form through wires and switches.

It should be emphasized, again, that only closed systems are completely describable. To the extent that one or more of the enterprises compounded in human organizations are telesitic, the communication systems subserving them will necessarily be open. Since only fully closed (or closable) systems are rationalizable via deduced "information" systems, the applicability and usefulness of computers and their related data systems, as they exist today, are only partial. That is, they are fully applicable only to those tasks and enterprises which are determinate and completable. Under any other conditions, their applicability is limited.

THE ENTERPRISE ⟷ ENVIRONMENT LEVEL

Those who have contemplated the enterprise⟷environment level of analysis over the years have frequently been tempted to analogize directly from the organism⟷environment interface. But there are some differences.

1. As indicated before, it is useful to conceive of a human organization as a compound enterprise. The phenomena of communication and intercommunication are not *basically* different in this context; but they must be viewed as occurring *within the context* of a contrived social organization having rationalized task functions, data systems, decision prerogatives, etc. In addition, every complex enterprise has a life of its own; that is, as a result of the actions taken by its members on behalf of the enterprise, it is continuously in the process of evolving—irreversibly. A final overlay is that of the enterprise's telesitic existence. Its goals or ends (or its *raison d'etre*), and the means thereto, are chosen by one or more members, or by all of the members tacitly (as a byproduct of their behaviors). This establishes the need for an additional communication system, one which links the enterprise with the relevant domains of its environment. What is observable at this level, then, is a complex hierarchy of communication systems which may or may not articulate one with another.

2. At this level of a fourth-order system, what must be organized are capacities for creating, maintaining, altering, or utilizing intercommunicative state-relationships between the enterprise and its relevant environmental domains. Because few "contrived" enterprises are developed and organized from the outside in, as "evolved" organizations are, they are in constant danger of "losing touch" with their. environments, which are continuously changing as a result of the telesitic behaviors of other enterprises, of the evolving self-organization of those environments, and the like.

The internal operations of an enterprise can be controlled; relationships with its environments cannot be controlled, but must be strategically coped-with. This may be one reason why "management scientists" and "operations researchers" have so little of substance to say about this level of analysis. Because telesitic behavior alters both the enterprise and its environment, is morphogenetic for both and for the state-relationships that interlink them, and is neither completable nor determinate, the consequences are hardly "scientizable," even probabilistically. But this does not mean the underlying processes are not understandable.

3. A further factor to be contended with is that the same ends can be reached via different means and from different sets of circumstances where living systems are concerned (*equifinality*), and that similar sets of circumstances can consequent in different ends (*multifinality*). Such conditions place extreme limits upon the possibilities for arriving at "laws" of organizational behavior. But approaching such complex phenomena as communication concomitants and byproducts may prove to be especially fruitful.

Implications

One implication is that, because the basic phenomena of communication are what they are, living (open) systems and their environments are interdependent. What this means, in turn, is that the success or failure of an enterprise is a function not of the enterprise alone (as is so often assumed), but of the nature of the state-relationships that obtain between the enterprise and the various relevant domains of its environments. Thus "profit" is not a measure of enterprise effectiveness, but of the efficacy of its state-relationships. No enterprise can be more efficacious than its subserving communication systems.

A second implication is the fact that our deeply embedded scientistic orientations have led us to think in terms of "riskless" change. This is fallacious. The only out-of-risk living system is that one which is being perfectly controlled by its environment. *Any* exercise of telesitic capacities carries with it the risks of disequilibrium and even of failure. Telesitic choices are made on the basis of information-about, and hence carry with them all of the imperfections and potential risks of morphogenetic communication.

Associated Technologies

There are very few technologies appearing at this level of analysis that have not been appropriated from the other levels. There is currently some interlocking of computers amongst buyers and sellers, government agencies, etc. for purposes of expediency. But these are capabilities which exist within enterprises.

In the years just ahead, however, new technologies will emerge to enhance and facilitate the communication systems of the enterprise *qua* enterprise. These will greatly modify the conceptions of enterprise design and functioning which we now hold. The impetus for these changes will come from our increasing cognizance and understanding of the basic nature of communication and communication systems for the functioning of all living systems.

THE TECHNOLOGICAL LEVEL

The technologies of communication and intercommunication can be and often are studied apart from the basic phenomena to which they are applied. For example, descriptive linguistics focuses upon one particular technology of intercommunication—language forms and patterns. Similarly, the study of media characteristics and codes, deriving from the "communication" and information theory formulations of scholars such as Shannon and Wiener, is the study of but one aspect of the technology of human intercommunication.

These are perfectly valid and useful endeavors. However, the technological mystique so deeply imbedded in our culture, along with the remarkable faith we seem to put in scientism, have led some researchers and perhaps a great many laymen to assume that the "secrets" of human communication will ultimately be revealed through these studies of the technology. There is seductive appeal but considerable danger in attributing too much relevance (for human communication and intercommunication) to the mathematical models, the formulae, and the other trappings connected with purely technological studies. It may be useful to study and refine the horse harness, but one would hardly expect to find therein the "secrets" of the horse's behavior (or the driver's, for that matter).

Much more care needs to be taken to avoid the confusion that often exists between the phenomena of communication and the technologies employed.

What I have attempted here is to suggest an empirically sound conceptual frame of reference for approaching and comprehending the fundamental nature of human communication and intercommunication. To the extent that these reformulations are acceptable and useful, the frame and the substance of the behavior sciences will be subject to radical changes, both in method and approach. It is likely that the failure to build those sciences on a firm understanding of this one of the two basic life processes has contributed to the fact that little real progress has been made.

To accommodate these basic reformulations in our thinking will require widespread and continuous searches for their implications for all of man's thinking and his behavior—which are both cause and effect of his communication and intercommunication—and of their social and institutional byproducts.

REFERENCES AND SUGGESTED READINGS

1. Ashby, R., *An Introduction to Cybernetics*. New York: Science Editions, Wiley, 1963.
2. Beer, S., "Below the Twilight Arch—A Mythology of Systems," in *Systems Research and Design*, ed. by D. P. Echman. New York: Wiley, 1961.
3. Berelson, B. and G. Steiner, *Human Behavior: An Inventory of Scientific Findings*. New York: Harcourt, Brace and World, 1964.
4. Buckley, W., ed., *Modern Systems Research for the Behavioral Scientist*. Chicago: Aldine, 1968.
5. Goffman, E., *Encounters*. Indianapolis: Bobbs-Merrill, 1961.
6. Grinker, R., Sr., ed., *Toward a Unified Theory of Human Behavior*, 2nd ed. New York: Basic Books, 1967.
7. Langer, S., *Mind: An Essay on Human Feeling*, Vol. I. Baltimore: The Johns Hopkins Press, 1967.
8. Lynd, H., *Shame and the Search for Identity*. New York: Science Editions, Wiley, 1961.
9. Monane, J., *A Sociology of Human Systems*. New York: Appleton-Century-Crofts, 1967.
10. Polanyi, M., "A Conversation With Michael Polanyi," *Psychology Today*, 1:12, 1968.
11. Rokeach, M., *The Open and Closed Mind*. New York: Basic Books, 1960.
12. Ruesch, J., *Disturbed Communication*. New York: Norton, 1967.
13. Ruesch, J. and G. Bateson, *Communication: The Social Matrix of Psychiatry*. New York: Norton, 1951.
14. Thayer, L., *Communication: Concepts and Perspectives*. New York: Spartan Books, 1967.
15. ———, ed., *Communication: Theory and Research*. Springfield, Ill.: C.C. Thomas, 1967.
16. ———, "Communication: Tool, Game, Ecology," paper presented to the Communication Colloquium, University of Wisconsin-Milwaukee, 1968.
17. ———, *Communication and Communication Systems*. Homewood, Ill.: Irwin, 1968.
18. Wheelis, A., *The Illusionless Man*. New York: Norton, 1966.

2

Zoology

HUBERT FRINGS

DEFINITIONS AND PROBLEMS

AN exact definition of animal communication is not possible—indeed, may never be possible.[7; 12, pp. 5–18; 26] It is generally agreed, however, that an operant definition can be formulated. Communication between two animals is said to occur when one animal produces a chemical or physical change in the environment (*signal*) that influences the behavior of another. The study of animal communication has received no generally accepted single name, being engaged in by students in many fields: sensory and nervous physiology, ecology, animal behavior (ethology), and comparative psychology. Sebeok [24; 26] has suggested the term *zoosemiotics* for this field of research, but it is still too early to see whether this will be adopted generally.

While some students of animal behavior would restrict communication to intraspecific relationships only, others would include any case in which the behavior of one animal influences that of another, thus including warning colors, and the like. An interesting case in point is that of echolocation: the ability of some animals—for example, bats and porpoises—to locate unseen objects by reflected pulsed sounds. Some consider this a form of autocommunication; others consider it not communication at all. We shall not discuss echolocation here, not because it is unworthy of discussion or should necessarily be excluded from communication, but for the much more prosaic reason that there are enough other matters to occupy us.

Up to now, studies on animal communication have not in themselves led to generalizations that aid our understanding of human communication. When comparisons between human and animal communication have been made, they have invariably been by someone trying to decide whether animals actually have languages, and the criteria used have been those proposed by students of human language (cf., for instance, Hockett in Ref. 14 and Count in Ref. 26). Studies on animal communication are still generally empirical and have not resulted in many theoretical concepts. As for the question of animal language, one's view of its existence or nonexistence depends entirely upon the criteria he selects as critical, and these vary from worker to worker. Luckily the matter does not concern us practically, and studies proceed fruitfully without a decision.

GENERAL DESCRIPTION OF ANIMAL COMMUNICATION

As with all communication systems, three essential parts are necessary: (1) an individual that produces some chemical or physical change, the *sender,* also called source, addresser, and so forth; (2) a chemical or physical entity produced, the *signal;* and (3) an individual that receives the signal and responds to it, the *receiver,* also called reactor, addressee, and the like. Each of these may be studied scientifically.

Two facets of the sender's activities have received special attention: (1) what might be called the *motivation* of the sender, that is, those internal states and external stimuli that initiate production of signals; and (2) the *mechanisms of signal production* and the effects of environmental factors, such as temperature, upon these. As an example of the first, it is well known that signals involved in communication during reproduction of mammals and birds are generally produced only at times of sexual activity, and are often evoked by such features of the environment as day length, presence of other individuals, and the like. As an example of the second, the best-studied cases are probably production of acoustic signals by various insects. Since insects are poikilothermal, the rate of production of sound by males is directly related to temperature, creating an interesting situation, for the feature of greatest significance in the signals is the emission rate. Thus females, the receivers, must also have behavioral adjustments to correct for this inexactness in the males.

The chemical or physical properties of signals have also been studied, often by chemists and physicists as well as zoologists. Where chemical signals, such as sex odors of insects, may be useful for control of pests, these studies have been especially numerous.[10; 11] Some attention, but much less, has been given to the range of transmission of various signals and the effects of the environment on this.

Two facets of the receiver's activities have been the subject of special study: (1) the nature and functions of *receptor organs* and (2) the induced *behavioral responses.* Much more work is needed on the first, for the limits and properties of receptors are known for only a very few animals, and poorly known for most of these. It is by no means safe to assume, as many have done, that the critical features of a signal reaching an animal are those that impress themselves most upon man. Some insects (e.g., honeybees) receive ultraviolet light, and others (e.g., moths and some grasshoppers) are sensitive to ultrasonic sounds. Furthermore, the responses of receptors of animals other than man are by no means necessarily similar to those of the receptors of man. For example, many insect phonoreceptors act as filtering units, rectifying the fundamental acoustic frequencies, here used as carrier waves, to produce nerve impulses determined only by temporal patterns of the sound pulses. Without precise information on receptive capacities, studies of the receiver's behavior may lead to erroneous conclusions.

No really new experimental techniques have been evolved for these studies.[25] The usual physiological methods are used for studies on mechanisms of production and reception of signals; the usual methods of study in animal behavior are adopted for that aspect. Perhaps the only characteristic feature of many studies on animal communication is the extensive use of constructed or recorded dummies—models of body structure or animal sounds—to stimulate potential or suspected receivers. Even this, however, stems directly from earlier ethological work. Students of animal communication, however, are usually much more interested than ethologists in the exact chemical and physical nature of the signals; therefore, many become involved in chemical and physical analyses. There is no question that all aspects of research in animal communication have been greatly aided by recent developments in microchemical methods, tape recording, and cinematography.

PLACE OF COMMUNICATION IN ANIMAL LIFE

Communication between members of a species, at least for most higher animals, infuses every aspect of existence from birth to death. Most young vertebrates react almost at hatching or birth to food and alarm signals of the parents, and these reactions increase in precision and variety as life progresses. To these are added, in maturity, sexual reactions generally governed by complex communication signals. While most invertebrates do not live in such close social units as do vertebrates, they too usually have signals for reproduction and often for other aspects of life. We may, for convenience, classify communication systems into those involved in nonsexual activities and those involved in sexual activities.

Nonsexual Activities

Species identification is an important aspect of life for most animals. For many (e.g., some fish and birds, social insects, and barnacles), members of the same species form specific *aggregations*. This obviously necessitates recognition of other members of the same species, generally through specific body patterns or sounds which act as aggregational signals. For many others (e.g., some birds, spiders, and marine annelids), individuals of the same species practice *dispersion*, except during reproduction, each with its own *territory*. Since members of other species are usually not excluded from the territory, this too necessitates species recognition. In this case, the signals are mostly chemical or acoustical, the most studied being the territorial songs of birds.

Social facilitation between members of aggregations is common among animals. Warnings of danger, by alarm or distress signals, are found among social insects, fish, birds, and mammals. These are usually acoustical, but may be chemical. Most birds, for instance, have staccato calls that they emit when they sight a cat or other predator, which cause other individuals of the species to flee. In a few cases, a special type of alarm signal occurs, first discovered in grasshoppers and now known for a few birds. In this case, an individual leaving a group utters a special sound if there is no danger, the *departing call,* to which the others respond by remaining. If the departer leaves suddenly, without giving the signal, the others leave also. In highly developed social animals (e.g., honeybees, and many birds and mammals), signals are developed that serve for *guidance* to food or to homes. Among the most studied of these are the guidance signals of honeybees, through which scout bees alert hive-mates to the presence of food at a distance from the hive and communicate to them the distance, nature, and direction.

Sexual Activities

Attraction and *recognition* of a mate are generally the first steps in reproduction. Few species, apparently, depend merely upon chance wandering to bring the sexes together; almost all animals have means whereby at least one sex attracts the other through signals, mostly chemical or acoustical. Birds, grasshoppers, and crickets with songs, and mammals and moths with odors, to mention only a few, combine attraction and species identification in specific signals. Even in protozoans, chemical attraction of mating partners—conjugants—has been found. Slime molds, whose name reflects their questionable position as animals, have chemical signals that bring individuals together for reproduction. In these organisms, individual "animals" are amoebalike forms creeping about on the forest floor. To reproduce, they come together and fuse into a multinucleate mass. One individual releases puffs of a chemical, now known for at least one species to be cyclic adenosine monophosphate, to which others respond by crawling to the "caller" and fusing with it. Amazingly enough, it is not the chemical itself that identifies the species, but the rhythm of puffs. This is actually a more sophisticated use of chemical signals than that of many mammals, which simply give off a continuous scent.

Courtship behavior is, for most higher animals at least, a preliminary to *mating,* and in both activities, communication signals are prominent. Courtship usually serves two purposes—confirmation of species and sexual identification, and arousal of the mating partner. The most elaborate courtship patterns are found among birds, mammals, fish, insects, spiders, and mollusks. Since the partners are usually near each other, almost any type of signal may be used. Thus birds have both visual signals (posture, flashing colors) and sounds (courtship duets). Jumping spiders and crabs have poses or dances by which the male identifies himself to the female and arouses her to mating pitch. Male crickets and grasshoppers, after calling in the female by a so-called ordinary, or calling, song, change to a courtship song when the female is in sight. Male web-spinning spiders of some species pluck the strands of the female's web and thus identify themselves and diminish her normally aggressive reactions, so that mating can take place. Males of one group of flies prepare balloonlike structures to present to the females. Male tree-crickets produce a secretion from a gland on their back on which females feed during mating. Certain land snails shoot pointed projectiles, fancifully called "love-darts," into their partners before mating. Even animals such as oysters and marine worms, that cannot come together for mating, release chemicals into the water that induce others to discharge eggs or sperm for external fertilization.

Parent-young relationships, while not directly sexual, are related to sexual activities and may be considered to be derived from sexual acts. These relationships are also facilitated by communication patterns, at least among higher animals. Many invertebrates, and vertebrates such as amphibians, reptiles, and fish, usually have no contact with their offspring. However, social insects, birds, and mammals have intergenerational contacts, and these are carried out through communication signals.

In honeybees, as long as a queen is present in the hive, the workers— all her sexually incompetent daughters—usually produce no new queen.[3] But if the colony becomes too large or if the queen dies, the workers produce another queen, as if they know that the queen is insufficient or gone. The signal here is a chemical called Queen Substance (now known to be 9-oxodec-trans-2-enoic acid) given by the queen to the workers and passed by them from one to another. When enough of this is present to go around, the workers produce only more workers. When the supply decreases, they produce new queens.

Among birds and mammals, the development periods of offspring are to a great degree regulated by signals from the parents and feedback from the young. Often the reactions of the young are quite different from those of older animals, and adult reactions develop or are learned. The earliest reaction to alarm signals of baby birds and mammals is usually immobility. This changes, as the babies leave the nest or lair, to the adult pattern, usually flight. A young male bird may learn to imitate the song of an adult male, usually his father, generating a local tradition in song pattern.

Communication thus plays an important role in the life of almost every, if not every, animal. Generally, the degree depends upon the development of the sensorimotor capabilities of the animal. Sessile or pelagic beasts, such as sponges and jellyfish, seem to have few methods for communication, while mobile animals with well-developed receptors and nervous systems, such as bees, birds, and mammals, have all of life guided in large measure by communication systems. The exact nature of the systems likewise depends upon potentialities. Thus animals with well-developed eyes tend to have highly evolved visual communication signals, and those with well-developed ears tend to have highly evolved acoustical signals. Since almost all animals are sensitive to chemicals, systems based on these are the most widespread of all. The channels available, therefore, fundamentally determine the nature of the communication systems.

COMMUNICATIVE CHANNELS AND THEIR USES

Tactile

The tactile channel is restricted to animals in contact with one another. Other than that restriction, however, the potential variability of signals is very great, from simple contact to elaborate dances, especially favorable for analog-type codes. Tactile signals are used chiefly in courtship and mating, but a notable exception is the remarkable guidance system of honeybees, involving so-called dances. We may recognize three categories of tactile signals, employing (1) touching, bumping, and so forth, (2) vibration, and (3) so-called dancing.

Touching, bumping, and the like, in some form, are found throughout almost the whole animal kingdom as a part of courtship and mating. Even in man, the language of love is often tactile. Most other mammals likewise rub, stroke, or lick sexual partners. Even porpoises and whales nuzzle their mates. Conversely, ritualized fighting often takes the form of pushing and bumping. Similarly, in birds, mutual preening or solicitation of preening is an important part of courtship rituals. Allowing oneself to be preened or fed signifies suppression of aggression, and thus readiness for mating. It has been suggested that the dull colors and submissive postures of so-called parasitic birds, which lay their eggs in other birds' nests, turn aside the aggression that might otherwise be their lot.

Among insects, many species engage in mutual stroking· or titillation before mating. Some male insects, for instance, have special organs associated with their external genital organs that stroke the genitalia of the female in patterned fashion and cause the female organs to admit the male intromittent organ. Ants have an alarm system that is based on rapid and excited running about. Twining of mating pairs, with secretion of mucus envelopes, is usual in many species of leeches and slugs. We have already noted the love-dart of some land snails, seemingly an extreme example of tactile stimulation. From simple touching or stroking to puncturing, the sexual behavior of animals is permeated with tactile signals.

Vibration of a substrate is much less common as a signaling means than touching and bumping. As an example, we may note the warning rattle of frogs. Male frogs call in females by their breeding choruses in ponds and puddles. When the females contact the males, the males mount them. Actually, whenever anything frog-size contacts the male, he mounts it. Sometimes this is another male. In this case, the under frog vibrates his body with a warning rattle, and the upper one releases. Vibrations may be used, as are sounds, for sexual identification and courtship. Thus, in land leeches, a sexually ready animal taps the leaf on which it rests and so attracts another for mating. The most elaborate vibration signals are found in orb-web-spinning spiders. In most of these, the male is much smaller than the female, and the female attacks without hesitation any small creature that vibrates the web. It is necessary, therefore, for the male to identify himself to the female before entering the web. This he does by plucking the strands at the edge of the web in a specific rhythm. If his rhythm is correct and the female is receptive, she remains quiet—usually after a few abortive attacks—and he enters and mates with her.

Dancing is a term used for various patterns of movement and contact found in birds, insects, spiders, and so forth. So-called dances of birds, such as those of gooney birds, usually involve visual and auditory signals, but the partners do nibble each other. In scorpions, there is an elaborate mating dance involving ritualized back-and-forth movements by the partners. These seem basically to give the male a chance to pull the female across a spermatophore, which he has already deposited on the ground, allowing its hook to catch in her genital opening and thus to fertilize her.

By far the best-known and most carefully studied dances of animals are those of honeybees, discovered by von Frisch.[8; 9] These are used by scout bees to convey to their hive-mates information about food sources or suitable places for hive construction. We shall summarize only very, very briefly the impressive body of data that von Frisch and his students have accumulated about these dances.

If a scout bee has found food within about 50 meters of the hive, she performs a round-dance on the comb. In this, the bee runs excitedly to and fro in a circular pattern, bumping into other bees. This movement conveys the information that the food source is close. The degree of persistence and excitement gives information about the quality and quantity of the source, and the odor on the bee's body identifies the flower source. If the food has no odor itself (e.g., if it is an experimental food dish), the bee deposits its own odor on it. Thus informed, other workers can easily find the food by systematic coverage of a relatively small area.

If the food is at a greater distance, the scout performs a waggle-dance. In this, the bee runs for a short distance in a straight line, waggling the abdomen, then in a circle right or left, back to the starting point, after which she repeats the straight run, then around on the other side to start, and so on. The nature of the dance informs the bees that the distance is greater than about 50 meters. The exact distance to the food is indicated by the duration of the waggle run, and possibly by other items which vary simultaneously. The direction to the source is indicated by the direction of the straight run on the comb—directly upward indicating directly toward the sun, directly downward away, and angles between appropriate angles right and left. As before, the vigor and persistence indicate quality and quantity, and odors are used as markers.

This elaborate system is still being subjected to detailed analysis by von Frisch and his students [9; 16] and has been analyzed, in a preliminary fashion, using methods developed for communication systems of man. As the studies proceed, the complexity of this system is being unfolded, and data being obtained on inaccuracies and differences among strains of honeybees may soon lead to a full theoretical analysis. It is, without doubt, one of the most fascinating and highly developed communication systems in the animal kingdom, rivaling in complexity that of primitive peoples.

Visual

To so visually oriented an animal as man, this might seem to be the channel of choice. Actually, for animals in general, it is of restricted use, for the visual apparatus needed to receive coded light messages is found only in cephalopod mollusks, higher arthropods, and vertebrates. Visual signals, unlike tactile, can operate at a distance, but generally not a great distance. They are particularly suited for a digital type of code, unless highly developed eyes are present, and allow considerable variability and control. In short, where the proper receptors are present, visual signals become of great importance for close-range signaling. We may recognize three categories of visual signals, employing: (1) variations in body shape or color, (2) body postures and movements, and (3) production of light (luminescence).

Body shapes and colors of animals are usually so characteristic of species that taxonomists use them routinely for identification. In many species, males and females are differently colored, thus allowing visual discrimination of sex. Where animals have well-developed eyes, these clues to identity and sex form important parts of the social and sexual patterns. Thus, many mammals, most birds, many reptiles and salamanders, and most fish, display characteristic body patterns or colors in some phases of courtship or social relations. An interesting case of use of body-color pattern for sexual communication is found in certain fish that hold the developing eggs in the mouth for incubation. In these, the female takes the eggs into her mouth after she has deposited them outside. While she is picking up the eggs, the male, who has egg-shaped spots on his body near his cloacal opening, displays these near her. As she picks at them, he discharges sperm into her mouth, fertilizing the eggs. It is quite possible that some insects identify mates by body shape or color, but this has been little studied. It is known that certain crabs can identify the general form of the body of mates and react to this. The cuttlefish *Sepia* and some octopods can change color patterns rapidly, and males thus display special patterns to females in courtship.

Postures and movements add further variables to shape and size and, where eyes are well developed, form an important, and so far too little studied, facet of communication. We are most familiar with facial expression in man and other mammals, reflecting aggression or submission. These are matched by aggressive and sexual displays, usually involving intention movements—that is, movements adumbrating the actual activities —such as baring the teeth, displaying claws, or preliminary sexual movements. Alarm may also be communicated by special gaits or movements. Facial expression in birds is, to our eyes, rather limited. However, birds have many other visual signals, such as wing flashing, display of brightly colored tail feathers, and threat postures. In most birds, much of courtship, which can be very elaborate, involves displays of brightly colored areas or adoption of submissive or aggressive postures. In sea gulls, a typical pattern of flight over a source of food signals the presence of this to others. Many reptiles, likewise, use display in their courtship or defense of territory. The displays of male fish, often, as in sticklebacks, induced by the body pattern of the female, involve special postures and displays of bright areas by fin flashing. Male Siamese fighting fish, likewise, spread their brilliantly colored fins at the appearance of another male—a threat gesture—or at the appearance of a female—a courtship gesture.

Among invertebrates, visual displays are found only in those with well-developed eyes—insects, spiders, crabs, and a few mollusks. Male butterflies of some species have on their front wings striking flash patterns. When a male or female of the species appears, the wings are flicked apart, revealing the telltale markings. The wings thus act as semaphores, identifiying species and sex. Male jumping spiders and other hunting spiders with good eyes may use their eyes for signaling by moving a reflecting layer, the tapetum, back and forth, causing the eyes to flash. They also assume special postures and make patterned movements with their legs. In some male wolf spiders, as the front legs are held aloft before the female the internal pressure is increased causing the hairs on the legs to be erected in a brushlike fashion. These movements are usually rhythmic, and so are often called dances. Similarly, males of many species of crabs, such as fiddler crabs, display their large claws, usually by waving them in rhythmic patterns. These movements may be accompanied by sounds, as the appendages are thumped against the ground.

Luminescence requires a highly specialized system for production of cold light. This has been intensively studied by physiologists and biochemists, mostly because of interest in the phenomenon itself, rather than in behavior. Luminescence is rather widespread in animals, but in most cases our knowledge of the communicative significance, if any, is meager. A wide variety of invertebrates luminesce: fireflies and many other insects, a few millipedes, many crustaceans, some mollusks, a number of marine annelids, and many lower forms, such as protozoans, ctenophores, and coelenterates. In most cases, the significance of light production is unknown. There are, of course, a number of theories—mere illumination, warning, sexual signaling, and so on. In fireflies (really beetles, not flies) the males are generally winged, while the females are not. The males flash, as they fly, in rhythms characteristic of each species, and the females answer, often at set intervals of time after the male's flash. Thus, the sexes identify themselves and set up a mutual-attraction system. Luminescence could be involved in communication of other animals, particularly in ocean depths or open terrestrial areas, for signaling at considerable distances. How much this advantage has been exploited, if at all, is for future work to determine.

Chemical

Chemical signals, chiefly odors in terrestrial animals and similar substances in aquatic forms, are characterized by persistence and action at a distance. While many chemicals are quite evanescent, most dissipate slowly and so preclude rapid changes of temporal patterns. They are usually used as markers, rather than off-on signals. These have been given a special name, *pheromones,* by some biologists, chiefly those studying insects.[10; 11] The similarity of this word to the word *hormone* is intentional, supposedly indicating a similarity in mechanism of action. This seems, however, more an analogy than a homology. Chemical signals may not be pure chemical compounds, or they may act only with other signals.

Their supposed targetlike actions are not unique, for other communication signals may bring about the same results. For instance, the effects of chemical signals on development of sexual maturity or activity is emphasized by the originators of the term to justify a hormonelike designation. Yet, in many animals, visual or acoustical contacts, without odors, produce exactly the same effects. While the coining of the name gives a convenient term, and probably has led to some extra research, its use has also suggested a special character for these materials that is unwarranted. If an international single term shorter than *chemical communication signal* is desired, it would seem preferable to base it on a general root, such as *semant* (from the Greek, a signal) to which prefixes, such as chemo-, phono-, and photo-, could be attached. This usage would not suggest a separation of chemical signals from other types of signals which have the same effects, and it would avoid the almost certainly spurious suggestion of homology with hormones that the word *pheromone* suggests. We may recognize two categories of chemical signals, those employing: (1) body odors, and (2) special chemicals produced by glands.

Body odors for identification of species or sex are common among mammals, possibly fish and salamanders, and many invertebrates, particularly insects. In all of these cases, there is no sharp distinction possible between these and specially produced odors, for most body odors are glandularly produced. However, we can distinguish between the constant odor of the body of an animal and special odors produced only occasionally at certain spots on the body. In mammals, use of body odor for identification, particularly of species and in parent-young identification, is general. Ants and bees acquire the odor of the nest or hive, and this serves as a password. An individual without the colony odor is rejected, and one with the odor, even though of a foreign species, is accepted. Barnacles form aggregations consisting of only one species, apparently brought together by chemical signals released from settled individuals. Similar aggregations are formed by other aquatic invertebrates, presumably mediated by chemicals given off by the animals. Wolf spiders, which are wandering species, as the name suggests, have good eyes and their visual courtship we have already mentioned. They are, however, ordinarily as solitary as possible. Males locate females by following the silken draglines that the females lay down as they walk about. The males can, with receptors on their feet, detect the species and sex of the individual that laid down the dragline, even the direction taken, much as a dog can detect recent from older tracks. When the male has found the female by following her dragline and has placed himself in her view, he begins courtship posturing to identify himself to her.

Special chemicals produced by glands in the skin are widespread among animals. Perhaps all animals have them, and where unknown they merely need to be discovered. Among mammals, many have alarm scents or sexual odors produced by special glands, usually near the genital organs, or scents used for marking territories. Sometimes urine is used by mammals, as in dogs, as a territorial marker. Certain salamanders, when sexually ready, give off chemicals into the water that identify them to other members of the species. These animals may use their bodies or tails to stir the water and thus carry the chemical to the other individual. Some fish, when injured, give off a material from the skin, called *Schreckstoff*, a warning and alarming substance. It has been shown that release of this material into the water by marine fish attracts sharks, an interesting example of a little-studied facet of communication: the detection or deception of one species by another through communication signals.

Among invertebrates, chemical signaling systems are common, and are best studied by far among insects.[3; 8; 9; 10; 11; 12; 22] Of particular interest are the materials, usually secreted by females, that attract sexual partners. The high interest here arises from the possibility that these might be used for insect control. These sexual odors are surprisingly effective. Male moths have been attracted from distances up to five miles downwind. One investigator reports that a glass vial which had contained two female *Plodia* (cereal-infesting moths) for only four minutes still excited courtship behavior in males after lying open for two days. Some of these insect sex attractants have been prepared in pure form, and their chemical structure is known. Female silkworm moths give off an attractant (hexadecadiene $(10, 12)$-ol-1) which is still active in inducing male reactions when presented to them on a glass rod dipped in a solution containing 10^{-10} micrograms per milliliter. These facts well illustrate the persistence and carrying power of odors. There are many other examples of chemical use for communication by insects—alarm odors of ants and bees, marking odors of male bumblebees, guidance odors of ants and bees that are used to produce scent trails for cohorts, to mention a few.

Acoustical

As with visual signals, acoustical signals require the presence of rather specialized receptors. They are excellent for distances, easy to control for production of pulses and other time-related patterns, and offering almost infinite variability. Because specialized phonoreceptors are present only in vertebrates and insects, acoustical communication systems are practically limited to these, but in these groups they are second to none in importance. We may recognize three categories of acoustical signals, those employing: (1) incidental sounds, (2) stridulatory or other mechanically produced sounds, and (3) vocal sounds.

Incidental sounds are those that accompany activities other than special sound production. Thus, birds and insects cannot fly without wing sounds, large animals cannot walk without footfalls, fish cannot swim without swishing. In many cases, these sounds are merely incidental, or even accidental, and have no communicatory significance, but in others they are included in signaling systems. Two examples will suffice. In some birds, the whirring noise of the wings, as the animals fly up suddenly, is an alarm signal, causing other birds also to fly away. In mosquitoes, the flight sound of the female attracts males and induces mating. In the latter case, males can be induced to come to a tuning fork emitting a frequency of sound like that of the female's flight. The receptors are bulblike organs at the bases of the antennae, the Johnston's Organs, whose reactive characteristics are quite different from those of human ears. Some attempts by biologists to induce reactions in male mosquitoes have failed because the size relation of the sound projector was inappropriate. A female mosquito is small, and her wings produce sound fields with characteristic intensity patterns and wave forms. The male's receptors enable him to detect these, so the sound projector must approximate them. These facts illustrate the problems one may encounter in making adequate dummies for behavioral tests.

Stridulatory sounds are produced by drawing a toothlike structure over a filelike structure. These are produced by some fish and most grasshoppers and crickets. Other mechanically produced sounds are those made by: drumming in grouse and some grasshoppers; snapping the beak in birds; rattling or tail-swishing in reptiles; vibrating the air bladder in fish; thumping the ground in crabs, insects, and spiders; snapping tymbal-like areas of the body wall in cicadas. Together, stridulation and other mechanical methods of sound production comprise the largest and most varied group of acoustical signal-producing mechanisms in the animal kingdom. We can discuss only a few examples.

Grasshoppers and crickets are famous for their songs. Male short-horned grasshoppers (the familiar common grasshoppers or locusts) rub the hind legs against the wing covers, usually a set of teeth on the legs over a scraping ridge on the wing covers, producing rustling sounds. Male long-horned grasshoppers (often called katydids) and crickets have a file and tooth on the forewings and rub these together, producing generally musical tones, in some cases almost completely ultrasonic. Katydids may have highly specialized areas on the wings near the stridulatory apparatus, creating special acoustical conditions. All of these produce specific, temporally patterned sequences—their songs. The ordinary—or calling—song of the males attracts the females, which are variously tuned to the song (tuned receptors, receptors acting as filters, or specific behavior patterns). However, the males can produce other songs—rival's song if a male appears, mating song during copulation, warning notes, departing song when jumping but not in haste, and so forth. For one species of European grasshopper, 14 songs, separable in sound to man and in behavioral accompaniments, have been cataloged. For about 60 European species over 400 different songs have been found. The vocabulary is fairly large.

There have been many studies on insect sounds. In 1960 [5] we listed about 1,800 papers, and since then at least 800 more have appeared. The sounds of insects afford challenging material for physicists, as well as for students of animal behavior. The temporal coding patterns are various, basically trains of pulses produced by tooth impacts. In general, the receptors are resonant with the major frequencies, where such are present, but the nerve impulses finally produced are synchronous with the pulses. So the parameter most noted by man—frequency—is of little direct informational significance to the insects. Again, use of equipment for recording the projecting sounds—equipment that is almost always designed primarily for human speech and music—may give deceptive results, or none at all. For instance, in a European study, broadcasts of recorded grasshopper sounds through an ordinary loudspeaker were ineffective in inducing responses in females. It was necessary to use a special, corona-type speaker, with no inertia, so that the sounds could be sharply enough pulsed.

One factor of the environment affecting insect songs that has attracted considerable attention is temperature. Since insects have approximately the same temperature as the environment and singing is muscular, the chirp-rate is faster at higher temperatures than at lower. The exact nature of the relationship is still uncertain. This could create a problem for females, for their responses are to the temporal patterns of the songs. Actually their responses also vary with temperature, such that they respond to the rate appropriate for their body temperature. Experimentally, females at, let us say, 15 degrees Centigrade will not respond to the male song at 25 degrees Centigrade. In nature, of course, no such situation ordinarily arises.

Cicadas produce sounds by snapping areas of the body wall in and out, much as one can snap the bottom of a tin can. Each snap produces a pulse of sound. The frequency of snapping ranges from about 100 to 500 times per second, thus fusing the snaps for the human ear. The muscle driving this device is, like the flight muscles of insects, a special type, requiring only occasional neural feed-in to keep going at its own rate, determined by its innate rate and the constraints placed upon it by the tymbal. The muscle snaps the tymbal in, thus releasing tension on the muscle, causing it to relax, after which, as the tymbal snaps out, the muscle is again put under tension and again contracts. Nerve impulses are needed merely to start the train; once going, only occasional impulses keep it going until stopped. It is remarkable what a variety of sound patterns can be produced by so simple a device. Again the males sing, and the females are attracted; and there are other than the calling songs, too, such as protest notes.

These are the best-known insect musicians, but many others produce stridulatory sounds. Many beetles have ridges on the thorax against which they rub the wing covers, producing sounds that seem primarily to repel predators, but they may also be used in mating. Many species of ants and termites produce squeaks by rubbing together specialized areas of the abdomen and thorax. The significance of these sounds is unknown, but they are suspected of being used as alarm calls. Many insects can produce high-pitched buzzing sounds by vibrating the thorax with the wings closed. The best studied of these are the piping sounds of queen honeybees. All bees can produce sounds like these, and recent work makes it seem quite possible that the sounds produced by scout bees during the waggle run are the informational parameter rather than the more easily noted rates of turning. The queen pipes when another queen is present in the colony, or when a new queen is about ready to emerge. This seems to be a challenge to the new queen, and usually the new queen answers and a fight may ensue, or one queen may be driven away with part of the colony. Piping is equivalent to a territorial marker for the queen, therefore. Bees do not have ears and apparently receive the sounds as vibrations through the hive via their excellently developed subgenual organs—strands of tension-sensitive neurons extending across the leg joint and picking up the slightest movement of exoskeleton.

Vocal sounds are those produced, as in man, by passage of air over or through vibrating or resonating structures. Except for one case in insects —a moth that produces sound by driving air over a vibrating membrane near the mouth—voiced sounds are restricted to terrestrial vertebrates. The most studied are those of mammals and birds, and their use in communication in these groups is well known.

The singing of frogs and toads, produced by vibration of bladderlike parts of the mouth cavity, has likewise been noted from antiquity. The male sings, an almost universal situation among animals with acoustical communication systems. The songs are temporally structured, generally quite specific. While it has long been assumed that male choruses of frogs and toads in ponds on spring evenings call in females, it has only been recently that direct proof, through recordings, has been obtained. Besides the calling songs, frogs and toads also have various other notes, including warning and protest notes.

The variety of sounds produced by mammals has been appreciated by man as a "language" since earliest times. With the mobile lips and tongue of most mammals, the wonder is that these systems have not been much more highly developed. Considering the complex systems found in some insects with ridiculously simple sound-producing equipment, the paucity of separable acoustical signals produced by, let us say, dogs or cattle, is noteworthy. Perhaps the strong dependence of mammals upon smell or vision, and the fact that so many species are hunted or hunt, make sounds less valuable, for sounds tend, once released, to carry, and their origin is easily determined. The primates form something of an exception to this, for even in monkeys there is a variety of communicative acoustical signals. And man has taken advantage of the lips and tongue to develop subtle languages.

The songs and calls of birds have likewise attracted attention, even from nonscientists, since earliest times. The variety of sounds and the many patterns of songs of birds almost immediately suggest that they represent a protomusic; much of the earlier writing was in this vein. Actually the songs of male birds are territorial markers and signals to the females. Thus they correspond with the ordinary songs of male crickets and grasshoppers. The song gives notification of territory, identification of species (for the song of each species is usually distinct), identification of sex (for only the males sing), and in breeding season notification of readiness to mate. This is far from being mere music. Bird songs are probably the most studied of all animal sounds, but still much remains to be learned.

Generally the timbre and temporal pattern are the distinctive features of a bird's song. Some birds seem to have the song mostly innate, and even if raised in solitude sing like other males of the species; they do not try to imitate others that they hear. Other birds seemingly inherit only the general vocal structures and the patterns of the song. If raised in isolation, the males sing only a skeleton song. As soon as they can hear other males, they imitate them and ultimately build their own individual patterns as a sort of pastiche. Some, such as mockingbirds, carry this to great lengths, and the so-called talking birds, such as parrots and mynahs, mimic human sounds. In cases where young males learn the distinctive features of their songs from other males, generally their father, the way is open for development of local dialects, and a number of cases of these have been discovered—in meadowlarks, song sparrows, chaffinches, etc.

Far less studied have been the calls, or call notes of birds. These are generally short, often not at all musical in quality to us. Yet they are much more important in the daily lives of birds than are the territorial songs. Too few birds have been studied for generalizations to be very useful. Thorpe [29] lists 17 classes of call notes, based on reactions to these, including alarm, distress, and food-begging. Except for domestic chickens, there has not been any detailed study of acoustical systems in parent-young relations in birds, a most fruitful area, it would seem. Generally, parents and young are quite silent when humans are visible nearby, even, it would seem, when the observers consider themselves to be unobserved. However, if a microphone is concealed near a nest, with wires leading to a distant tape recorder, it quickly reveals to a listener the great variety of sounds of very low intensity that are used by both parents and young in normal activities.

Generally the call notes of birds are specifically distinctive, as are the songs. They are, however, usually shorter and much more simply structured, so that similarities among species are noticeable. Thus, alarm notes tend to be short and staccato, suggesting danger even to human ears. It is, therefore, relatively easy for different species living together to learn to respond to each other's calls; this cross-reactivity has been studied, particularly in crows and gulls. At the same time, calls lend themselves, as do songs, to the development of local dialects. Thus, herring gulls in Holland do not respond to the call notes of the same species recorded in Maine. A detailed, carefully monitored study of the call notes of a single species would probably turn up at least 25 to 50 separable categories, with a tremendous range in variability and intensity. So far no such complete study has been made.

An interesting case of cross-reactivity, bird-mammal, is that of the African honey guides. These small birds feed upon beeswax, but are apparently incapable of withstanding the stings of bees to get it. Instead, when a bird has found a bee colony, it seeks out a mammal, generally a badger-like animal, the ratel, and flies over it emitting a special call which induces the ratel to follow and thus get to the bees. There the ratel tears up the nest, eats the bees and larvae, apparently little affected by the bees, and leaves the wax for the honey guide. This system has been invaded by man too; honey guides often summon human beings the same way for the same purpose. There are many examples also of mammals being alerted by alarm notes of birds, and vice versa.

The development of the tape recorder and modern high-fidelity sound-projecting equipment has made possible scientific studies of bioacoustics that are in their merest infancy. Except for the lower aquatic invertebrates, acoustical communication systems are almost universal in animals, and along with chemical systems are the most important for informational transfer at a distance.

Other Possibilities

The ability of animals to find their way about where man cannot (e.g., bats and owls in the dark), and their aggregation, dispersion, or migration without signals that are obvious to us, have led to postulation of use of channels other than those already discussed. In the case of bats, the discovery of their use of ultrasonic pulses inaudible to man to guide their nocturnal flight made an extrasensory channel unnecessary as an explanation. This type of location of obstacles and prey, using a form of sonar (echolocation), has now been found also in porpoises, sea lions, and oil birds. Some biologists consider it to be a type of autocommunication. It involves no supernormal receptive capacities, except possibly extended frequency ranges for hearing.

Electrical and magnetic fields have been postulated many times as agents in animal behavior, but generally the evidence is negative. Recently, however, it has been shown that fish produce electrical discharges and have receptors for them. These are used as means for detecting objects in the external environment through alterations by the objects of the external fields. And, recently, reactions of various animals to magnetic fields have also been reported. It is difficult to see how an animal could produce magnetic signals, but the possibility is there.

It is rather surprising that there are no reported cases of communication in thermal channels. It must be admitted that thermal changes would seem to have little virtue over other more readily controllable types. Thermal changes are hard to produce (almost impossible in water). They would have very short ranges, and they do not lend themselves to pulsed coding. It is possible that changes in body temperature in mammals during sexual excitement (the common language notes these with the term "in heat") might be involved in courtship and mating, but so far no clear-cut evidence has been presented. Pit vipers have temperature receptors of astonishing sensitivity, capable of detecting differences of as little as 0.1 degree Centigrade between external objects. These are near the mouth and enable them to strike prey accurately. Similarly, mosquitoes respond to the heat given off by their hosts, and moths seem to respond to infrared emanations of food plants. But these cases would not represent communication in the usual sense. However, the generality of temperature sensitivity among animals and the existence of specialized thermoreceptors in many groups suggest that this channel for communication may be exploited too.

As for suggestions that animals communicate by a type of extrasensory perception, little can be said. Since ESP in man is not accepted by many scientists, and its presence in animals would be many times more difficult (if not impossible) to demonstrate, prudence dictates, for animals, the assumption of communication in channels whose presence is known.

Multichannel Communication

Most communication in animals involves more than one channel simultaneously. This is the familiar principle of redundancy, insuring signal transmission. We can mention just a few cases.

In most mammals, courtship is fairly elaborate, involving a number of communication systems. Odors and sometimes accompanying sounds are usual as distance attractants, bringing the sexes together and carrying information about the species, location, and sexual state. When the individuals are near each other, confirmation of identification involves at least specific odors and body forms or color patterns. This is usually facilitated by postures and movements: caressing, licking, or nuzzling and bumping, as well as by special sounds. If the possibility of detection of the "heat" of the female is included, it is obvious that the preparation for mating in this case takes advantage of all channels for communication.

Insect courtship is similar but by no means simpler. Attraction of the sexes usually comes about through chemical or acoustical signals, in the first case with the female usually as sender, in the second the male. Since all insects have body odors, it is quite possible that, even when sounds are produced, odors are important. When the presumptive partners are near each other, courtship may turn to visual signals, to other chemical and acoustical signals, or to a variety of tactile signals. In crickets, for example, males call the females in with a specific song. When the male and female are near each other, the male song changes; identification apparently involves both song and vision. In some singing grasshoppers, the system changes at this point from song to vibration of the plant on which the animals stand. The female tree-cricket approaches the male from behind (in many species of singing insects the pattern of the sound field, produced by erection of the wings or by sound reflectors, guides her), and feeds from a gland on his thorax. While she is thus engaged, the male, aided by tactile exciters, achieves copulation.

Courtship, of course, is not the only complicated signaling system in insects. We need only mention the guidance signals of honeybees, involving, as we have seen, chemical markers (primitive bees,[16] unlike honeybees, use only scent trails to guide their hive-mates), tactile stimuli, and possibly acoustical signals. The operant stimulus pattern transmitted by the dance of the scout through direction on the comb is the pattern of ultraviolet polarized light of the sky. All usual sensory channels are thus involved.

Another example of multiple-channel use is the alarm complex of many birds. Our knowledge of this is really quite fragmentary, but the indications are that every channel, except possibly chemical (and this has been suggested for starlings) is used. The simplest alarm signal is often sudden silent flight from a group. If one bird departs precipitously, the others do too. While this may be mostly visual, often accentuated by flashing of white wing bars or tail feathers, the whirring of the wings in this maneuver is also important. Other visual alarm signals involve a series of body postures communicating varying degrees of alarm. There are almost invariably also alarm notes, emitted generally when a bird, itself safely in a tree or in the air, sees approaching danger. The alarm calls of a species may be various, different for ground predators and for aerial predators. And finally there is often a type of call (the assembly or mobbing call) given when a bird sights a cat, owl, or hawk, which induces others to fly in and mob the predator. And these are not all. In crows and possibly gulls, as in some grasshoppers, there seems to be a call whose absence denotes alarm —the departing call. This is of low intensity, given by an individual that is leaving the flock without alarm. It serves to maintain the status quo, and is therefore hard to test for. If a bird flies away suddenly without giving this call, the others leave too. This is an example of absence of a signal communicating information. In essence, the queen substance of honeybees does the same; its absence signifies absence of the queen. Almost always, however, such signals are part of a complex of overlapping, multichannel communication systems.

EVOLUTIONARY SIGNIFICANCE OF COMMUNICATION

For most biologists, the key to speciation in animal evolution is isolation, allowing the development of separate gene pools in isolated populations originally the same species. For instance, two populations of a species—one on a continent, the other on an island separated so far from the continent that cross-breeding is impossible—gradually accumulate different mutations. Since the conditions of life are also different, variations within the populations have different survival values, and so different genes are favored. Gradually, the gene pools of these two populations diverge, until, at some point, even if individuals from the two populations come together, they are no longer able to produce viable offspring; they are two species.

It is obvious to all biologists that geographic isolation is effective in producing speciation in this way. But what about other types of isolation? If these are strict enough to absolutely prevent sharing of genes, they should function also. Many students of animal communication believe that differences in identification signals may be sufficient to keep populations of the same species from interbreeding, even though they live at the same place. We might imagine that the first evidence of differences within a once monospecific population could be what we have called *dialects:* small differences in signals which only some members of the population produce and to which only some react. Gradual intensification of the differences could occur through genetic changes or, in animals such as birds and mammals, through "inheritance" of learned traditions, as in song patterns learned by offspring from parents. Finally, the differences would become great enough that members of the two groups could not "recognize" each other as of the same species. At this point, even if they occupy the same geographic locality, they no longer share genetic material and are essentially isolated. From there the path to separateness of species is the same as in the case of geographic isolation.

Since behavior patterns are generally much more labile than morphological characters, any population of animals has many variants already present. In the case of a signaling system such as that of crickets, for instance, the individual males differ in rate, tonality, number of pulses, and so forth. If one works with a group of grasshoppers or crickets, recording their songs and later playing them over and over for study, he finds that he can identify each by the individuality of its song—slight elisions or extensions, various degrees of time regularity, subtle variation in tonality, and the like. Similarly, females vary in response to different aspects of the song. This could very well mean that the first steps toward speciation are taken when the signals of the sender deviate far enough from the norm that only correspondingly deviant receivers respond, gradually fixing the difference genetically and so creating the situation postulated for behavioral isolation. There is evidence of this now in crickets, frogs, and some birds. This matter is of such importance to zoologists that we can confidently expect much future work on such matters as the nature of signal variations, the inheritance of signal patterns, and the inheritance of and learning of behavioral responses.

PRACTICAL VALUES IN STUDIES OF ANIMAL COMMUNICATION

We might say just a word, finally, on possible practical (that is, anthropocentrically valuable) aspects of these studies.

The first use of communication signals for economic purposes was in pest control. At present, the most extensive use is probably of insect sexual odors (pheromones) to attract pests to their death.[10; 11] Male gypsy moths, for example, are attracted by the scent of females and can be trapped and killed. So far, attempts to use sounds produced by insects— with the possible exception of those produced by mosquitoes—have not been successful.[4; 6]

Since the discovery in 1954 that starlings could be driven from roosts by broadcasting recordings of their distress call, acoustical controls for birds using communication signals have been slowly evolving. At present, starlings, sparrows, crows, gulls, and a few other species of birds are being kept from places where they are not desired by broadcasts of their alarm or distress calls. The development has been somewhat impeded by misunderstanding of the actions of the signals, even by some scientists. It is not enough just to broadcast a call, no matter how effective, to control a pest bird. Similarly, the synthesis of a drug or insecticide, no matter how potent, does not automatically insure disease or pest control. The discovery of acoustical signals that influence bird behavior represents only a beginning. One must know the ecology and behavior, at least, of the pest birds before he can decide upon times and durations of broadcasts, placement of speakers, and other such considerations. Furthermore, the broadcast sounds must be "understandable" to the birds, which means consideration of acoustical and electronic aspects. These are often foreign to biologists. The biological aspects often seem unimportant to acousticians or electronics specialists. So the scene is set for attempts at acoustical control to fail through lack of appreciation of acoustical problems by one group, or of the subtlety of animal social life by the other. At present, in France and Germany, teams of workers are attacking the problems, and effective controls are being developed. In the United States progress has been slow, but there is increasing interest, for usually killing birds, even when they are pests, is considered undesirable, and alternative methods of control are not fully effective.

Studies on animal communication should also increase our knowledge of communication in general and may thus lead to better understanding or an extension of human means of communication. As an example, for the blind we doubly transform the spoken work, first to ordinary writing, then to a derived tactile system. But why? Why not a direct transformation of acoustical to tactile signals, taking full advantage of the special characteristics of the latter?

So far, studies on animal communication have led to few generalizations, and attempts at theoretical analysis have invariably started with ideas derived from studies on man, rather than the other way around. No doubt the diversity of animal communication systems has made it difficult to derive generalizations, and the tendency of zoologists to study only one group of animals has also contributed. As research proceeds, however, generalizations derived from studies on animals themselves and valid for all species should be formulated. A deepened understanding of human communication may be possible. Arguments over whether or not animals have language will then be seen to have no relevance, for the differences and similarities between human and animal communication will be obvious.

REFERENCES AND SUGGESTED READINGS

1. Armstrong, E. A., *A Study of Bird Song.* London: Oxford University Press, 1963.
2. Busnel, R. G., ed., *Acoustic Behavior of Animals.* Amsterdam: Elsevier, 1963.
3. Butler, C. G., *The World of the Honeybee.* London: Collins, 1954.
4. Frings, H., and M. Frings, "Uses of Sounds by Insects," *Annual Review of Entomology,* Vol. 3, 1958.
5. Frings, M., and H. Frings, *Sound Production and Sound Reception by Insects— A Bibliography.* University Park: Pennsylvania State University Press, 1960.
6. Frings, H., and M. Frings, "Pest Control with Sound," Parts I and II, *Sound,* Vols. 1 and 2, 1962–1963.
7. Frings, H., and M. Frings, *Animal Communication.* New York: Blaisdell, 1964.
8. Frisch, Von, K., *Bees—Their Vision, Chemical Senses, and Language.* Ithaca, N.Y.: Cornell University Press, 1950.

9. Frisch, Von, K., *The Dance Language and Orientation of Bees,* trans. by L. Chadwick. Cambridge, Mass.: Harvard University Press, 1967.

10. Jacobson, M., *Insect Sex Attractants.* New York: Wiley-Interscience, 1965.

11. Jacobson, M., "Chemical Insect Attractants and Repellents," *Annual Review of Entomology,* Vol. 11, 1966.

12. Johnston, J. W., Jr., D. G. Moulton, and A. Turk, *Advances in Chemoreception,* Vol. 1, *Communication by Chemical Signals.* New York: Appleton-Century-Crofts, 1970.

13. Kainz, F., *Die "Sprache" der Tiere.* Stuttgart: Ferdin and Enke Verlag, 1961.

14. Klopfer, P. H., *Behavioral Ecology.* Belmont, Calif.: Dickenson, 1970.

15. Lanyon, W. E., and W. M. Tavolga, eds., *Animal Sounds and Communication.* Washington, D.C.: American Institute of Biological Sciences, 1960.

16. Lindauer, M., *Communication Among Social Bees.* Cambridge, Mass.: Harvard University Press, 1961.

17. Marler, P., "Developments in the Study of Animal Communication," in *Darwin's Biological Work: Some Aspects Reconsidered,* ed. by P. R. Bell *et al.,* Cambridge, England: Cambridge University Press, 1959.

18. Marler, P., "The Logical Analysis of Animal Communication," *Journal of Theoretical Biology,* Vol. 1, 1961.

19. Marler, P., and W. J. Hamilton, III, *Mechanisms of Animal Behavior.* New York: Wiley, 1966.

20. Moulton, J. M., "Underwater Sound: Biological Aspects," *Oceanography Marine Biology Annual Review,* Vol. 2, 1964.

21. Reese, E. A., "Ethology and Marine Zoology," *Oceanography Marine Biology Annual Review,* Vol. 2, 1964.

22. Ribbands, C. R., *The Behaviour and Social Life of Honey-bees.* London: Bee Research Association, Ltd., 1953.

23. Roe, A., and G. G. Simpson, eds., *Behavior and Evolution.* New Haven, Conn.: Yale University Press, 1958.

24. Sebeok, T. A., "Animal Communication," *Science,* Vol. 147, 1965.

25. Sebeok, T. A., *Animal Communication: Techniques of Study and Results of Research.* Bloomington: Indiana University Press, 1968.

26. Sebeok, T. A., and A. Ramsay, *Approaches to Animal Communication.* The Hague: Mouton, 1969.

27. Tavolga, W. N., ed., *Marine Bio-acoustics.* New York: Pergamon Press, 1964.

28. Tembrock, G., *Tierstimmen: Eine Einführung in die Bioakustik.* Wittenberg Lutherstadt: A. Ziemsen Verlag, 1959.

29. Thorpe, W. H., *Bird Song.* Cambridge, England: Cambridge University Press, 1961.

30. Thorpe, W. H., and O. L. Zangwill, eds., *Current Problems in Animal Behaviour.* Cambridge, England: Cambridge University Press, 1961.

31. Tinbergen, N., *The Study of Instinct.* Oxford: Clarendon, 1952.

32. Tinbergen, N., *Social Behaviour in Animals, with Special Reference to Vertebrates.* London: Methuen, 1953.

3

Anthropology

ALFRED G. SMITH

To all approaches there are approaches in turn. Even the anthropological approach to communication is not a first step. Rather, let us step into the stream with a conception of anthropology itself, a conception specific to the needs of studying human communication.

A STUDY OF HUMAN RESPONSES

When author James A. Michener was trying to understand the people of Spain, he had to learn the significance of the phrase *"Viva yo."* He recalled that "some time ago there was a competition for the cartoon which best expressed the Spanish character, and the winner, without a close second, was one showing an arrogant little boy urinating in the middle of the street and spelling out the words *'Viva yo,'* which could be translated as 'Hurray for me,' except that the guts of the phrase is implied in the second half, 'and to hell with everyone else.' A comprehension of the Spaniard's addiction to *viva yo* will help anyone trying to make his way in Spain. When the little car barrels right down the middle of the highway, forcing everyone else into the ditch, you don't swear at the driver. You say *'Viva yo'* and you understand what happened and why." [28, pp. 56–57]

But suppose one tries to make his way not in Spain but in Japan? The self-assertive *"Viva yo"* is quite different from the Japanese concept of *enryo*. This concept, according to anthropologists Bennett, Passin, and McKnight, is "loosely translatable as 'hesitance' or 'reserve.'" [6, p. 230] It is part of the traditional Japanese way of showing respect to superiors, submitting to social proprieties, controlling oneself, and maintaining a behavioral reserve. The traditional Japanese used the concept of *enryo* particularly when duties and relationships were unclear.

Thus the 'shyness' [of the Japanese student] or reserved behavior often found on the American campus can be due either in the fact that the Japanese views Americans, or certain Americans, as superior people; or to the fact that he is simply not sure how to behave in American social situations, regardless of status." [6, p. 231]

Viva yo and *enryo* represent two different ways of making one's way, and not necessarily differences between Spaniards and Japanese. Many Japanese urinate in the street, and many Spaniards are reserved. These are not necessarily national or group differences, nor are they differences between people who are self-assertive and those who are submissive. All people are a mixture of both. Different ways of making one's way are simply different responses.

There are a thousand and one responses to human circumstances. Neanderthal man made physical responses; sometimes his molars were ground down by his rough diet, and from that it can be inferred that his bowels must also have responded to that diet. Many North American Indians responded to a grievance by committing suicide as a form of revenge. In every period of human history and in every region of the earth, man has responded biologically and socially to the environment he lived in. Some men have toughened their intestines, some have bowed humbly, and others have marched in protest.

The male responds if a blond he admires bats her eyelashes at him. An American responds when he sees Neil Armstrong stepping onto the moon. The addict responds to heroin, and both student and faculty to a confrontation on campus. Some responses, for example, that to the blond, could be immediate while others might be delayed. Some are inherited and others are learned. Some are parts of characteristic sets of responses, parts of fixed-action patterns. Like a bicycle rider on a corduroy road, man responds to stimuli from his environment in order to maintain his balance and momentum.

Anthropology is the study of these responses. To some extent this conception of anthropology is novel. It is also fruitful, and it relates anthropology more closely to the study of human communication. Anthropologists often claim that anthropology is the study of man. [17; 24] If it were the study of total man it could claim the lion's share of attention. But that claim is either an affectation or a delusion. The claim is too brash and vain, too broad and vague.

Some social scientists claim that anthropology is the study of *primitive* man. [8, p. 9] That could include monkeys and apes, Americans, Russians, and other semiprimitives. Where does one draw the line between the primitive and the advanced?

Other anthropologists claim that anthropology is the study of culture or of race. But race and culture, like man and primitive man, tend to be regarded as entities—as fixed things. The sciences, however, recognize that the specialist in each field can best study processes rather than entities. The most fruitful subject of inquiry is not things, but actions; not man nor culture, but human interaction.

Because human responses are processes, let us begin by examining anthropology as the *study* of human responses. That conception leads to the anthropological approach to communication, the subject of this chapter.

ANTHROPOLOGY AS NATURAL HISTORY

The study of human responses is valuable to man in order for him to get along with his fellowman and to understand himself. There are those who specialize in specific kinds of responses: economists who study how people respond to a rise in prices or to automation in industry; psychologists who study responses to approval, to ambiguity, or to isolation. The anthropological approach is a part of this common enterprise. What these studies hold in common far outweighs their differences, the differences being less in what is studied than in how it is studied. To illustrate: The physicist and the physiologist study the color red in quite different ways. The physicist begins by measuring wavelengths, while the physiologist dissects the rods and cones of the retina. The difference is in method and orientation. Some specialists also study human responses by measuring them. A sociologist, for example, might administer a questionnaire about drugs to a hundred sophomores and then scale their responses. Poll-taking and attitude measurement, however, are not basic methods of study by the anthropologist. Other specialists conduct experiments. A psychologist might remove part of a rat's brain to study the effect on its responses. But the conducting of experiments is not a prevalent basic method of study for the anthropologist either. He has taken an apple off another tree.

The anthropologist studies human responses by using the methods and orientations of natural history. Some anthropologists might shake their heads at this, yet the natural-history approach has been the most common among anthropologists for the last 100 years.[39, chap. 1; 10, pp. 281–289, pp. 243–259; 22, pp. 172–178] Natural history is an ancient science that studies and compares plants, rocks, and animals. It used to mean collecting and identifying caterpillars and pine cones, and it generally entailed excursions into the country. Anthropology, like natural history of old, is one of the more humane branches of science.

In various museums of natural history—such as in New York, Chicago, and San Diego—stuffed birds, preserved insects, animals, plants, and rocks are displayed either in an evolutionary order, or by means of variations and comparisons. The anthropologist observes and describes human responses in a similar way.

Contemporary natural history is more concerned with living birds and insects than with dead ones, and it is primarily concerned with their behavior. A naturalist and ethologist like Konrad Lorenz [25] observes aggressive responses among birds and other animals, and Niko Tinbergen [38] observes the male stickleback fish staking out a nesting territory and changing its colors from dull gray to red, white, and blue in order to attract the female sticklebacks in the spring. There is a gradual and natural progression from the study of responses in birds and fish to the study of human responses. For example, Stuart A. Altmann [1] spent two years on an island off the coast of Puerto Rico studying a colony of rhesus monkeys, recording their behavior. George B. Schaller [32] did the same with the mountain gorilla of Africa. In a similar way, the anthropologist is a naturalist and ethologist of human communication.

THE NATURAL CONTINUUM OF RESPONSES

Like the fish, the bird, and the monkey, man responds to his environment—physically, socially, biologically, and symbolically. One kind of response can hardly be distinguished from another. Responses do not come in different colored packages: blue for biological and brown for symbolic; green for primitive and yellow for advanced. When the little boy spells out *viva yo* in the street, that is both a physical and a social response. There is a natural continuum.

When the anthropologist studies human communication, he assumes there is unity in responses. The responses of a mountain gorilla and of a Neanderthal man, of a Spaniard and of a Japanese are first cousins to each other. It is difficult to tell, and it seldom matters, whether a response is a product of nature or of nurture, whether it is genetically inherited or learned in a library, whether it is conscious or unconscious. A man communicates as well with an involuntary blush as with a calculated speech. Thus, a natural continuum is assumed. The same methods and orientations of natural history are used to describe and compare verbal responses, body movements, spatial relations, and many other forms of communication that are even less obvious. The same methods are used in the study of monkeys and people.

The idea of a natural continuum broadens vision and, incidentally, increases tolerance. It prevents us from making sharp distinctions between the normal and the deviant, the primitive and the civilized, the emotional and the rational. The principles of behavior of a schizophrenic patient in a mental hospital are the same principles that govern the behavior of the average saleslady in a dress shop. At least there is a natural continuum of responses.

In the study of human communication, the idea of a continuum indicates that communication processes cannot be separated from other processes; it indicates that agriculture, commerce, and warfare are also forms of communication.

Consider, for example, the introduction of a money economy into a community in East Africa. It changes all the processes of communication. Such communities used to practice *lobola,* the giving of cattle by a boy's family to a girl's family as a kind of bride price. *Lobola* compensated the girl's family for the loss of her services, as she would no longer cook for them, draw water, or make pots. It also compensated them for the investment they had made in her, the equivalent of the American investment in ballet lessons, braces on the teeth, and a hope chest. *Lobola* always took the form of cattle, because these were the prized possession among East Africans.

With the introduction of a money economy, everything is changed. First, money becomes the most important medium of contact with the outside world and increases that contact. With money, anyone in the community can write to Sears Roebuck in Chicago and order anything from a refrigerator to a corset. People can buy magazines, radios, and other sources of information, thus enlarging the world to which they respond.

Second, money changes responses in the local world of the community. Suppose a father refuses to give cattle for his son's bride. Perhaps he does not approve of the girl, or wants his boy to marry into another family, or wants the boy to keep working only for him. With the introduction of a money economy, the boy can go off and get a job, perhaps in the mines or on a plantation, and earn the money for the *lobola* cattle. Thus in a money economy, parental authority is reduced and a boy's response to his father is changed.

Responses become more impersonal. Traditionally, the boy works beside his father, erecting a new corncrib or tending a sick calf. If he goes off and gets a job, he might send a little money home each month, but that is much more impersonal than father and son building a wall together. And working for wages on a plantation also makes responses much more impersonal there. Father and son relations are replaced by employer and employee relations. There are employers and employees rather than fathers and sons.

Third, money becomes the covert common denominator for all things. Goods and services that used to be unmeasurable and incommensurable, such as a cow, a family heirloom, and a day's work, can all be evaluated in shillings. And in a money economy, a man can hide all his wealth in a sock under his mattress, while formerly his wealth—his house, his cattle, and his other goods—was on public display. This changes the whole process of bargaining and trading. Before, one could estimate how much the bride price should be, but now it is not so easy to tell how wealthy each family is and where the bargaining should begin.

Human responses are not isolated and detached—unrelated to family or friends. When a boy sees a picture of a bicycle in a mail-order catalog, his response is related to tending his father's sick calf, to the possibility of wages for labor, and to courting a girl. Communication processes are inextricably connected to all the other processes of living—to urinating in the street or to building a wall. Anthropological approaches to communication are the natural history of the continuum of human responses.

Nevertheless, some anthropologists look only for a special kind of response. Some emphasize biological responses, while others emphasize social ones. Cutting across this dichotomy is a second one: Some anthropologists emphasize the history of responses, while others emphasize comparisons among responses. These divisions yield four different kinds of anthropologists. Many biologically oriented anthropologists are concerned with man's adaptations in the course of biological evolution from a fish to a primate. Other biologically oriented anthropologists emphasize the similarities and differences among men today—differences in skin color, in hat size, and in blood type. In the same way, many socially oriented anthropologists follow a historical course of study, while others follow a comparative one. The history of social adaptations and responses is largely a matter for archaeologists. Since many ancient societies have left no written records, the anthropologist literally has to dig for his data, scavenging for potsherds in an Indian mound, his hands blistering and his back aching. And from that mound and its relics, he has to deduce how human beings responded to their environment in the past.

Cultural and social anthropologists may compare the habits of a band of Australian aborigines with those of an African tribe. The concerns of such cultural anthropologists include what different peoples know and feel and what they are anxious about. This can sometimes be deduced from language, art, folklore, and religion. Despite differences between the biological approach and the cultural approach, between historical and comparative approaches, the aim of anthropology as a whole is to understand the continuum of human responses.

WHAT ANTHROPOLOGISTS LOOK FOR

It is all very well to say that anthropologists study human responses as a part of natural history, but what do these anthrolopogists actually look for? Individual anthropologists study human communication through specific forms of responses. For example, Ray L. Birdwhistell [9] studies the use of body motion, or kinesics, in communication; Edward T. Hall [18; 19] studies spatial relations, or proxemics; Eliot D. Chapple [12; 13] has emphasized the rhythms of interaction; Ward H. Goodenough's [15] componential analysis dissects the structure of verbal categories; and Dell H. Hymes [20; 21] has related linguistics to ethnography by describing a speech community and its verbal repertoires. But what kinds of observations do these anthropologists make in general? What do they look for?

Looking for Nothing

Anthropologists look for four things. First, they look for nothing. When an anthropologist begins to dig, he does not know what he is going to find or what may be relevant or crucial in a particular case. He may find something quite different from anything yet known to man. Therefore, he expects anything—and nothing in particular.

Consider an anthropologist who specializes in the study of verbal responses and who comes across the Bimbams, a group of people who have never before been studied. Does he look for nouns and verbs, infinitives and participles in the Bimbam language? No, perhaps the Bimbams do not distinguish these parts of speech, but make other distinctions instead.

Anthropologists do not begin their observations with prepared questions or with hypotheses to be tested in the classic tradition. Such questions and hypotheses can distort the information that, say, the Bimbam may give. A preformulated hypothesis is what courtroom lawyers speak of as "leading the witness." It prejudices the testimony. And it is not in the tradition of natural history.

Ordinarily, anthropologists do not set out to prove that *lobola,* for example, is an African form of capitalism or of male chauvinism. Yet it is, of course, dangerous to look for nothing. When questions and hypotheses are not explicitly stated, they may still be there, hidden beneath the surface like the agenda of a "free and unstructured" committtee meeting or a line of questioning that unobtrusively leads the witness. The unstated hypothesis or question is the most insidious and prejudicial of all.

Therefore, paradoxically, it takes much knowledge and experience to look for nothing. Ignorance and inexperience lead us to look at other people's responses as projections of our own. If we know only Freudian psychology, everything becomes Freudian to the point of distortion. If we know only English, and only one way of analyzing the structure of English, when we encounter the Bimbam language we will be prejudiced by our ignorance. We will be unable to look for nothing.

Looking for Differences and Distinctions

The second thing anthropologists look for is differences and distinctions. The Eskimo and the Zulu build houses that are round, while the English and the Iroquois build houses that are rectangular. Human responses differ. There are differences and distinctions not only between groups, but also within groups. There are distinctions made between what is summer work and what is winter work, what is sacred and what is profane, between plebeians and patricians, and between generations. In fact, the more advanced a group is, the more differences there are within it. English-speaking groups include bus drivers, priests, captains of finance, and spot welders. In comparison, the Eskimo are undiversified as a group. An anthropologist does not want to impose a preconceived set of distinctions on his findings. He does not know what differences and distinctions he will come across, but he generally assumes that he will find some.

Basically, he believes in the self-structured field. The bases of that structure are differences and distinctions. Variations and dissimilarities lay before our eyes the structure of language, of courtship, and of all other patterns of response. In English, for example, a difference between nouns and verbs is revealed by the fact that adding an *s* to one creates a plural (hat, hats), but to the other creates a singular (sit, sits). In East Africa, there is a difference between the *lobola* for the oldest daughter and for the younger ones, which is generally revealed by the number of cattle given. The anthropologist looks for no particular structure, but he expects differences and distinctions to reveal one.

Anthropologists have generally found antitheses and binary oppositions in their studies of groups. This is particularly true today, although there is a long historical tradition behind it. Bachofen [2] noted the distinction between matrilineal and patrilineal; McLennan [26] between exogamous and endogamous; Morgan [29] consanguineal and affinal and also classificatory and descriptive; Baudouin de Courtenay [4] and Pike [30] etic and emic; van Gennep [41] rites of passage and of intensification; Bateson [3] schismogenesis or polarization of ethos; Linton [24] ascribed and achieved status; Benedict [5] continuities and discontinuities in child-training; Redfield [31] folk and urban societies; and Levi-Strauss, [23] the raw and the cooked categories in myths. These are only ten examples of the hundreds of differences and distinctions that anthropologists find in social relations, language, mythology, and other habitual responses. When they find these distinctions, they often formulate theoretical points of departure after the fact. In other words, they discover their approach after they have arrived.

Looking for Contexts

In studying the natural history of the continuum of responses, anthropologists not only look for nothing and for differences and distinctions, they also look for contexts. Benjamin Lee Whorf, a student of anthropology who also worked for a fire insurance company, found that factory workers were careful of fire hazards around gasoline drums, but around empty gasoline drums they smoked and tossed about cigarette stubs. Wrote Whorf:

> Yet the empty drums are perhaps the more dangerous, since they contain explosive 'vapor.' Physically the situation is hazardous, but the linguistic analysis according to regular analogy must employ the word 'empty,' which inevitably suggests lack of hazard. (42, p. 75)

Whorf found differences and distinctions in the workers' responses and then looked for the context of each response. He found that part of the context was simply linguistic. Looking for contexts is based on the assumption that responses are not isolated and detached, without family or friends.

Looking for contexts is a matter of seeing relationships and searching out meanings. When an anthropologist digs for arrowheads in an Indian mound, he is not interested in the arrowheads for their own sake, not according to the canons of scholarship. When an anthropologist studies the body movements of two Japanese greeting one another, he is not concerned with a singular incident. Any event, of itself, is meaningless for the anthropologist. Things have meaning only when they are related to other things. How is the arrowhead related to the technology and the economy of the Indians? How are the two Japanese related to one another, and what is the occasion of their meeting? Contexts give meanings.

An anthropologist does not look for just any context. He looks at responses in their own contexts. He does not want to *give* things a meaning, he wants to *find* a meaning within the contexts of responses. He hears a Zulu click, for example, and he relates that sound to its own context, to the other sounds of Zulu language. He does not relate it to the sound of English because that is not the click's own context. Relating Zulu to English sounds means seeing another language in terms of the linguistic differences and distinctions of English. That projects the structure of English on Zulu, and for an English-speaking anthropologist, that is a form of self-centeredness. Ethnocentrism and linguacentrism are cardinal sins for the anthropologist.

Nor does he study those responses in the context of anthropological theories and hypotheses. That, too, would distort the response; it would lead the witness. Anthropologists look for things in their own contexts, believing in the self-structured field and the self-meaning field.

In anthropology, seeing things in their own contexts is part of seeing cultures as wholes, seeing the contribution of each individual response to an entire repertory of responses. Anthropologists look for contrasts and distinctions in a repertory of responses in order to see the pattern of those responses, and that pattern becomes the context in which each of the individual responses has meaning. Some anthropologists assume that each culture has a unique system of perceiving and organizing the world, that it has a special cognitive code. [40] Some anthropologists are also concerned with emotional or affective codes and with codes of human interaction. [33] These codes are the responses' own contexts.

All scholars study things in their own contexts. In physics, that is in a sense what is called "field theory"; students of business administration call it "systems theory." Anthropologists relate each response to its own environment.

Looking for Freedom and Order

The fourth thing anthropologists look for when they study responses is freedom and order. In some situations, there are responses that *must* be made; in other situations, there are responses that *may* be made. This is a matter of redundancy and entropy, and in human communication, the two are always intertwined.

Without freedom, we would be bound to routines and traditions. We would have no choices and options. We would respond to new things in old ways, and we would not learn anything. Without order, we could not know anything. We could not know that summer follows spring. We could not know what response would be effective or appropriate in a given situation. For us, the world would be chaos.

What are the freedoms and the constraints that frame any response? To understand the Spanish boy writing out *viva yo,* the anthropologist looks for the latitude the boy has and also for his restrictions. The fashion designers of New York and Paris are in part creative and deviant and in part traditional. The anthropologist asks, "Which part is which?" When all the children in one family learn the same responses, each child's response in a given situation is still different. The anthropologist asks, "How?" This present sentence is constrained by the structure of English, yet it is a sentence that has never been made before. Every response is both redundant and entropic.

There are traditions and norms in responses, and there are also variations and changes. Anthropologists generally find order and custom where people need security and predictability in their relations. And they find that changes and variations follow relatively unchanging and invariant traditions. [27; 36]

APPLYING ANTHROPOLOGICAL APPROACHES TO COMMUNICATION

Now how useful are anthropological approaches to communication? We may just as well ask, "How useful are mathematical approaches to algebra?" An utter tautology. How appropriate is a legal approach to jurisprudence? A sheer redundancy. Like teaching fish to swim!

Anthropology and communication are not solitary islands separated by deep waters. We need no bridge to span a chasm between them, nor even stepping-stones from one to the other. To negotiate an approach there would be like breaking down doors that were already open.

Nevertheless, let us break them down by taking a second look at the main points made earlier. The first point was that anthropology is a study of human responses. Now we can also regard the study of communication as a study of human responses.

A more widespread view is that communication is the eliciting of a response.[7, p. 16; 14, p. 289] A television commercial communicates when it induces people to buy Dimple's Dumplings. But the idea of eliciting responses can present awkward problems involving the nature of purposes and intentions.

We can avoid some problems by viewing the study of communication as a study of human responses. That view is akin to Goyer's [16] operational approach and to Thayer's conception of communication as taking something into account.[37, pp. 26ff] And as we have seen, this can also be a view in anthropology. In fact, when an anthropologist is on a South Sea island, it is easier for him to see people responding to each other, to see them communicating, than it is to see their culture, their heredity, or some other hypostatized quiddity.

The second point made earlier was that anthropology studies human responses with the same methods and orientations used in studying communication. Although most communication studies also use other methods, such as experiments, some have used the relatively unstructured approach of natural history. It has been used particularly in studying monkeys and apes, but in studying human interaction as well.[34] It should be further used to compare and classify communication patterns around the world. We have anthropological classifications by kinship system, by level of energy utilization, and by language group for the Navaho, for the Nuer, and for other peoples; but we have no comparable classifications by communication type. The natural history of communication and the science of comparative communication both need to be fostered.

Third, as anthropology studies the continuum of human responses, so does communication. Instead of fragmenting the world and balkanizing our concerns by making sharp distinctions between biological, social, and humanistic responses, we can better understand them as a continuum. There are also natural continuums between graffiti and poetry, between the physical expression of human aspiration in a ballet and the mating dance of the stickleback fish. They are all well-founded and legitimate forms of communication, each significant in its own context and all part of the human spectacle.

The fourth point described what anthropologists look for. The simple empiricism of natural history and its relatively open and unstructured approach lead anthropologists to look for nothing, for differences and distinctions, for contexts, and for freedom and order. Or, in more ontological terms, they look for the self-structured and self-meaning field. Communication studies can be equally free of prestructuring and closure. When we look without anticipating what we will see, the world opens up and expands. We could see whales in the desert, languages that have no verbs, emotions that have never been known before. And when we think we see new responses, we also have to consider how we see them. When we conceive of a field as open, we emphasize the process of looking at it as much as the content at which we look. Thus Richard W. Budd has shown that the most productive study of communication is "an open learning experience." (11, p. 32)

But how relevant is any of this in a world beset by wars and galled by inequality in cities that have become uninhabitable? Anthropological approaches to communication can do more than study facts for their own sake. In at least two ways, they are relevant to the problems we face as citizens.

The questions we pose and the problems we face are largely determined by the way we look at the world. A paranoid person, for example, asks, "Why is everyone looking at me?" The person in love hopes he can give enough. Generally we try to answer questions using the same viewpoints from which these questions arose in the first place. We leave where we came in, unable to get outside of ourselves, on a treadmill leading nowhere. Anthropology, however, teaches us Hausa, Hottentot, and Hopi points of view, giving us broader perspectives in which to reorient ourselves. It gives us alternatives to our own habitual ways of looking at things, and when we are faced with problems we need to perceive alternatives. By providing a catharsis through perspective, anthropology helps resolve our daily perplexities.

Even when anthropological approaches do not solve our problems directly, they can help more generally in the long run. Botanists help us to increase the quantity of corn we can grow per acre, not by studying corn directly, but by studying photosynthesis and genetics, by uncovering basic principles that can later be applied for the betterment of corn. In the same way, anthropologists can uncover basic principles about communication that may be used for the betterment of man.

REFERENCES AND SUGGESTED READINGS

1. Altmann, Stuart A., "Sociobiology of Rhesus Monkeys," *Journal of Theoretical Biology*, Vol. 8, 1965.
2. Bachofen, Johan Jacob, *Das Mutterrecht.* Basel: Benno, Schwabe, 1861.
3. Bateson, Gregory, "Culture Contact and Schismogenesis," *Man*, Vol. 199, 1935.
4. Baudouin de Courtenay, J., *Versuch einer Theorie der phonetischen Alternationen.* Strassburg, 1895.
5. Benedict, Ruth, "Continuities and Discontinuities in Cultural Conditioning," *Psychiatry*, Vol. 1, 1938.
6. Bennett, John W., Herbert Passin, and Robert K. McKnight, *In Search of Identity: The Japanese Overseas Scholar in America and Japan.* Minneapolis: University of Minnesota Press, 1958.
7. Berlo, David K., *The Process of Communication.* New York: Holt, Rinehart and Winston, 1960.
8. Bierstedt, Robert, *The Social Order.* New York: McGraw-Hill, 1957.
9. Birdwhistell, Ray L., *Kinesics and Context.* Philadelphia: University of Pennsylvania Press, 1970.
10. Boas, Franz, *Race, Language and Culture.* New York: Macmillan, 1940.
11. Budd, Richard W., *Communication, Education and Simulation,* Institute for Communication Studies, University of Iowa, 1970, prepublication copy.
12. Chapple, Eliot D., *The Interaction Chronograph: Its Evolution and Present Application.* New York: American Management Association, 1949.
13. Chapple, Eliot D., *Culture and Biological Man.* New York: Holt, Rinehart and Winston, 1970.
14. Dance, Frank E. X., *Human Communication Theory.* New York: Holt, Rinehart and Winston, 1967.
15. Goodenough, Ward H., "Componential Analysis," *Science*, Vol. 156, 1967.
16. Goyer, Robert S., *Communication, Communicative Process, Meaning: Toward a Unified Theory,* Special Report No. 20, Center for Communication Studies, Ohio University, 1969.
17. Haddon, Alfred C., *The Study of Man.* London: Murray, 1908.
18. Hall, Edward T., "A System for the Notation of Proxemic Behavior," *American Anthropologist*, Vol. 65, 1963.
19. Hall, Edward T., *The Hidden Dimension.* Garden City, N.Y.: Doubleday, 1966.
20. Hymes, Dell H., "Introduction: Toward Ethnographies of Communication," in *The Ethnography of Communication*, ed. by John Gumperz and Dell H. Hymes; *American Anthropologist*, Vol. 66, Pt. 2, 1964, special publication of the American Anthropological Association.
21. Hymes, Dell H., "On Anthropological Linguistics and Congeners," *American Anthropologist*, Vol. 68, 1966.
22. Kroeber, Alfred L., *An Anthropologist Looks at History.* Berkeley and Los Angeles: University of California Press, 1963.
23. Levi-Strauss, Claude, *The Raw and the Cooked.* New York: Harper & Row, 1969.
24. Linton, Ralph, *The Study of Man.* New York: Appleton-Century, 1936.
25. Lorenz, Konrad, *On Aggression.* New York: Harcourt, Brace, 1966.
26. McLennan, John Ferguson, *Primitive Marriage.* Edinburgh: Adam and Charles Black, 1865.

27. Mead, Margaret, *Continuities in Cultural Evolution.* New Haven: Yale University Press, 1964.

28. Michener, James A., *Iberia.* New York: Random House, 1968.

29. Morgan, Lewis H., *Systems of Consanguinity and Affinity of the Human Family.* Washington, D.C.: Smithsonian Institution, 1870.

30. Pike, Kenneth L., *Language in Relation to a Unified Theory of the Structure of Human Behavior.* The Hague: Mouton, 1967.

31. Redfield, Robert, "The Folk Society," *American Journal of Sociology,* Vol. 52, 1947.

32. Schaller, George B., *The Mountain Gorilla: Ecology and Behavior.* Chicago: University of Chicago Press, 1963.

33. Smith, Alfred G., ed., *Communication and Culture.* New York: Holt, Rinehart and Winston, 1966.

34. Smith, Alfred G., *Communication and Status.* Eugene, Oreg.: University of Oregon, 1966.

35. Tax, Sol, Loren C. Eiseley, Irving Rouse, and Carl F. Voegelin, eds., *An Appraisal of Anthropology Today.* Chicago: University of Chicago Press, 1953.

36. Textor, Robert B., *A Cross-Culture Summary,* New Haven: Human Relations Area Files, 1966.

37. Thayer, Lee, *Communication and Communication Systems.* Homewood, Ill.: Irwin, 1968.

38. Tinbergen, Niko, "The Curious Behavior of the Stickleback," *Scientific American,* Vol. 187, 1952.

39. Tylor, Edward Burnett, *Primitive Culture.* London: Murray, 1871.

40. Tylor, Stephen A., ed., *Cognitive Anthropology.* New York: Holt, Rinehart and Winston, 1969.

41. van Gennep, Arnold, *The Rites of Passage.* Chicago: University of Chicago Press (1908), 1960.

42. Whorf, Benjamin Lee, "The Relation of Habitual Thought and Behavior to Language," in *Language, Culture, and Personality: Essays in Memory of Edward Sapir,* ed. by Leslie Spier *et al.* Menasha, Wis.: Sapir Memorial Fund, 1941.

4

General Semantics

RICHARD W. BUDD

GENERAL semantics, as an area of study, focuses upon the relationship between the language people use and how they think and behave. The area needs to be differentiated from *semantics,* which deals primarily with words and their meanings, and from *linguistics,* which is concerned with the analysis of language structure. In addition to integrating elements of both semantics and linguistics, general semantics offers a theory of behavior upon which an operational philosophy that is essentially "hygienic" in nature is built. One of the basic tenets of general-semantics theory is that an individual's assumptions, beliefs, and attitudes are a function of the structure of his language, and that his perception and behavior will be affected more or less in direct relationship to his susceptibility to influence by that language structure. In its operational philosophy, general semantics proposes a systematic method and a set of working principles designed to provide the individual with a set of guidelines for personal adjustment. In a very direct sense then, general semantics is, in its entirety, a model of and a prescription for the process of human communication.

FOUNDATIONS OF GENERAL SEMANTICS

Alfred Korzybski, a Polish mathematician and engineer, was the formulator of the principles subsumed under the title "General Semantics." The area of study was so named by Korzybski in his monumental work *Science and Sanity,*[18] first published in 1933. But the foundations of general semantics were laid several years earlier by Korzybski in his first major work, entitled *Manhood of Humanity,* published in 1921. It was in this volume that Korzybski offered his observation that man was a "time-binder." * Humans, he wrote compared with other life forms, have the unique capacity to pass along accumulated knowledge from one generation to the next; each new generation builds upon that knowledge and passes it along to the succeeding one. Korzybski theorized that since man was a time-binder, the progress that he could make from generation to generation should increase exponentially. At the same time, he was distressed by what he considered a sharp difference between the rate of progress in science and technology, each of which seemed to advance at an increasingly rapid pace, and that in areas of human affairs such as politics, philosophy, and education, areas which Korzybski felt had been stifled and were, at best, chaotic in their development.

The crucial link in Korzybski's time-binding notion was language, the human invention which made possible the accumulation, storage, and eventual retrieval of knowledge. He attributed the great disparity between progress in the scientific and nonscientific domains to the differing ways in which people talked about, and thus thought about, problems in both areas. It was his contention that the language of science matched the facts of science. In other words, Korzybski felt the assumptions implicit in the language of science (its structure) to be in close accord with the structure of reality being examined by science, or, as he was fond of analogizing, the "map" (language) fairly well represented the "territory" (empirical facts). He did not find this relationship to hold true in everday human affairs. To the contrary, Korzybski found most human endeavors beset by unquestioned traditions, routinized habits, and unchallenged beliefs about "human nature" and about causes and effects which, to him, were inconsistent with the laws of nature. Further, Korzybski was concerned that most of mankind were unaware that their lives were governed by these "false-to-fact" doctrines and truths, which he attributed to a faulty relationship between the structure of our language and the structure of reality.

Korzybski summed up the relationship between language and behavior as follows:

> A language, any language, has at its bottom certain metaphysics, which ascribe, consciously or unconsciously, some sort of structure to the world. . . .

* Korzybski classified life forms in terms of what they could *do,* as opposed to the classical philosophical categorization by what man *is.* Anatol Rapoport cites this shift as crucial to an operational discipline. Korzybski classified plants as "chemical-binders," because they convert solar energy into organic chemical energy (first dimension of life); animals, while possessing chemical-binding characteristics, move from place to place and are "space-binders" (second dimension of life); man the time-binder possesses chemical- and space-binding characteristics, but language and the capacity to store language permit him to bind time (third dimension of life).

Now these structural assumptions are inside our skin when we accept a language, any language. . . . We do not realize what tremendous power the structure of a language has. It is not an exaggeration to say that it enslaves us through the mechanism of semantic reactions and that the structure which a language exhibits, and impresses upon us unconsciously, is automatically projected upon the world around us. (18, pp. 89–90)

Korzybski maintained that the structure of our language affects the functioning of our nervous system, and he expressed concern that our language was too often "false-to-fact"—that the structure of our language did not adequately represent the structure of empirical reality. In fact, he was convinced that the structure of our language caused us to see and understand things by the names we gave them. This defining before seeing, or "projection," as he called it, was counter to the way the human nervous system ought to operate. As he put it:

To achieve adjustment and sanity and the conditions which follow from them, we must study structural characteristics of this world *first*, and, then only, build languages of similar structure, instead of habitually ascribing to the world the primitive structure of our language. (18, p. 59)

Drawing from his background in mathematics (which Korzybski believed to be the only language with a structure similar to that of the human nervous system) and engineering, and heavily influenced by Einsteinian physics, biology, neurology, psychology, and psychiatry, Korzybski formulated a "corrective theory" and method for developing adequate "language-to-fact" relationships, which he first called human engineering and, later, general semantics.

BASIC PREMISES OF GENERAL SEMANTICS

The whole structure of general semantics has been built upon a single basic assumption: that reality is to be conceived of as a *process*. This basic notion of modern science postulated that the universe is in a constant state of motion, its elements in a perpetual state of change and changing relationships. More than two thousand years ago, Heraclitus stated the concept quite simply: One may not step in the same river twice. Wendell Johnson,* one of Korzybski's major interpreters, further observes:

. . . One may not step in the same river twice, not only because the river flows and changes, but also because the one who steps into it changes too, and is never at any two moments identical. (16, p. 23)

---

* Wendell Johnson was my teacher, colleague, and friend from 1960 until his death in 1965. Much of my understanding of general semantics came from working and teaching with him. Throughout this chapter, I have tried to indicate the material in the text that represents his own thinking and writing. Considerably more than has been footnoted undoubtedly should have been, since I borrowed liberally from his mind during those years.

> For once we grasp clearly what has been "known" for centuries and what is, in fact, the central theme of modern science, that no two things are identical and no one thing is ever twice the same, that everywhere is change, flux, process, we understand that we must live in a world of differences. (16, p. 25)

As was noted earlier, the notion of a process reality, with its consequences of change and differences, occupies a central role in general-semantics theory. At the time these notions were introduced by Korzybski, they represented a major break with tradition. Korzybski underscored this break with the past by referring to his new system as "non-Aristotelian."

Korzybski based his non-Aristotelian system on three basic principles: (1) the principle of *nonidentity* (A is not A); (2) the principle of *nonallness* (A is not all A); and (3) the principle of *self-reflexiveness*. Korzybski's premises were called non-Aristotelian because they were markedly different from the basic assumptions of Aristotle (which Korzybski felt had been internalized by Western society and were largely responsible for false-to-fact evaluations): (1) the law of identity (A is A, or whatever a thing is, it is); (2) the law of noncontradiction (everything is A or not-A); and (3) the law of the excluded middle (nothing is both A and not-A).

The first of these three non-Aristotelian principles, the principle of nonidentity, says, to use Korzybski's analogy, "the map is not the territory," the word is not the object it stands for. As Johnson interprets Korzybski:

> . . . the name given to a fact, or any statement made about the fact, is not identical with that fact.
> Since "the word is not the object" is so utterly indisputable, we tend very strongly to develop an illusion of complete understanding. Moreover, we find it most difficult to believe anyone has ever doubted it or has ever believed that the word is not the object.
> The identification of which we speak is that seen, for the most part, in those instances in which people *act as if* the word were the object. (16, p. 172)

As an example of identity, Johnson points out that for many years one did not use the word *syphilis* in conversation. Despite the fact that medical science had developed a means of controlling, and perhaps even eliminating the disease, little was accomplished in bringing syphilis under control because the "taboos" of society operated to prevent discussion, much less public information campaigns.

> People acted toward the word *syphilis* very much as they did toward what it presumably represented. They sought to avoid not only syphilis, but the word *syphilis*. Their behavior was remindful of the primitive word magic, in accordance with which it is naively assumed that by controlling the word, one controls the thing it stands for. (16, p. 172)

The second of Korzybski's premises, the principle of nonallness, supplements and, to a large extent, subsumes the first. It states that the map does not represent all the territory. Anatol Rapoport writes:

> . . . no matter how good a map you make, you cannot represent all of the territory in it. Translated into terms of language, it means that no matter how much you say about some "thing," "'event," "quality," or whatnot, you cannot say *all* about it. [23, pp. 19–20]

The second non-Aristotelian premise suggests that in terms of ordinary human behavior, we become aware, we perceive, through a process of abstracting, which in turn is a process of leaving out details. Our best description of any object or event, for example, at least in everyday life, simply does not include a detailed account of the object's atomical structure, "the mad dance of whirling electrons," or its relationship to other objects in the universe. Since the process of abstracting is central to an understanding of general semantics, the notion will be presented in some detail later in this chapter.

The third premise states, in essence, that we employ language for talking about language, we make statements about statements, we make evaluations about evaluations. Johnson points out that the infinite regress is a case of self-reflexiveness gone wild. "How miserable I am when I think about how miserable I am"; "How worried I am when I think about how worried I am." At the same time, the self-reflexive nature of language, as we shall see later, makes possible the making of abstracts of abstracts, which is at the heart of the development of scientific theory.

THE PROCESS OF ABSTRACTING

The literature of general semantics is shot through with the notion that our everyday language, unlike the language of science, is often false to fact. Much of the criticism leveled at general semantics centers on this very notion. Do general semanticists have a corner on knowing what is fact and what is not? It is perhaps unfortunate that the false-to-fact notion has been expressed the way it has by so many general semanticists, for at first blush it does seem to imply that there is a knowable reality and that what general semantics is all about is fitting our language structure to the structure of reality. Perhaps some of the confusion can be sorted out by understanding how general-semantics theory views fact.

Among the main generators of credibility in modern society are statements something to this effect: "Look at the facts," or "The facts show." Behind such statements lies the assumption (and perhaps a hope of the susceptibility that we will believe) that facts are facts, and, at the least, everyone knows a fact when he meets one.

What we call facts, writes Johnson,[16, p. 93] change "so that yesterday's statistics become today's fairy tales." Every fact appears different, depending upon whether you are labor or management, tenant or landlord, the manipulated or manipulator. Facts, says Johnson, are a matter of social agreement. In summary, writes Johnson,[16, p. 94] any given fact is (1) necessarily incomplete (since it is impossible to know *all* the fact about anything), (2) changeable, (3) a personal affair, and (4) useful to the degree to which others agree with you about it.

Einstein, who had a strong influence on Korzybski's formulations, offers an observation quite consistent with Johnson's:

> The belief in an external world independent of the perceiving subject is the basis of all natural science. Since, however, sense perception only gives information of this external world or of "physical reality" indirectly, we can only grasp the latter by speculative means. It follows from this that our notions of physical reality can never be final. We must always be ready to change these notions. . . . [7, p. 156]

As noted earlier, however, many writers in general semantics, in their efforts to simplify Korzybski's basic notions, do not present a clear picture of the relativity of fact or reality. We have belabored the issue here because it seems crucial to an understanding of the process of abstracting as a viable model of human communication.

The notion of abstracting, as it relates peculiarly to general semantics, was first modeled by Korzybski in *Science and Sanity,* where he called it the "structural differential." Adaptations of this model appear in virtually every major book written about general semantics, among them the "process of abstracting," [16] "the abstracting process," [29] the "abstraction ladder," [13] to name a few. The alterations in drawings or titles have clarified Korzybski's original presentation of the notion but have not impacted the basic concept.

Growing out of Korzybski's three basic, non-Aristotelian principles, the notion of abstracting states simply that there are limitations upon our ability to "see" the world around us, and that our language restricts us even further when we attempt to communicate our observations to others. Following Korzybski's original formulation, most writers have presented the notion in terms of levels of abstraction, with a clear-cut division between the nonverbal and verbal levels. For reasons mentioned earlier, I feel more comfortable using Johnson's adaptation of Korzybski's structural differential than any of the others.

The Nonverbal, Unspeakable World of Not-words

"We live in two worlds, which must not be confused, a world of words, and a world of not-words," wrote Irving Lee.[19, p. 16] His statement simply reiterates one of general semantics' basic themes: The phenomenon of language is different from the nonverbal phenomena we represent by it. The part of the abstracting process with which we deal in this section concerns those "preverbal" levels of our observations and experiences.

As I have pointed out, there are limitations upon what we are able to see, feel, hear, smell, and taste. The facts we are able to observe at the *macroscopic,* neural level are, we know, incomplete—an abstract of a more detailed reality. In order to see beyond the limits of that which we can experience directly, we must use some extension of our neural system (e.g., microscope, telescope, magnifying glass, electronic-sensing equipment) to extend the range of our senses (referred to as the microscopic level). In Figure 4.1, the relationship between these two levels, in terms of abstracting, is shown by the differing number of dots within the two circles. We are able to observe considerably more at the microscopic level, with the aid of instruments, than at the macroscopic level of direct sensing. Our "first-order facts" at the macroscopic level are, then, abstracts of what we are able to observe at the microscopic level. But even at the microscopic level there are limitations (the closed circle on both levels indicates a finite set of possible observations). With the invention of each new and more powerful telescope, for example, scientists find things they were unable to see before.

Beyond the microscopic level lies the *submicroscopic* level. Korzybski called it the "event level." Johnson, in his classes in general semantics, called it the "beable" level—that which *might exist* in a process reality to explain what we are able to observe only partially at the upper two levels. His label "beable" clearly places the submicroscopic world in the inferential class. Johnson uses a quote from Einstein and Infeld's *The Evolution of Physics* [9] in a slightly different context than the one used here, but it aptly addresses itself to the philosophical and epistemological questions embedded in any discussion of reality, be it of the process or any other variety.

> In our endeavor to understand reality we are somewhat like the man trying to understand the mechanism of a closed watch. He sees the face and the moving hands, even hears the ticking, but he has no way of opening the case. If he is ingenious he may form some picture of a mechanism which could be responsible for all the things he observes, but he may never be quite sure his picture is the only one which could explain his observations. He will never be able to compare his picture with the real mechanism and he cannot even imagine the possibility or the meaning of such comparison. But he certainly believes that, as his knowledge increases, his picture of reality will become simpler and simpler and will explain a wider and wider range of his sensuous impressions.

This section of this chapter is under the heading "nonverbal, unspeakable world" simply because such direct experiences as are covered here cannot be transformed into words. You can tell someone *about* your toothache, but all the words in the dictionary will not make him *experience* the toothache. Verbal communications simply describe experiences, they are not the experience being described. Korzybski said, "Whatever you say a thing is, it is not." More likely, when someone describes his toothache to us, what we feel, or perhaps more accurately what we recall, is a toothache we once had.

The World of Words

The core of general-semantics theory and the study of language and behavior lie at the conceptual interface of language and reality—of the "world of words" and the "world of not-words." The greater share of what we know about the world around us—the basis for our beliefs and disbeliefs, for the way we act, comes to us through words. Further, general semantics points out, the greater portion of what others tell us (and we tell others) is not words about facts, but is, rather, words about words. Reports of our direct experience (sensing) account for very little of the intercommunication among most of us. Herein lies the *raison d'être* of general semantics. Commenting on these observations, Johnson writes:

> Nevertheless, firsthand reports of direct experience must form the basis of our entire language structure, unless we are to live in a gravely disordered relationship to the world of non-verbal reality. (16, p. 113)

Most general semanticists do not appear to mean by this, as criticism frequently seems to indicate, that what we say must always have as a referent some immediate experience or object or person that can be offered as tangible evidence to back up our words. What does seem important is that our statements, through a series of interconnected relationships, eventually be tied to "facts" derived from the levels of observation referred to in the preceding section on nonverbal levels. For as Johnson points out:

> Language is never so boring, however, or so ineffectual, as when it is kept on the level of sheer enumeration of first-order facts. In order to say anything significant, one simply has to rise above that level, and the higher above it one can rise, the more significant one's remarks become—provided the steps taken in rising, so to speak, are taken in orderly fashion and can be traced back to the level of factual data. (16, p. 114)

A good example of what is being discussed here is the *atom*. Atoms are not tangible things. There is no direct referent for an atom. An atom is one of those ingenious constructs of which Einstein spoke, a "picture of a mechanism" which *could* be responsible for the things which man has been able to observe. Clearly, however, scientists have been able to trace the concept back to the level of factual data.

Now, general-semantics theory argues that this crucial relationship between language and reality is a *structural* relationship. The heart of Korzybski's thesis is that if we are to achieve personal adjustment and productive social organization, *the structure of a language must correspond to the structure of reality.*[18, p. 58] Korzybski, and those who have written about general semantics since, believe there is ample evidence to the contrary— that the structure of our everyday language does not correspond very well to the structure of reality. The evidence presented in the literature of general semantics is drawn from comparisons of the structure of language with the structure of reality, employing as a criterion for that analysis the basic assumption presented earlier: Reality is to be conceived of as a process. The notion of a process reality implies two basic characteristics of structure: (1) change and (2) differences. The second is the child of the first.

Structural Comparison and Change

As was noted earlier, no two things are alike, and no one thing is ever twice the same. A fact, says Johnson, occurs only once. This, of course, is not true of words in our language. We use the same words over and over again, although we certainly do not always intend for them to mean the same thing each time we use them. And there is the rub. If the structure of language were to match the structure of reality (as reality is here defined), each word, like each fact, would occur only once. As Johnson puts it:

> Reality is process-like; language by comparison is static. The world in which we live and we who live in it change faster than does the language we use to speak about the world and ourselves. So it is words become generalized because the conveyer belt of time brings under their spell a changing inventory of "meanings." [16, p. 117]

This is not to deny that language changes. One need only stay up and watch an old late movie, or curl up for an evening with one of Shakespeare's plays, to understand that it does. But crucial to the point made here is that, at a rather fundamental level, our language is slow to change.

Perhaps the major problem, in a sense, has less to do with the words that are spoken than with those of us who use the words. Because the words we hear others say now seem to be the same as words we have heard before, *we* make the assumption that what we understand is basically the same as that which we have always understood. "There is nothing new under the sun." "What you are saying is basically the same as what I heard So-and-So say." "I would never have believed he could do such a thing. He was always such a nice boy." It is in this same response pattern that we feel comforted when we deal with a company that has been in business "since 1845," while perhaps the only thing about the company that is 180 years old may be the artifacts hanging on the walls. General semanticists believe that an unawareness of the disparity between the relatively slow pace of change in language and the higher rate of change in technology and social life can lead to personal maladjustment and, ultimately, to a state of persistent disillusionment.

> There are maladjusted individuals—and societies—who live as though they looked upon the present as a temporary deviation from the past. Their norm being of yesterday, they treat the here and now as though it were a condition of abnormality.
>
> The essential forms of our language were devised by ancient men who were remarkably unfamiliar with present-day knowledge. Because they had not been driven to assume the superdynamics of the submicroscopic realm which we accept, the world in its visible aspects seemed far more static to them than it does to us. In devising our language, they created a world of words that implied a relatively static world of not-words. (16, p. 120)

Structural Comparison and Differences

As noted above, change necessarily gives birth to differences. In the preceding section, the major point was that there is a fundamental difference between the structure of language and the structure of reality, because of the static nature of language relative to a process reality. Here we compare most specifically the infinite differentiation inferred to exist in a process reality with the ability of our language to reflect such differentiation. In short, what are some of the problems brought on by having at our disposal a finite language for speaking about an infinite reality or, at the least, for having an infinite number of ways to conceive of that reality?

To begin with, one word may mean many different things, and several different words can often mean the same thing. This particular problem can take two quite different forms. First, it can be confounded by the "Dictionary Dans" of the world, who insist on the "one word, one meaning" approach. Hayakawa writes:

> Everyone, of course, who has ever given any thought to the meanings of words has noticed that they are always shifting and changing in meaning. Usually, people regard this as a misfortune, because it "leads to sloppy thinking" and "mental confusion." To remedy this condition, they are likely to suggest that we should all agree on "one meaning" for each word and use it only with that meaning. (13, p. 60)

While we can all read that quote with some amusement, we cannot read it without reflecting upon the number of quarters we have won—or lost—betting with a friend on what "a word really means," and having resolved that bet by going to the dictionary. This particular problem would perhaps be easier to deal with if we were at least consistent in our responses to words. We are, however, more likely to vigorously defend those words we have internalized with all sorts of intense feelings (e.g., *Communist, Negro, right, wrong*), and show considerable flexibility toward others about which we don't care.

The other form this problem takes (although it may be of the same genre) is that one word is often used to refer to a variety of behaviors or activities or assumed attributes. The basic problem here is that the users of such words are unaware that the words could have any other meanings except the ones they carry around in their own heads. The list of such words is inexhaustible: *beauty, democracy, love, freedom, intelligence, male chauvinism,* and so on. Incredibly enough, such words have consumed an embarrassing number of pages in leading scholarly journals, not to mention the time taken up at PTA, congressional, professional, or neighborhood meetings that would better be spent on crucial human problems.

General-semantics theory attributes these and similar problems to the structural differences between language and reality. Most writers in the field pinpoint the problem as stemming from Aristotle's third law that nothing is both A and not-A. Our language basically tends to be *two-valued,* to take an "either-or" form reflecting two categories: win-lose; for-against; right-wrong; real-fantasy; liberal-conservative; Republican-Democrat; labor-management; love-hate; intelligent-stupid; success-failure. At best, we add a third, "middle-of-the-road" category, which we generally think of as being "unprincipled" or "wishy-washy." The nub of the problem, again, is traced to our attempts to categorize an infinite-valued reality in terms of a two-valued (or three-valued) language structure.

This pattern repeats itself on a slightly higher level of analysis in the disparity between the structures of reality and language, or what Korzybski calls a problem of "ordering," and Johnson refers to as the "organization" of language. The grammar used to classify words in our language, in any language, is also used to organize and classify reality; rules essentially invented for organizing words into classes and syntactical relationships are not necessarily the best rules for organizing reality.

In our grammar, nouns name things (persons or places), adjectives impute qualities, verbs establish relationships between things and the qualities. One of the consequences of this organization is discussed by Ruben:

> In classificational thinking, things (nouns) do things (verbs) to other things (nouns), in a unidirectional, unidimensional fashion. The paradigm is: "This (one) thing caused that (one) thing." Our thinking, our literature, and our vocabularies are replete with examples. It is common, for example, to say, "You made me mad," "Smoking causes cancer," or "You don't understand what I am telling you." In each instance a single factor causes some *thing* to happen. (25, p. 7)

The structure of the language used in Ruben's examples guides us toward (insists upon) the classical cause-and-effect model. Embedded in this kind of language structure is the assumption that things (persons or places) themselves possess the qualities, and that such qualities, are, in a manner of speaking, "observer-free." What is more, such "truths" appear to be self-evident from the use of the verb "is," traceable to Aristotle's law of identity (A is A; whatever a thing is, it is). The simple statement, "Marcia is immoral," is often regarded as a fact of nature, rather than being seen as a creation of the speaker; the *is* in the sentence would seem to make it so. *Is* implies that the immorality resides in Marcia. Perhaps she is even "possessed" by it. That the "immorality" could—depending upon the observer—range anywhere from chewing gum or smoking on the street to giving birth to an illegitimate child, seems irrelevant once the *is* and the label are affixed. The statement about Marcia ignores a very basic point. The "immoratliy" being talked about does not belong to her alone, but, as R. D. Carmichael [4] has pointed out, is a joint product of the observed and the observer. The evaluation of Marcia tells us as much about the speaker as it does about Marcia, if not more. To paraphrase Wendell Johnson, there is no immorality in nature; immorality is a human invention and is a matter of evaluation. Immorality may only be the difference between what you demand of others and how others behave for themselves.

A number of writers of general-semantics books have taken a great deal of space to punish, as it were, the word *is*. But again, perhaps we should be less concerned with the word as such, and more concerned about its users. The first paragraph of this chapter pointed out that general semantics was basically concerned with one's susceptibility to influence by the language structure. The implication of this particular section is not so much that the structure of the language be altered—although this seems to be one of the less-thought-out goals of general semantics—but that in using language, one develop an awareness of its structural implications for enabling (or disabling) oneself to see the world around one.

The Verbal Levels of Abstracting

In an earlier section we diagramed the nonverbal levels of the process of abstracting. In the past several pages, the discussion has focused upon comparisons between the structure of reality and the structure of language. The nature of this relationship might be better understood by completing the diagram of the process of abstracting.

Figure 4.1 developed three levels of abstracting—macroscopic, microscopic, and submicroscopic—all preverbal. Figure 4.2 adds a fourth level of abstraction, which Johnson called the first-order verbal level of

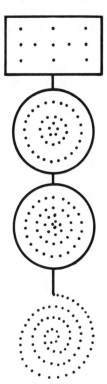

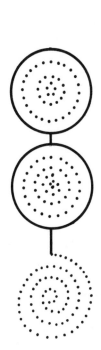

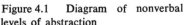

Figure 4.1   Diagram   of   nonverbal
levels of abstraction

Figure 4.2   Diagram of nonverbal
levels and first-order verbal level of
abstraction

abstraction,[16, p. 127] or, more simply, the level of "labeling" or "description." On this level, our preverbal observations, feelings, and experiences
are named or labeled and described. The experience being described *is not*
the experience itself. As we move from the nonverbal to the verbal level,
we leave out detail, as shown in the diagram by the smaller number of dots
in the rectangle. We simply cannot say *all* there is to say about what we
have seen or felt, because our observation, made at either the macroscopic
or the microscopic level, according to the theory developed earlier, is
only an abstract of reality. Descriptions at this level are specific and exhaustive, involving definitions of definitions. Relationships between facts
do not occur on this level; relationships between events are "higher-order"
abstractions. Writes Johnson:

> It is to be understood, then, that there are certain words which accord-
> ing to their accepted usages, may not be used on the first-order verbal level
> of abstraction. They do not serve to name or label particular observable

facts. They represent relationships among facts, or they refer to constructs of inferential data. (16, p. 130)

Since the discussion is leading toward the higher levels of abstraction, it will be useful at this point to complete the diagram of the process of abstracting. In Figure 4.3, three more verbal levels, called "inference levels," have been added. Each higher level shows fewer dots than each preceding level, indicating the further omission of detail and the attendant increasing of generalization. At the top of the diagram is an *ETC.* representing the self-reflexive nature of the process of abstracting: Every abstraction can be further abstracted.

A simple example drawn from Hayakawa's popularized version of general semantics (14) might help clarify the notion of the abstracting process.

> Bessie is a living organism, constantly changing, constantly ingesting food and air, transforming it, getting rid of it again. Her blood is circulating, her nerves are sending messages. (14, p. 166)

Using Figure 4.3, follow the levels of Bessie the cow from the bottom up. To the physicist, Bessie is the "mad dance of electrons" mentioned earlier. She is a dynamic, ongoing process (submicroscopic level). At the microscopic level, she is a mass of tissue, cells, corpuscles, and the like. Many of the details of the process-cow are left out. At the macroscopic level, where we see and sense the cow, she is shape and movement, color and texture, noise and odor, although, again, much detail from the previous level is left out.

At the descriptive level, the word "Bessie" is the label we give to that which we observe. She is a specific cow, the cow of our experience. But since the word is not the experience itself (they are, in a sense, two different phenomenon), we have, in effect, supplanted the experience, "leaving behind," in a manner of speaking, a great wealth of experiential detail. At the next level, we might talk about "cows," since Bessie has a great deal in common with other animals of similar description (some people might go so far as to say cows are cows; when you've seen one, you've seen them all). Specific characteristics of Bessie, our cow, are left out; we begin to lump together common characteristics—to generalize. At inference₂ level we might talk of Bessie as "livestock," and only those characteristics she has in common with other farm animals are included. And so it goes, from livestock to "farm assets" to "assets" to "wealth" to "economic indicators," etc.

We come now to the one remaining aspect of the diagram—perhaps its most crucial aspect—the line and arrow running from the highest inference level to the submicroscopic level. It is important to recall at this juncture that the submicroscopic level, according to Korzybski and others, is the event level, the level of the posited process reality. Figure 4.3

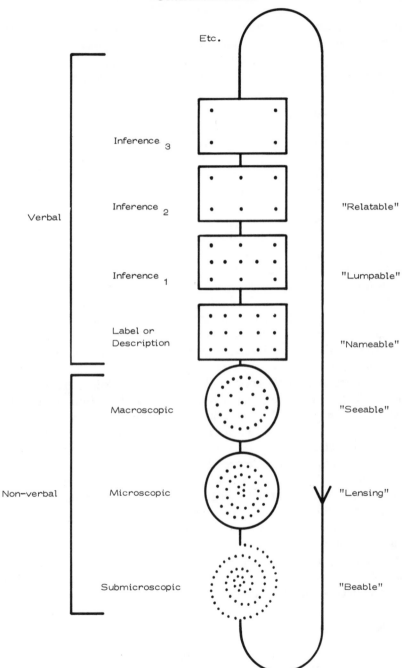

Figure 4.3   Diagram of the process of abstracting
From Wendell Johnson, *People in Quandaries* (New York: Harper, 1946), p. 135.

makes it abundantly clear that the submicroscopic level is, essentially, an extremely *high* level of abstraction. It means that the process reality, the basic premise upon which general-semantics theory is built, is a construct, an inference of the highest order: an assumption. Johnson underscores the circularity of the process of abstracting thusly:

> The statement which each man gives to his highest-order inferences—the way, that is, in which he describes the unobservable aspects of reality, the inferential data—determines his manner of investigating what is observable on the microscopic and macroscopic levels. The particular observations he makes and the particular observations he fails to make are determined mainly by the assumptions on the basis of which he undertakes to make observations. (16, p. 136)

Embedded in this statement of Johnson's is perhaps the real value for coming to more than a superficial understanding of the process of abstracting. He says, in effect, that each of us proceeds on a set of assumptions about reality, and, regardless of how carefully these assumptions are stated, they will be different for each of us, depending upon our purposes, our perspectives, our capabilities, and our competencies. Of equal importance, and perhaps a key anchor point for better understanding human communication, is the notion that what we observe and what we fail to observe are determined by the assumptions under which we operate in making our observations.

Perhaps one of the less subtle understandings to be gained from all this is that whenever we make some observation, we abstract from the totality of the event "to be seen." In so doing, if one accepts the basic premise of abstracting, we must also then leave some things out. It was Kenneth Burke who wrote: "A way of seeing is also a way of not seeing—a focus upon object A involves a neglect of object B." (3, p. 70) The key communicational question, then, has been raised. If Mr. A and Mr. B come to the same event with different assumptions, based on different purposes and different competencies (as we know they will), what promise does an intercommunication encounter hold for them, as their variant "realities" (which each has developed for himself communicationally) come face-to-face? At an operational level, general semantics provides a method for analyzing such problems and, in a prescriptive sense, gives a set of working principles to cope with those problems.

On Abstracting and Coping

For general semanticists, there is decidedly a right way and a wrong way to abstract. Korzybski claimed, as noted earlier, that most of us in our everyday lives do it wrong. Science, on the other hand, does it right, as demonstrated by its comparatively rapid progress. We have already noted that the abstracting process is circular. What is thought to occur on the submicroscopic level (the "beable" level) is inferred from what we can see or experience. That is to say, the atoms and electrons which scientists talk about are objects which have never been seen or touched. From what scientists have been able to observe on the microscopic and macroscopic levels, they have inferred that which they think must exist on the submicroscopic level (the process moves correctly in the direction indicated by the arrow in Figure 4.3). An atom is nothing more than a verbal construct. This is not to say that atoms are fanciful inventions belonging to the same category as good fairies and evil spirits; the survivors of Hiroshima and Nagasaki can tell us differently. The difference is that the verbal construct of an atom, used to explain the behavior of matter on the submicroscopic level, has proved to have a high degree of *predictability*. Until this construct proves to be too imprecise for use in science, and until further observations indicate that the concept of atoms and electrons is more complex than previously imagined and thus requires revision, its acceptance is productive. Fairies and spirits, on the other hand, have little predictability, but are easily blamed for events after the fact.

Our inferences, then, are only as good as our observations, our observations as good as our reality, and our reality as good as our inferences. Proper abstracting, according to general-semantics notions, requires moving up and down the "abstraction ladder": observations first, followed by careful description, followed by inferences. The well-adjusted person, however, understands that his inferences are only assumptions and he will move "back down" to the nonverbal levels to test his inferences through continued observation. Korzybski and his followers describe this "adjusted" behavior pattern as an *extensional* orientation—a predisposition to inspect the territory first and then to build the conceptual maps to correspond with it. A not-so-well-adjusted person—and Korzybski believes that includes most of us to some degree or other—does not tend to see first and then define, but to define first and then see. (Walter Lippmann discusses this and related notions in *Public Opinion*. The statement above is simply a paraphrase of Lippmann's observation.) Korzybski refers to this behavior pattern as an *intensional* orientation. To be intensional in orientation is to become more involved in the map, and the expense of the territory—perhaps, in extreme conditions, to assume that the map (the feelings, thoughts, deep-seated beliefs) *is* the territory.

What general semantics as a method strives toward is, at the least, an *awareness of the process of abstracting* and, at best, an understanding that our realities are temporary, communicationally created assumptions subject to continuous revision. Being aware simply means that the individual is more likely to do the revising himself, rather than have the rug of change snatched without warning from beneath his feet. This notion is made somewhat more clear in Figure 4.4, in the "short-circuited" abstracting process.[16, p. 138] The diagram is intended to represent the individual who fails to recognize that a high-level abstraction such as "Marcia is immoral" is an assumption, but rather assumes it to be a statement of fact. Any observations at the macroscopic or microscopic level are treated as irrelevant. Any abstracting done bypasses the nonverbal levels of abstracting.

> This is the mechanism of the "closed mind," of the old dog that cannot learn new tricks. It is represented in the behavior of the Indian who dances in a particular way in order to make the corn grow well, regardless of the corn crops that have followed his dancing in the past. To him the god who will refuse to make the corn grow if he does not dance is not an assumption to be tested but a fact to be respected. Since, to him, it is not an assumption, the way the corn grows has no bearing on its truth or falsity. (16, p. 140)

While it is always easier to talk about Indians or aboriginal tribes in some distant country, the pattern is readily discernible closer to home. Someone once said "structure is the residue of function." Endless numbers of human organizations continue to follow rules, procedures, and traditions that no longer facilitate their functions. (Schools divided by grades, grades divided by subject matter, universities divided into departments, the President officially elected by the electoral college, are some obvious examples.) On the individual level, we still go through all sorts of interaction rituals which deny us our honesty and our individuality, paying the price in frustration and ulcerated stomachs. But this, some semanticists feel, is the small of it. Wendell Johnson, for example, devotes six chapters of *People in Quandaries* [16] specifically to the more serious problems of schizophrenia, paranoia, hysteria, and other disorders which, general semanticists contend, grow out of and are defined through language. Thus it is that general semantics was earlier labeled a "hygienic" philosophy.

The Working Devices

The working devices of general semantics, organized for the most part by Korzybski in *Science and Sanity,* are more preventative than curative. They are, as we shall see, only reminders—aids to coping. Using the devices is one thing; understanding why one is using them is quite another. Korzybski lists five such extensional devices:

> (1) *Indexes.* The index is designed to expand the language and focus on differences. The function of indexing in language is not unlike the use of serial numbers on automobiles or numbers on the shirts of our football players. While they are all cars or all football players, it becomes useful to be able to tell them apart. So with language, the device $love_1$, $love_2$; or

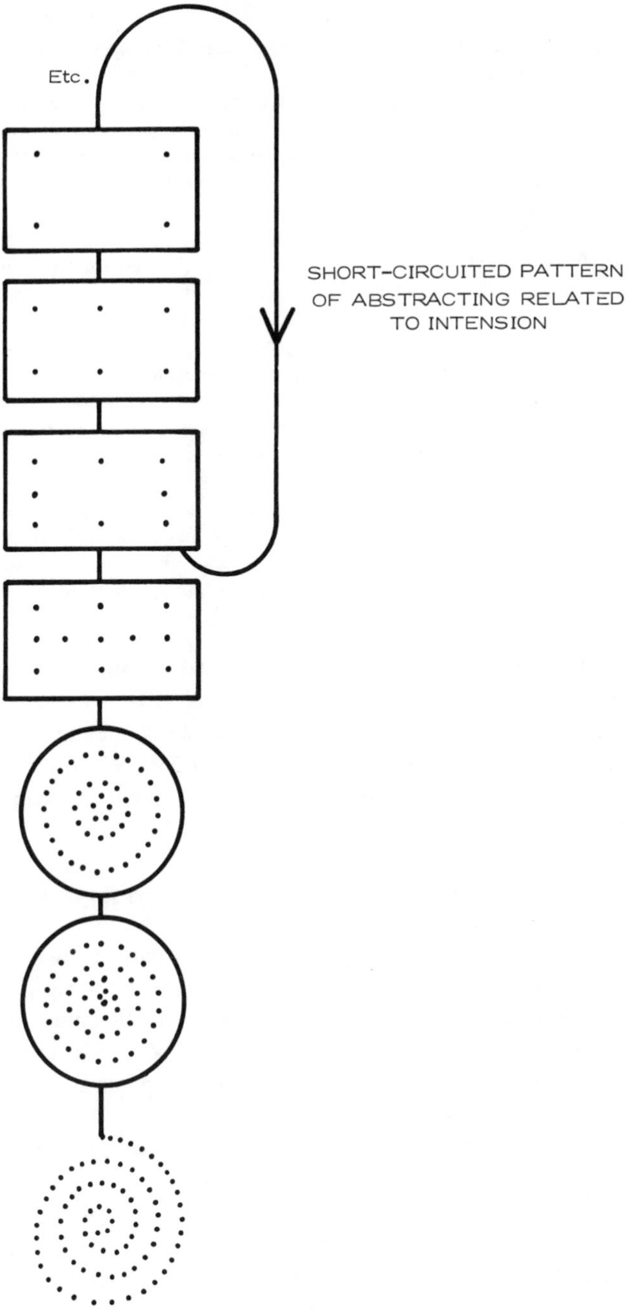

Figure 4.4   Diagram of "short-circuited" process of abstracting
From Wendell Johnson, *People in Quandaries* (New York: Harper, 1946), p. 139.

peace₁, peace₂ might well alert us against making unwarranted, perhaps disastrous, generalizations.

(2) *Dates.* Dates are a specialized form of the index; they index time. I_{1972} am not I_{1954} (and remembering that may help prevent me making a fool of myself at some time). And although the "since 1845" business establishment would like us to believe so, The Emporium₁₉₇₂ is not The Emporium₁₈₄₅.

(3) *Etc.* The good grammarian refuses to accept etc. as a "word." Its use grows from Korzybski's principle of non-allness. Stated simply, it means, "I haven't said all that could be said about X." It can be used effectively in conjunction with item 1 above: beauty₁, beauty₂, etc.

(4) *Quotation Marks.* Terms are placed in quotes, writes Johnson, to remind both the speaker and the listener that they are to be evaluated with regard to their false-to-fact implications. [16, p. 214] The quote marks permit us to use the language without implying the absoluteness of certain terms. For example, quote marks have been used extensively in this chapter, frequently with the word "reality."

(5) *Hyphen.* The hyphen is used in much the same way as quote marks, to remind us of the systemic nature of "process reality." As Korzybski pointed out, our language permits us to separate things verbally which cannot in reality by separated. Einstein, for example, refers to "space-time," which he considered to be inseparable notions.

There are a number of other devices offered by other writers in general semantics which will not be dealt with here. But, whether or not they would qualify as working devices (or extensional devices, as Korzybski called them), two questions which often cut effectively through "semantic flack" were frequently employed by Johnson: What do you mean? and How do you know?

GENERAL SEMANTICS FROM ANOTHER VIEW

It would be a gross oversight not to spend at least a few pages taking a more global view of general semantics, both as a scholarly pursuit and as a pragmatic social force. If there is one thing general-semantics theory and principles has not been, from *Science and Sanity* on, it is noncontroversial. As an area of study, it has spanned the range of potential responses, from basking in the adulation of those who believe it a panacea for all the ills of all mankind to wincing under the intellectual whips of those who find it a hollow, murky haven for naïve charlatan-scholars.

In a not uncommon pattern, many of the admirers of general semantics have also been the authors of basic general-semantics books, not the least of whom is Korzybski himself. Both *Manhood of Humanity* and *Science and Sanity* are couched in rather imperative tones from which one draws a real sense of urgency. In an effort to interpret and spread Korzybski's notions, a number of his commentators reflect this urgent tone (the last chapter of Johnson's book, [16] for example, is entitled "The Urgency of

Paradise"), bringing on a frequent criticism that general semantics seems more of a religion than a rational approach to the study of language and behavior. Thayer writes in the introduction to his recent reader in general semantics:

> My major criticisms of the present state of general semantics—that it is for many of its central spokesmen more of a religion than an intellectual discipline; that its disciples often exhibit a kind of "intellectual imperialism"; that it is static, closed, and proprietary; that it is myopic and naive— have not changed essentially with the additional contact I have had with it, through its proponents and dissidents, during the development and editing of this book. (28, p. viii)

While this remains, as Thayer notes, a major criticism of general semantics, it hardly seems appropriate to dismiss the entire area of study because of the overzealousness of a few writers who have found it necessary to publish accounts of their personal salvation through general semantics. The misfortune for general semantics is that scholars who have studied it enough to find it lacking, have done very little about it. Criticism of general semantics, like that of a great many other disciplines, tends to be reactive in the sense that it focuses upon what is wrong with the discipline; the critics rarely assume a proactive stance by taking the further step toward reconceptualization of the field.

The subissues raised in Thayer's critique seem to provide a far more central and solid base for mounting criticism of general semantics. General semantics has not progressed markedly or been substantially revised since *Science and Sanity* was first published. For the most part, general semantics$_{1933}$ is general semantics$_{1972}$. The irony is that Korzybski himself hoped and publicly called for such revision. At a deeper level of analysis, it can easily be construed as a gross violation of the principles Korzybski himself advocated that the dozen or so major books published since 1933 are highly redundant. It is, for example, difficult to believe that Korzybski said *all* there is to be said about language and behavior, or that forty years have not brought about changes that his conceptualization did not take into account.

It might be useful for the student of general semantics to, at some point, find out how well general semantics might withstand examination by its own principles. The outline for such a test was provided by Korzybski:

> Because of the cumulative and non-elementalistic character of human knowledge, a mere challenge to a "principle" does not carry us far. For expediency, assumptions underlying a system have (1) to be discovered, (2) [to be] tested, (3) [to be] eventually challenged, (4) [to be] eventually rejected, and (5) [finally] a *system,* free from the eventually objectionable postulates, has to be built. (18, p. lxiii)

Once again we may be jockeying ourselves into the position of blaming general semantics rather than some of those who write and talk about the principles subsumed under that name. In view of that, it seems only fair to point out J. Samuel Bois's definition of general semantics, which has stimulated my final observation. Wrote Bois, "A definition of general semantics can be given in two words: *up-to-date epistemology*." [1, p. 12] Perhaps one of the most serious deficiencies of most basic general-semantics textbooks is that they are markedly lacking in considerations of epistemology, much less up-to-date ones. One of Thayer's observations was that general semantics is essentially a closed area of study. Those pursuing the discipline might find considerable value in expanding their conceptualization of general semantics to include more of the theories of epistemology, the sociology of knowledge, general systems theory, symbolic interactionism, and a variety of other related areas which have, for the most part, been ignored in classical studies of semantics. (Anatol Rapoport serves as one of the better examples of a scholar who has used much of what general semantics has to offer as a point of departure in his work.)

From another view this and other similar criticisms of general semantics might reasonably be called "shooting fish in a barrel." General semantics may not be a discipline at all; it may simply be an elaborate methodology. If this is true, it would help explain why it appears static and closed; for with a methodology, there is really only one step beyond the mastery of its principles—that is, behaving as if one understood them. From this perspective, perhaps general semantics can only have its intended social impact on an each-one (general semanticist), teach-one (nonsemanticist) basis.

If, indeed, general semantics is a methodology (and this issue should be explored), it should be suggested that general semantics could (or has) become not non-Aristotelian, as Korzybski proclaimed, but rather, neo-Aristotelian.

REFERENCES AND SUGGESTED READINGS

1. Bois, J. Samuel, *The Art of Awareness*. Dubuque, Iowa: Brown, 1966.
2. Boulding, Kenneth, *The Image*. Ann Arbor: University of Michigan Press, 1950.
3. Burke, Kenneth, *Permanence and Change*. New York: The New Republic, 1935.
4. Carmichael, R. D., *The Logic of Discovery*. Chicago: Open Court, 1930.
5. Chase, Stuart, *The Tyranny of Words*. New York: Harcourt, Brace, 1938.
6. Chisholm, Francis P., *Introductory Lectures on General Semantics*. Chicago: Institute of General Semantics, 1944.
7. Einstein, Albert, *The World As I See It*. London: Lane, 1935.
8. Einstein, Albert, "Physics and Reality," *The Journal of the Franklin Institute*, Vol. 221, 1936.

9. Einstein, Albert, and L. Infeld, *The Evolution of Physics*. New York: Simon & Schuster, 1938.
10. Einstein, Albert, *Ideas and Opinions*. New York: Crown, 1954.
11. Hall, William T., *The Silent Language*. New York: Doubleday, 1959.
12. Haney, William V., *Patterns of Communication*. Homewood, Ill.: Irwin, 1960.
13. Hayakawa, S. I., *Language in Thought and Action*. New York: Harcourt, Brace, 1939.
14. Hayakawa, S. I., ed., *Language, Meaning and Maturity*. New York: Harper & Row, 1954.
15. Hayakawa, S. I., ed., *The Use and Misuse of Language*. New York: Fawcett, Premier Books, 1962. (Paper edition of 14.)
16. Johnson, Wendell, *People in Quandaries*. New York: Harper, 1946.
17. Korzybski, Alfred, *Manhood of Humanity: The Art and Science of Human Engineering*. New York: Dutton, 1921.
18. Korzybski, Alfred, *Science and Sanity*, 3rd ed. Lakeville, Conn.: The International Non-Aristotelian Library Publishing Company, 1948. (First Edition, Dutton, 1933.)
19. Lee, Irving J., *Language Habits in Human Affairs*. New York: Harper, 1941.
20. Rapoport, Anatol, *Science and the Goals of Men*. New York: Harper, 1950.
21. Rapoport, Anatol, *Operational Philosophy*. New York: Harper, 1953.
22. Rapoport, Anatol, *Fights, Games, and Debates*. Ann Arbor: University of Michigan Press, 1960.
23. Rapoport, Anatol, "What is Semantics," in *The Use and Misuse of Language*, ed. by S. I. Hayakawa. New York: Fawcett, Premier Books, 1962. (Also in 14.)
24. Rogers, Carl, *On Becoming a Person*. Boston: Houghton Mifflin, 1961.
25. Ruben, Brent D., *A Model of Communication and Human Organization: Toward a Unified Theory of Education*. Iowa City: The University of Iowa, 1970.
26. Ruesch, Jurgen, and Gregory Bateson, *Communication: The Social Matrix of Psychiatry*. New York: Norton, 1951.
27. Ruesch, Jurgen, and Weldon Kees, *Nonverbal Communication*. Berkeley: University of California Press, 1956.
28. Thayer, Lee, ed., *Communication: General Semantics Perspectives*. New York: Spartan Books, 1970.
29. Weinberg, Harry L., *Levels of Knowing and Existence*. New York: Harper & Row, 1959.
30. Weiss, Thomas M., and K. H. Hoover, *Scientific Foundations of Education*. Dubuque, Iowa: Brown, 1960.
31. Whorf, Benjamin L., *Language, Thought, and Reality*, ed. by J. B. Carroll. New York: Wiley, 1956.
32. Young, J. Z., *Doubt and Certainty in Science*. New York: Oxford University Press, 1950.

5

General System Theory

BRENT D. RUBEN

FUNDAMENTALLY, general systems is a science of organizing and organization. Since communication is the means through which human organizing and organization occur, it occupies a central role in general system thinking.

Unlike most of the disciplines represented in this book, there are no departments of general systems in present-day colleges. It is not a self-sustaining discipline, but rather a conglomeration of scholars from a diversity of fields, who contribute to and draw upon a growing collection of concepts, propositions, and understandings.

For those interested in human communication, a general system approach has much to offer. It presents a way of thinking about living things—as living systems—and focuses attention on the fundamental life processes that all living things have in common: the metabolism of matter-energy and the metabolism of information.[46, p. 338] From this perspective, communication is basic to the activity of all living things and, therefore, central to the emergence and survival—the total functioning—of human beings, their friendships, families, organizations, and societies.[61, p. 17]

There are a number of interesting inferences that can be drawn from this central framework. Among them is that human communication is not a one-way process, as suggested by a sender-message-channel-receiver-oriented model, but rather a multidirectional phenomenon with no distinguishable beginning or end.

Another concept that can be generated from system thinking is that what is normally thought of as perfect or effective communication implies

95

the control and manipulation of a receiver of messages by the sender. The more effective is the communication, the more like tape recorders—and one another—become the message recipients. In an educational context— where creativity and diversity are desirable, the best teacher-student relationship turns out to be, therefore, one in which the teacher fails to communicate to the students.

A third notion of relevance for human communication is that the individual and the reality he experiences are codetermining phenomena, such that the way an individual thinks determines what he sees, hears, touches, and so on; and conversely, that what he sees determines how he will think. As a consequence, what we see in, and say about, other people (and things) says far more about us than about them.

But general system theory is not so much a set of neat propositions as it is a way of thinking about things. To make use of it in human communication requires a commitment to spending some time acquiring a framework for understanding its goals, scope, and basic concepts. It is here that we will begin, and because it is useful, we will look first at the background.

Background of General System Theory

General system theory has a rich and lengthy heritage. Aspects of it can be traced to Aristotle, for example, who stated in *Politics* that a state is composed of villages, which are in turn made up of households, which contain families.[32] Conceiving of things in terms of wholes and interrelated parts is a basic concept in the general system framework of today.

This element of general system theory* is also reflected in our daily language and our thought patterns. We use terms such as *universe, society, community,* and *individual* to classify reality into units consisting of parts or components. Dictionary definitions of these terms help to illustrate my point. A common meaning of *universe* is the comprehensive system—the total of all things. The universe is said to consist of, among other things, societies. *Society* refers to groups of related and interdependent people who constitute communities. In most human societies and communities, there are smaller constituent units called families, which are composed of a parent, or parents, and their children—individuals.

Many other trappings of the modern system approach date back little more than twenty or thirty years, to the early work of Ludwig von

---

* Sometimes *general system theory* is referred to as *general systems theory* or *General System(s) Theory* and the three distinguished from less formal terms like, *general system(s) thinking, the system(s) approach,* and *the system(s) perspective.* This tends to muddy already polluted water; therefore, all are used interchangeably in this chapter.

Bertalanffy,[15, pp. 256-258] Norbert Wiener,[73; 75] Shannon and Weaver,[59] and von Neuman and Morgenstern. Of these, only Bertalanffy was directly concerned with system theory *per se,* but all shared an interdisciplinary orientation and a concern for organization and communication.

General system theory has been greatly influenced by developments in related fields. Particularly significant in this regard were the contributions of Norbert Wiener, whose highly impactful book entitled *Cybernetics* appeared in 1948. Information theory, and in particular, the work of Shannon and Weaver, *The Mathematical Theory of Communication,* published in 1949, also had an important effect upon developments in system thinking. A third major thrust came in the area of game theory from contributions of von Neuman and Morgenstern in 1947, in *Theory of Games and Economic Behavior.*

The more recent history of general system thinking dates back to 1954 and the founding of the Society for General Systems Research, and to 1956, when the society began publishing *General Systems,*[16] the major journal in the field. It was largely in and through the society and its journal that the present form of general system thinking was molded.

In the words of the original statement of the society, its major functions were to:

> (1) investigate the isomorphy of concepts, laws and models in various fields, and to help in useful transfers from one field to another; (2) minimize the duplication of theoretical effort in different fields; (3) encourage the development of adequate theoretical models in fields which lack them; (4) promote the unity of science through improving communication among specialists. [14, p. 15]

Writing for the first volume of *General Systems,* Bertalanffy, credited by his peers as the father of modern general system theory, explains the impetus for the development of a general theory in this way:

> Modern science is characterized by its ever-increasing specialization, necessitated by the enormous amount of data, the complexity of techniques, and a breakdown of science as an integrated realm: The physicist, the biologist, the psychologist, and the social scientist are, so to speak, encapsulated in a private universe, and it is difficult to get a word from one cocoon to the other.
>
> There is, however, another remarkable aspect. If we survey the evolution of modern science, as compared to science a few decades ago, we are impressed by the fact that similar general viewpoints and conceptions have appeared in very diverse fields. Problems of organization, or wholeness, of dynamic interaction, are urgent in modern physics, chemistry, physical chemistry, and technology. The same trend is manifest in gestalt theory and other movements as opposed to classical psychology, as well as in modern conceptions of the social sciences. These parallel developments in the various fields are even more dramatic if we consider the fact that they are mutually independent and largely unaware of each other. [13, p. 1]

Not only were there parallel developments in the fields Bertalanffy mentions, but there were also parallel efforts under way aimed toward cross-disciplinary unification. Commenting upon this trend in *Communication: The Social Matrix of Psychiatry,* an important volume on communication and organization, Ruesch and Bateson point out:

> The convergence of physiology, ecology, and ethology—fields that study the organism's transactions with his physical and social environment—have resulted in the emergence of general systems theories of the biological sciences. The convergence of psychiatry, psychology, sociology, and anthropology—fields that study man's behavior alone and in groups—has led to what is now known as behavioral science. The convergence of administration, social organization, group management, and group therapy—fields that share in common the tendency to steer, organize, or change social behavior—have resulted in a theoretical body of knowledge concerned with social operations. (57, p. vii)

The foregoing was written a number of years ago; in current conception, the scope of general system theory is considerably broader than suggested by Ruesch and Bateson, finding application not only in physiology, ecology, and ethology, but in many other disciplines as well.

Scope

Contrary to what must be a logical inference from much of what has been said thus far, general system theory is not seeking to become a single theory designed to replace all the specialized theories of particular fields. As Boulding points out:

> Such a theory would be almost without content, for we always pay for generality by sacrificing content, and all we can say about practically everything is almost nothing. Somewhere, however, between the specific that has no meaning and the general that has no content there must be, for each purpose and at each level of abstraction, an optimum degree of generality. It is the contention of the General Systems Theorists that this optimum degree of generality in theory is not always reached by the particular sciences. (17, p. 11)

There is no clear-cut agreement among general system writers as to where that optimum level is; likewise, there is no single answer as to how it might be found. Boulding (17, p. 131) has outlined what he considers to be two alternatives. The first proceeds by examining the universe to identify certain general phenomena which are found in various disciplines, and then it seeks to build up generalized theories taking into account these phenomena. The second begins by arranging the various empirical fields in a hierarchy based upon the complexity and level of abstractness of the phenomena with which they deal. Ashby, who shares a similar view, also suggests two ways of proceeding:

One [method] . . . takes the world as we find it, examines the various systems that occur in it—zoological, physiological, and so on—and then draws up statements about the regularities that have been observed to hold. . . . The second method is to start at the other end. Instead of studying first one system, then a second, then a third, and so on, it goes to the other extreme and considers the set of all conceivable systems and then reduces the set to a more reasonable size. [1, p. 2]

These alternatives circumscribe the range of research approaches utilized in general system theory. For our purposes, what is most important is the set of concepts and the basic framework for conceiving of organizing and organization which have emerged from this research.

What follows is a brief summary of basic system concepts and terminology, included because it is essential to understanding the language and framework of human communication in system perspective. The first section deals with those terms related to system *structures;* the second section considers systems in terms of their *processes.*

SYSTEM STRUCTURES

System

The concept of the *system* is the unifying idea around which revolve the goals and methods of the general system perspective. The term implies wholeness and suggests the presence of parts in relationship.

Roy Grinker, in *Toward a Unified Theory of Human Behavior,* provides the following perspective on the concept of the system:

The reader may be somewhat bewildered by the use of the term "system" applicable to the biological, psychological, cultural or social aspects of life-in-process. A "system" is considered to be some whole form in structure or operation, concepts or functions, composed of united and integrated parts. [29, p. 370]

In further discussion, he states that "its parts are in continued activity in relation to each other and to the whole. . . ." [29, p. 370]

Bertalanffy [13, p. 3] has defined a system as a set of elements which stand in interaction. With a slightly different emphasis, Churchman [23, p. 11] characterizes the system as made up of sets of components that work together for the overall objective of the whole.

The most illustrative of the various definitions is provided by Hall and Fagen. [30, p. 18] They define a system as "a set of objects together with relationships between the objects and between their attributes." They point out also that their definition implies that "a system has properties, functions or purposes distinct from its constituent objects, relationships and attributes." They use a series of examples to clarify their definitions:

Objects are simply the parts or components of a system, and these parts are unlimited in variety. Most systems in which we are interested consist of physical parts: atoms, stars, switches, masses, springs, wires, bones, neurons, genes, muscles, gases, etc.

Attributes are properties of objects. For example, in the preceding cases, the objects listed have, among others, the following attributes:

atoms—the number of planetary electrons, the energy states of the atoms, the number of atomic particles in the nucleus, the atomic weight.
stars—temperature, distances from other stars, relative velocity.
switches—speed of operation, state.
masses—displacement, moments of inertia, momentum, velocity, kinetic energy, mass.
springs—spring tension, displacement.
wires—tensile strength, electrical resistance, diameter, length.

The *relationships* to which we refer ·are those that "tie the systems together." It is, in fact, these relationships that make the notion of "system" useful . . . we take the attitude that the relationship to be considered in the context of a given set of objects depend on the problem at hand. . . . [30, p. 18]

Subsystems or Components

Systems can be divided up conceptually into subsystems or components. In discussing this concept, Churchman [23, p. 64] describes subsystems in terms of the various activities that are performed within a system. Applying this scheme to an educational situation, for example, components would include teachers, classrooms, books in the library, and so on.

According to J. G. Miller,[46, p. 218] "The totality of all the structures in a system which carry out a particular process is a subsystem." Like Churchman, Miller contends that a subsystem or component is identified by the process it performs.

Suprasystem

The components or subsystems of suprasystems are systems. In Miller's terms, "the suprasystem of any living system is the next higher system in which it is a component or subsystem." [46, p. 218] According to this definition, every system has a suprasystem except the universe.

Boundary

Boundaries hold together the components which make up a system. According to Miller,[46, p. 342] where systems are living things, boundaries are regions at the outside edges of a system, which protect them from environmental stresses and exclude or admit various sorts of matter-energy and information.

In discussing boundaries of systems made of living things, Miller offers the following description:

> System boundaries at various levels are quite different. Cells have walls; organs have covering membranes or capsules; organisms have skin, fur, scales, feathers, hair, exoskeletons, and other structures. All these have many gaps in them through which matter-energy and/or information can pass.
>
> When functioning normally, boundaries selectively filter, admitting desired inputs and blocking out excessive, dangerous or unwanted . . . inputs. [46, p. 342]

Environment

Systems are embedded within physical, spatial, temporal, and sometimes symbolic sets of conditions called environments. Environments characteristically affect the systems which interact with them and are, in turn, affected by those systems. Miller says:

> The immediate environment is the suprasystem minus the system itself. The entire environment includes this plus the suprasuprasystem and the systems at all higher levels which contain it. [46, p. 218]

With a slightly different emphasis, Churchman [23, p. 63] describes environment as a set of conditions that are relevant, but not directly under the influence of a system.

An Example

Some of the basic system structure concepts can be meaningfully illustrated by examining briefly a typical living-room stereo system. When we talk about a stereo sound system, we generally take that to imply a whole—a unit consisting of various components, or subsystems, integrated with one another to perform operations that no single component could itself accomplish.

Minimally, such a system would consist of a record changer (or turntable), stylus (or perhaps a cartridge tape player), amplifier, and two speakers (or a set of headphones). In nontechnical terms, the function of the system is to detect sound from a source (record, FM station, or tape, for example), amplify and thereby reproduce it loudly enough so that a human ear can hear it from the speakers or headphones.

Subsystem boundaries are the several wood or metal encasements which protect each component from the environment, while allowing appropriate and necessary transactions between them via wires connected to terminals of each subsystem. To make our example neat, let us say that all of the components are housed in a single console, which could be thought of as

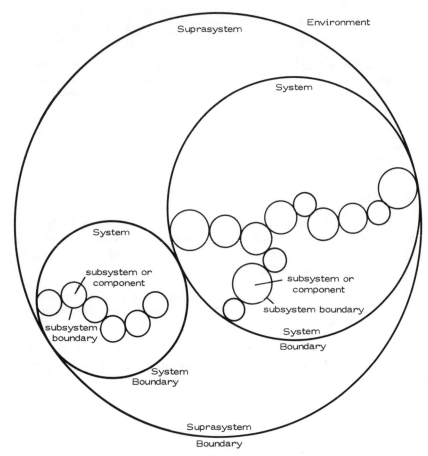

Figure 5.1   System structure

the system boundary. For purposes of this example, we can say that the room in which the stereo operates is the immediate environment of the system.

Level of Analysis

In the foregoing example, we used the term *system* to refer to the sum, or aggregate, of the components—the turntable, amplifier, and so on. It is important to point out that entering at this level of analysis, though common, is arbitrary. That is, we could just as well consider the turntable as the system, and the set of components the suprasystem. If we had done that, we would have described the components or subsystems of the turntable. Or the turntable components might have been referred to as systems, and so on. Several levels down, we might have referred to the automatic record rejection system.

If we want, we can think of suprasystems as composed of systems, composed of subsystems or components, composed of subcomponents or subsubsystems, made up of subsubcomponents, and so on ad infinitum, or we could alternatively conceive of this state of affairs as a *hierarchy of encompassing systems*,[17: 60] ranging in this case from the simple to the complex.

Selecting the appropriate level of analysis from the hierarchy depends upon one's purpose and perspective. That which is usefully viewed as the system or whole from one point of view is useless or irrelevant from another. Since we are frequently not consciously aware of selecting a level of analysis at all, we often make the choice more by accident than by design.

Examples are as abundant as our willingness to think of them. Kim [31, pp. 143–144] illustrates this point by a football game. The perspective and purposes of the quarterback are different from those of the defensive tackle, the coach, the general manager, or the fans. Each has a concept of the football system appropriate to his purposes and based upon how he sees, and is organized with, that system—upon his perspective. There is no single level right for all purposes. Each level of analysis highlights some phenomena and obscures others.

Take an example from another situation: The level of analysis at which a salesman operates is likely to be quite different from that utilized by the president of the same company.

Understanding this about level of analysis can serve to dispel some of the mysticism associated with system thinking. One realizes that the way system, subsystem, boundary, and environment get defined depends mostly upon the level of analysis one selects—and that that decision depends largely upon how one conceived of the situation in the first place. This is an extremely important point—one which draws upon system thinking to explain system thinking. Specifically, it involves the notion of the codeterminacy between the individual's mind and his reality, discussed in an upcoming section entitled "Individual Communication System." Reread this paragraph after having completed that section.

SYSTEM PROCESSES

Living Systems

The distinction between *open* and *closed* systems is extremely valuable in understanding human communication. Living systems are units of living things and are more-or-less open systems. Open systems are so named because they exist only through continual exchanges with the environment.[14, p. 32] They maintain themselves through a continual inflow and outflow, a building up and breaking down of components.[14, p. 39] This process is known as metabolism. J. G. Miller [46, p. 338] has pointed out that there are two types of metabolism basic to the functioning of all living systems: the metabolism of matter-energy* and the metabolism of information. Living systems organize themselves only in and through these two processes. Some processes also involve both together.)

Lee Thayer, an important contributor to the interface of general system thinking and human communication theory, has extended and elaborated upon Miller's basic notion of information metabolism, which Thayer terms *communication:*

> Communication may thus be conceived of as the dynamic process underlying the existence, growth, change, the behavior of all living systems—individual and organization. Communication can be understood as that indispensable function of people and organization through which the organization or the organism relates itself to its environment, and its parts and its processes one to the other.
>
> Communication is as fundamental to the living system—the individual or the organization—as is ingestion and consumption of "food" and "fuel" to run its physical and physiological machinery. [61, p. 17]

In contrast is the closed-system model, which comes from conventional physics and is directly applicable to things in the physical and mechanical realm. These systems are termed "closed" because they function in isolation from their environment. Bertalanffy [14, p. 39] cites as an example of a closed system the domain of physical chemistry, which, he points out, is concerned with reactions, their rates, and the chemical state which eventually comes about in a closed container where several reactants are brought together.

One interesting characteristic of closed systems is that their eventual state is always determinable from the initial conditions.[14, p. 40] In the case of a process involving chemicals in a closed vessel, the final concentrations of the reactants can be calculated from a knowledge of the initial concentrations. If either the starting conditions or the process is altered, the final state is also changed.[14, p. 40] This is not the case for open systems, where the same final state may be reached from different initial conditions and in different ways. This characteristic of open systems is termed *equifinality.*

---

* "Metabolism involves an interchange of material between living organisms and the environment, by which the body is built up and energy for its vital life process is secured. Within the body of the individual both constructive and destructive processes take place. The incorporation of materials is known as anabolism and the breaking down of these materials for the release of energy contained in them is catabolism." *The Complete Book of Science* (New York: J. J. Little & Ives Co., 1959).

This distinction reflects a more basic difference between the two types of systems: Closed systems are conceived as behaving according to the second law of thermodynamics, and open systems are not. This law states that in a closed system, a quantity called *entropy* increases to a maximum and eventually stops when the conditions of the system are random, chaotic, and deteriorated, as the system loses organization and structure. The process of a closed system then, is one of continual deterioration.

Open systems work differently. In these systems, an increase in organization and a decrease in entropy is thermodynamically possible, since the systems interact and exchange matter-energy and information with their environments. [14, p. 150]

While the open-system model has obvious relevance for understanding the organization and communication processes of living things, the applicability of a closed-system framework is indirect. Though all living systems are open and interact with their environments, in terms of communication, not all seem to exhibit the same degree of openness. Some, in fact, become more or less isolated from their environments and undergo processes analogous to the loss of organization and structure of chemicals in a closed vessel. [57; 72] Sometimes, this general deterioration even leads to total chaos and a breakdown in the system structure, as in the case of a mental breakdown, divorce, or revolution. The second law of thermodynamics and elements of the closed-system model can provide new ways to think about such phenomena in terms of organization and communication.

Feedback Systems

The classification of systems in terms of feedback is common, due primarily to the widespread application of feedback systems in electronics, biology, and social sciences. Also, the basic elements of the feedback system are the core of the science called cybernetics, originated primarily by Norbert Wiener, and concerned with self-steering and self-regulating devices. [2; 8; 9; 73] Such mechanisms have been essential to the development of the computer, guided missiles, and other "intelligent" and "automatic" machines.

In the context of human communication, feedback has been used to refer to information about the outcome of communicating that is rechanneled back the source for further use. The notion is that the source can then modify his manner of communicating, based on a knowledge of how effective or successful he has been.

This basic conceptualization has been applied to mass communication as well as to face-to-face interaction. A difference sometimes cited between the two, however, is that feedback in mass-communication situations is often delayed (for example, television ratings or letters to the editor), whereas in interpersonal interaction, feedback may be immediate.

The concept has also been used widely in the context of the encounter group, where it refers to reports a T-group participant receives from others in the group about how he has affected them—"come across." Presumably, once the "feedback" is gotten, an individual can make comparisons between what he intended to communicate and what actually happened. When the two don't match, he can make changes to become more effective interpersonally.

These applications capture the most obvious aspects of the concept of feedback systems, but miss some of the deeper conceptual structure. In a generic sense, feedback refers to a portion of a system's output which is fed back or recycled to the system as input, thereby affecting the functioning of the system such that it is able to regulate itself and reach a preset or adaptive goal.[31, p. 1]

The origins of the concept can be followed back to the sixteenth century.* The more recent history traces to the work of James C. Maxwell on the steam engine governor. The governor works as follows:

> An engine turns at an increasing speed; the arms are mounted on pivots so that they are free to rise by centrifical force as they revolve; the arms operate a valve which admits power to the engine, so that the valve is closed in proportion as the arms rise and the speed grows. [31, p. 18]

Stafford Beer's description [8, p. 29] of the governor reflects the basic propositions implicit in the current conception of the feedback system. The contemporary view utilizes a series of specialized concepts including *input, output, control, goal,* and *deviation* in addition to *feedback.*

Input and output refer to directions of flow to and from a system or subsystem across its boundaries. Goal refers to a desired state of a system which is either present and predetermined, or emerges out of the activity of the system. Control is the consequence of the comparison performed between the actual output level and the desired level or goal. Feedback is the information with which this comparison is made.

Suppose we were going to bake a cake. We would begin by turning the oven temperature control (thermostat) to 375 degrees, and then we would turn the oven on. The 375 degrees represents our desired output state or goal. The oven heating elements turn on and begin to output heat, a portion of which is monitored by the thermostat (as input). The thermostat will keep the elements turned on until the actual output corresponds to the desired goal. When both equal 375 degrees the oven will temporarily turn off and will remain off until, once again, the thermostat detects a discrepancy or deviation between the oven output temperature and the desired output temperature (375 degrees). When a difference is detected, the oven

---

* In discussing the background and basic concepts of feedback and feedback systems I draw heavily upon the work of John Kim.[31]

will be turned back on and remain on until the gap between the present input goal and the oven output has been eliminated.

The thermostat and other cybernetic self-regulating, self-steering, or control systems, as they are variously termed, operate by detecting gaps, differences, *errors,* and *deviations.*[31] Systems which look for deviation, error, or difference which they are designed to counteract, eliminate, or equalize are traditionally termed *negative feedback systems.*

Magorah Maruyama [42] has proposed another conceptualization of system processes which he refers to as "the second cybernetics," since positive rather than negative feedback is involved. (Maruyama prefers not to use the terms *negative* and *positive,* but for our purposes here they serve to clarify the nature of his contribution to cybernetic thinking.) In the excerpt that follows, he provides us not only with a description of his concept, but also with a sense of the scope of application of "the first cybernetics."

> Since its inception, cybernetics was more or less identified as a science of self-regulating . . . systems. Thermostats, physiological regulation of body temperature, automatic steering devices, economic and political processes were studied under a general mathematical model of deviation-counteracting feedback networks.
>
> By focusing on the deviation-counteracting aspects . . . cyberneticians paid less attention to the systems in which the effects are deviation-amplifying. Such systems are ubiquitous: accumulation of capital in industry, evolution of living organisms, the rise of cultures of various types, interpersonal process that are loosely termed as "vicious circles" and "compound interests. . . ." [42, p. 164]

Maruyama [42; 40; 41] termed these deviation-counteracting (negative) feedback processes, *morphostasis.* Deviation-amplifying (positive) feedback processes, he termed *morphogenesis.* These concepts differ from the less complex notions of negative and positive feedback processes in that Maruyama's terms describe relationships which are mutually causal rather than one-way.

This represents a significant modification of the earlier feedback system framework. The classification solved a number of problems associated with the elementary feedback models and thereby provided an alternative to the more mechanistic conceptions of feedback in human processes.[14, p. 191] Such things as play, exploratory behavior, and creativity could now be better accounted for.

In the perspective of the elementary negative feedback system these phenomena were classed as "error" to be corrected out, since they represented a gap or deviation from normative behavior (the desired goal).[65; 55]

Additional refinements were embodied in this new classificational scheme. In the models of the first cybernetics the direction of feedback was understood to be one-way—from output to input; and feedback was presumed to exist and operate within a single system and therefore more or less in isolation from the environment and other systems.[31]

According to the refined framework, feedback is understood to imply at least a two-directional and mutually causal relationship involving two interconnected systems. Kim,[31, p. 31] after Ashby, proposed that feedback could appropriately be conceived to exist "when two or more interacting systems are mutually related to each other through input and output." One system's input is another's output, and vice versa; and the model becomes, in Maruyama's terms, one of multilateral mutual causality.

This conception is useful in several ways for thinking about human communication. In the first place, the model can be understood to indicate that communication always implies a relationship between two or more interacting systems. It suggests further that these communication relationships are mutually causal and multilateral, and that such mutually causal communication relationships involve mutual control and manipulation of the two components in relationship, each by the other.

Traditional feedback-oriented communication models viewed the process of human communication as one-way, cause-effect relationships—where sources (or initiators or senders) create messages, which they transmit over one of various channels, and cause a variety of effects in the receiver. Feedback was conceived of as that information which the source used to monitor his effect.

In contrast to this view, a mutually causal framework calls attention to the fact that it is logically sound, and probably more useful operationally, to say that it is the receiver who causes messages to have their meaning and significance and it is therefore the receiver who causes communication to have effects upon him.

From this perspective, it also becomes clear that defining communication effectiveness from the point of view of the sender often leads in paradoxical directions. In the case of the student-teacher communication pattern, for example, effective communication from the source's point of view is having the students learn exactly what a teacher intends. The perfect solution for this communication problem is a classroom filled with tape recorders—or students who act like them. Whether we intend it or not, an attendant consequence of perfect communication is homogenization. Ironically, creativity can therefore be thought of as a consequence and instance of ineffective communication.[65; 55]

But one need not take quite such an extreme position to find value in the concept of human communication as multilateral, mutually causal systems. One need only recall a typical argument between two individuals, each bantering with the other, and in so doing, perpetuating and perhaps intensifying the argument in a spiraling cause-and-effect fashion.[72, pp. 96–98]

It is interesting to note that the notion of feedback is not crucial to the mutually causal system perspective since, as you may recall, the concept of feedback implied a one-way process and suggested a source-oriented view of communication. What is feed*back* to the source is feed-*forward* to the receiver. A letter to the editor, for example, is feedback from the point of view of the newspaper, but feed-forward from the perspective of the audience member writing the piece.

HUMAN COMMUNICATION SYSTEMS

Up to this point, we have reviewed general system thinking. We looked briefly at the background, goals, and scope of general system theory, reviewed basic concepts related to system structure, and discussed several classifications of system processes. In the remaining pages, we will turn our attention to human communication systems, drawing upon those aspects of general system thinking which seem most generic in their relevance to human communication.

Information and Communication Systems

To begin with, we need to distinguish between *information systems* and *communication systems*. Lee Thayer provides a view that is well suited to our purposes. His differentiation is between communication systems on the one hand, and data systems (termed "information systems" here) on the other:

> There are at least two useful distinctions to be made. . . . Data systems [information systems] map the flow of *data* to and from humans or machines from the point at which that data is generated or disseminated, to the point of its intended destination. Data systems [information systems] are rational systems designed by people, deduced from some set of rational criteria of system efficacy.
>
> *Communication systems,* by contrast, are defined by the data acquisition —consumption practices (rational or not) of the consumers of the output of that system, whether by intention or accident. [61, p. 116]

Thayer makes a further distinction between the nature of the two sorts of systems, which helps to clarify his notion of each:

> . . . people may be *informed* by the data systems [information systems] which serve them. But people are *in-formed* within their communication systems. [61, p. 117]

The stereo system discussed earlier in this chapter was a good example of an information system. The structure and process of that system was discussed primarily in terms of the flow of data and messages from one component to another. The general goal was the detection and amplification of sound that is loud enough to be detected by the human ear. If we add to that system a human being—a listener—the system would move closer to the definition of a communication system. However, as long as the primary focus is upon the mechanical flow of messages—even with a listener included as one of the components—it would still be termed an information system. Only when the significances, competencies, purposes, functions, and desires which the listener brings to the situation were defined as a crucial aspect of the system, would it meet the definition of communication system.

Where an important question for examining an information system is, "How does it work?" the question of importance for the communication system is, "How are people using it?" It follows that the most effective information system might be an extremely ineffective communication system. The finest reproduction of classical music, for example, is worthless to the listener who enjoys only folk rock.

Many people who study human communication focus their attention upon information systems—upon the flow of messages from one place or one person to another. Unfortunately, this perspective misses much that is relevant for understanding human communication in system perspective. No amount of study of the postal system, linguistics, or cross-cultural communication—message flows—is likely to provide an adequate understanding of the significance that a letter from a boy in Princeton, New Jersey, to an intimate friend in London, England, will have for the two of them.

Communication System Framework

What follows is a skeleton model of a human communication-system framework, which builds upon and reflects many of the ideas presented in those two volumes.

To begin with, we propose conceiving of the totality of human enterprise as a suprasystem—a complex and interrelated hierarchy of systems and their components—organized and organizing itself and its parts one with the other. The systems making up the suprasystem—individuals, friendships, marriages, business organizations, people riding an elevator together, fraternities, strangers passing on a street, universities, or societies —are continually in process and thereby maintain and modify previous patterns of organization within and among one another.

This suprasystem, together with the environment, can be thought of as an ecosystem (ecological system), since the individual systems and components within depend for their survival, growth, and change upon their ability to fit themselves with one another and with the environment. The ecosystem notion implies that there are two fundamental life systems through which all organization and organizing occur: matter-energy systems and communication systems. The complexity and intricacy of pathways and interconnections necessary to even maintain these systems are impossible to enumerate, and difficult even to conceive of. In *The Origin of the Species,* Darwin examined the relationship between red clover and the bumblebees which pollinate it, in an attempt to suggest the intricacy and elaborateness of such ecological systems. Farb refers to the story as an "ecological classic."

> Darwin discovered that bumblebees, because of their long tongues, are the only insects which can effectively pollinate the deep red clover flowers From this he argued that the success of red clover in England can be attributed to the fact that bumblebees are so prevalent there. He then went on to quote an authority who had found that there were more bumblebees' nests in the vicinity of villages and towns than elsewhere because field mice, which eat bumblebee combs and larvae, are scarce around towns. And why are field mice scarce? Because towns usually harbor large numbers of cats which prey upon the field mice and keep the population down. Here a German scientist took up the argument: cats, he said, were thus proved responsible for the prevalence of red clover in England; red clover, a staple food of British cattle, could be ecologically linked to the British navy, whose staple diet was bully beef; hence cats could be given ultimate credit for Britain's dominance as a world power. Thomas Huxley then went even one step further: he suggested, half humorously, that since old maids were well known to be the principal protectors of cats throughout England, the fact that Britannia ruled the waves might logically—and ecologically—be traced right back to the cat-loving tendencies of her many spinsters. (25, pp. 35–36)

As Farb points out, the "cat-and-clover" story is obviously overdrawn and implies a one-way cause-and-effect relationship, but the interconnections discussed serve to illustrate the far-reaching ecological interrelationships and interdeterminancies that inextricably bind together systems and subsystems within the ecosuprasystem.

The story also indirectly makes the point that biological and social existence depends upon living systems organizing themselves metabolically and informationally with their environments and with the other living systems in it. For man, this is a particularly complex phenomenon, because unlike lower organisms whose relationships with their environment and other living things are largely determined genetically, man can and literally must organize himself through participation in communication systems.

To understand how this occurs, we need to consider two different levels of analysis of human communication systems, and the manner in which systems at these two levels relate to each other. The first we can call the individual communication system. The second is the multiperson communication system.

Individual Communication System

Man can and must invent whatever significances he attaches to himself, his environment, and the people in it. It is this capacity of communication, and the consequent, wide-ranging potential for individual uniqueness, that most clearly distinguishes man from other living things.

Human individuals have no way to experience their milieu other than in and through participation in communication systems. This participation is mandatory. It is in becoming organized through participation that man comes to comprehend and give significance and meaning to his experiences. Human sensory receptors are sensitive to light, sound, and pressure —and not to reality. One hears and sees those things which one has become organized to experience, in the same manner as one can eat and metabolize those foods that one is biologically organized to accommodate. Thayer's description of this parallel is a good one:

> Looking is a matter of registering light waves; perceiving a matter of having translated those light waves into an idea or image, into something manipulable not by the eye but by the mind. Listening is a matter of registering sound waves; hearing is a matter of having translated those sound waves into a meaningful pattern or an image, into something, again, manipulable not by the mechanics of the ear, but by the mind.
>
> Information is not something which inheres in the objects and events of man's world. Information is what a man endows those objects and events with. Man literally in-forms himself. He may be constrained or even destroyed by his environment. But its meaning . . . its significance . . . its utility for him . . . these are ultimately properties of him. Information is thus the lifeblood of his awareness, his consciousness, his knowledge of his environment, in the same way that the highly refined and translated products of metabolic process are the lifeblood of his body. An indigestible or undigested herb is either as useless or as troublesome to man as is being unaware or unable to inform himself adequately of some event in his environment which might have vital consequence for him. [66]

The process of becoming organized has multilateral mutually causal consequences, since how man becames organized determines what he sees, hears, believes, comes to know—his sense of what reality is, which in turn determines how he can become organized. And it is in this way that we get what we see.

Man creates the reality and environment he knows and at the same time, probably, the mind by which he knows it and therefore himself. While there is certainly a great deal more to be learned about the way the mind develops,[33, p. 6] it appears that it organizes itself in and through participation in the individual communication system, as the child, and later the adult, seeks to make sense of his life encounters. As Delgado explains:

The newborn baby is not capable of speech, symbolic understanding or directing skillful mobility. It has no ideas, words, or concepts, no tools for communication, no significant sensory experience, no culture. The newborn baby never smiles. He is unable to comprehend the loving phrases of his mother or to be aware of the environment. We must conclude that there are no detectable signs of mental activity at birth and that *human beings are born without minds.**

Pertinent also is Delgado's further point that the mind can best be defined as the *"intracerebral elaboration of extracerebral information,"* implying the interrelatedness and codeterminacy of mind and experienced reality. Both can therefore be viewed as structural residues of participation in the processes of the individual human communication system, as can beliefs, attitudes, and personality.

Vickers captures the essence of this point:

Insofar as I can be regarded as human, it is because I was claimed at birth as a member by a communicative network, which programmed me for participation in itself.**

Multiperson Communication Systems

At a different level of analysis are communication systems involving more than one person. The most obvious examples that come to mind are families, clubs, fraternities, universities, societies, and the like; however, a group of people riding an elevator or two strangers passing on the street are also examples of multiperson communication systems. Wherever organization between two or more persons exists, there is an instance of multiperson human communication systems.

Organization in these systems occurs through interaction between individuals whereby significances are created and maintained. The exchanges may involve words, money, gestures, eye glances, flags, or automobiles. Participation in multiperson communication systems is mandatory. At a given time each of us is a participant in a multitude of such systems.

The basic unit of the multiperson communication system is two or more individuals organized with one another, intentionally or by accident. Elaborations of this basic structural relationship indicate a variety of configurations in terms of level of complexity and the degree of organization. At one extreme is the simple and minimally organized system composed of several individuals riding together on an elevator. At a more complex and

---

* José M. R. Delgado, *Physical Control of the Mind* (New York: Harper & Row, 1969), p. 45. See also the chapter of this volume by Delgado entitled, "Neurophysiology: An Approach to Human Communication."

** Geoffrey Vickers, "The Multivalued Choice," in *Communication Concepts and Perspectives,* ed. by Lee Thayer (New York: Spartan Looks, 1967).

organized level is the multiperson relationship involved when one individual negotiates past another on a sidewalk. At a still more complex and intricately organized level is a system like friendship, and at an extreme in terms of complexity and intricacy of interrelationship is a multiperson system like society.

Peter Berger's view of society provides a good example:

> Every individual biography is an episode within the history of society, which both precedes and survives it. Society was there before the individual was born and it will be there after he has died. What is more, it is within society, and as a result of social processes, that the individual becomes a person, that he attains and holds on to an identity, and that he carries out the various projects that constitute his life. Man cannot exist apart from society.*

This description not only suggests something of the nature of society viewed as a multiperson communication system, but also raises the question of the relationship between society and the individual. For our purposes here, the generic issue is a larger one, having to do with the relationship of the individual not only to society, but to all other human, multiperson communication systems as well.

Like the relationship of mind and the reality it experiences, the relationship between the individual and the multiperson communication system is mutually causal. The raw data with which the human individual organizes himself (and in the process, develops a mind and a concept of reality) are products and consequences of the various multiperson communication systems which he encounters. Each has a reality of its own and its own tokens of significance, with which the individual comes to organize himself. Not only does each multiperson system have a part in the creation or positing of reality, but each also plays an important role in setting the agenda for the individual's encounter with nature as well.

For example, we do not experience trees or rivers at random. They are encountered in social context. Trees are for parking strollers under or for taking rides through in the fall or for climbing; rivers are for swimming or for fishing or for boating—or if they are spanned by bridges, for crossing in cars.

The other side of the coin is that while the individual is organizing himself to participate in various multiperson systems, he is helping to sustain them by contributing to the production of the raw data with respect to which other individuals must organize themselves.

It is in this sense that the input to the individual system is the output of the multiperson system, and, conversely, the output of the individual sys-

---

* Peter Berger, *The Sacred Canopy* (Garden City, N.Y.: Doubleday, 1969), p. 1.

tem is the input to the multiperson system. The relationship between the two is also codetermining in the sense that the individual mind is both a producer and a consumer of multiperson reality.

CONCLUSION

We could—and perhaps we ought to—spend years exploring the implications of this fundamental notion about the nature of human organization. We are victimized by our ignorance of these matters, whether we understand that it is happening or not. How often, for example, do we involve ourselves in the age-old activity of consulting with our closest friends, relatives, peers—those with whom we have become most closely organized— to assess the propriety of our actions and to validate our thoughts? In a literal sense, when we do this we are talking to ourselves.

Or how often do we search for failure to communicate in the person who is speaking rather than in the listener? If you do not understand this chapter is it *I* that have failed? How often do we find ourselves blaming others for the way we comprehend reality?

The fundamental nature of this mutually causal communication suprasystem of which we are all a part is so basic and complex as to defy mastery by generations of men who have sought to institutionalize—through churches, schools, prisons—the balance or "match" between the individual and the multiperson system. Our vocabularies would be greatly restricted if suddenly we had to eliminate words like "criminal," "sociopath," "pervert," "genius," "creative," and "insane" that we use to refer to "mismatches." We never have figured out what to do about diversity.

And as our youth are anxious to point out, most of our institutions reflect a morphostatic perspective—they are designed to eliminate and counteract mismatch, rather than to tolerate or amplify differences between individuals. It remains to be seen, however, whether those who clamor the loudest for deviation-amplifying or tolerating relationships can resist the temptation to replace old morphostatic institutions with new ones when an opportunity for change presents itself.

We are desperately in need of better ways to conceive of and cope with these sorts of issues. We need to look again and with a new scrutiny at ourselves and what we are about. And if we believe it a worthy goal, to strive to make a difference in the course of human affairs. And if we attempt to make that difference as a consequence of planning, then we can ill afford the luxury of having at our disposal any less than the most powerful ways for conceiving of man and the processes of human communication.

I think that general system thinking can provide such a tool.

REFERENCES AND SUGGESTED READINGS

1. Ashby, W. Ross, "General Systems Theory as a New Discipline," *General Systems*, Vol. 3, 1958.
2. Ashby, W. Ross, *An Introduction to Cybernetics*. London: Chapman, 1961.
3. Bahm, Archie J., "Systems Theory," *General Systems*, Vol. 14, 1969.
4. Bakke, E. Wight, "Concept of the Social Organization," in *Modern Organization Theory*, ed. by Mason Haire. New York: Wiley, 1959.
5. Bateson, Gregory, "Cybernetic Explanation," *The American Behavioral Scientist*, Vol. 10, 1967.
6. Bateson, Gregory, "Pathologies of Epistemology," paper prepared under Career Development Award (K2–21, 931) of the National Institute of Mental Health, Oceanic Institute, Hawaii.
7. Beer, Stafford, "Below the Twilight Arch," *General Systems*, Vol. 5, 1960.
8. Beer, Stafford, *Cybernetics and Management*. New York: Wiley, 1959.
9. Beer, Stafford, *Decision and Control*. New York: Wiley, 1966.
10. Bennis, Warren G., "Towards a 'Truly' Scientific Management," *General Systems*, Vol. 7, 1962.
11. Berrien, F. Kenneth, *General and Social Systems*. New Brunswick, N.J.: Rutgers University Press, 1969.
12. Bertalanffy, Ludwig von, "General System Theory—A Critical Review," *General Systems*, Vol. 7, 1962.
13. Bertalanffy, Ludwig von, "General System Theory," *General Systems*, Vol. 1, 1956.
14. Bertalanffy, Ludwig von, *General Systems Theory, Foundations, Developments, Applications*. New York: Braziller, 1968.
15. Bertalanffy, Ludwig von, "An Outline of General System Theory," *British Journal of Philosophical Science*, Vol. 1, 1950.
16. Bertalanffy, Ludwig von, and A. Rapoport, eds., *General Systems*. Washington, D.C.: The Society for General Systems Research, 13 vols., since 1956.
17. Boulding, Kenneth E., "General Systems Theory—The Skeleton of Science," *Management Science*, Vol. 2, 1956.
18. Boulding, Kenneth E., "Political Implications of General Systems Research," *General Systems*, Vol. 6, 1961.
19. Boulding, Kenneth E., "Toward a General Theory of Growth," *The Canadian Journal of Economics and Political Science*, Vol. 19, 1953.
20. Buckley, Walter, *Modern Systems Research for the Behavioral Scientist*. Chicago: Aldine, 1967.
21. Buckley, Walter, *Sociology and Modern Systems Theory*. Englewood Cliffs, N.J.: Prentice-Hall, 1967.
22. Caws, Peter, "Science and System," *General Systems*, Vol. 13, 1968.
23. Churchman, C. West, *The Systems Approach*. New York: Dell, 1968.
24. Emery, R. E., ed., *Systems Thinking*. Baltimore, Md.: Penguin, 1969.
25. Farb, Peter, *Ecology*. New York: Time-Life, 1963.
26. Gardner, John W., *Self-Renewal*. New York: Harper & Row, 1965.
27. Gerard, R. W., "A Biologist's View of Society," *General Systems*, Vol. 1, 1956.
28. Gray, William, Frederick J. Duhl, and Nicholas D. Rizzo, *General Systems Theory and Psychiatry*. Boston: Little, Brown, 1969.
29. Grinker, R. R., Sr., ed., *Toward a Unified Theory of Human Behavior*, 2nd ed. New York: Basic Books, 1967.

30. Hall, A. D., and R. W. Fagen, "Definition of System," *General Systems*, Vol. 1, 1956.
31. Kim, John Y., "Feedback and Human Communication," unpublished doctoral dissertation, University of Iowa, 1971.
32. Kim, John Y., "A Thought on Systems," Institute for Communication Studies, University of Iowa, 1969. (Mimeographed.)
33. Laszlo, Ervin, *System, Structure, and Experience*. New York: Gordon and Breach, 1969.
34. Laszlo, Ervin, ed., *The Relevance of General Systems Theory*. New York: Braziller, 1972.
35. Lawson, Chester A., "Language, Communication, and Biological Organization," *General Systems*, Vol. 8, 1963.
36. Lektorsky, V. A., and V. N. Sadovsky, "On Principles of System Research," *General Systems*, Vol. 5, 1960. "O Printsipakh Issledovania Sistem," trans. by A. Rapoport from *Voprosy Filosofii*, No. 8, 1960.
37. Lysloff, George O., "Semantic Categories and Hierarchy of Systems," *General Systems*, Vol. 14, 1969.
38. MacKay, Donald M., *Information, Mechanism and Meaning*. Cambridge, Mass.: M.I.T. Press, 1969.
39. Maruyama, Magorah, "Metaorganization of Information," *Cybernetica*, No. 4, 1965.
40. Maruyama, Magorah, "Morphogenesis and Morphostasis," *Methodos: Language and Cybernetics*, Vol. 12, No. 48, 1960.
41. Maruyama, Magorah, "A Postscript to 'The Second Cybernetics,'" *American Scientist*, Vol. 51, 1963.
42. Maruyama, Magorah, "The Second Cybernetics," *American Scientist*, Vol. 51, 1963.
43. McClelland, Charles A., "Systems and History in International Relations," *General Systems*, Vol 3, 1958.
44. Meadow, Charles T., "The Analysis of Information Systems," in *Dimensions in Communication*, 2nd ed., ed. by J. H. Campbell and H. W. Hepler. Belmont, Calif.: Wadsworth, 1970.
45. Mesarovic, M. D., *Views on General System Theory*, New York: Wiley, 1964.
46. Miller, James G., "Living Systems: Basic Concepts; Living Systems: Structure and Process; Living Systems: Cross-Level Hypotheses," *Behavioral Science*, Vol. 10, 1965.
47. Milsum, J. H., "Technosphere, Biosphere, and Sociosphere," *General Systems*. Vol. 13, 1968.
48. Monane, Joseph H., *A Sociology of Human Systems*. New York: Appleton-Century-Crofts, 1967.
49. Platt, John, "Hierarchical Restructuring," *General Systems*, Vol. 15, 1970.
50. Pringle, J. W. S., "On the Parallel Between Learning and Evolution," *Behavior*, Vol. 3, 1951.
51. Ramsoy, Odd, *Social Group as System and Subsystem*. New York: Free Press, 1963.
52. Rapoport, Anatol, "Methodology in the Physical, Biological and Social Sciences," *General Systems*, Vol. 14, 1969.
53. Rapoport, Anatol, "Modern Systems Theory," *General Systems*, Vol. 15, 1970.
54. Rice, Charles E., "A Model for the Empirical Study of a Large Social Organization," *General Systems*, Vol. 6, 1961.

55. Ruben, Brent D., and Albert D. Talbott, "Communication, Information and Education Systems," a paper presented to the 17th Annual Conference of the National Society for the Study of Communication, Cleveland, Ohio.

56. Ruesch, Jurgen, Epilogue to the 2nd edition of R. R. Grinker, ed., *Toward a Unified Theory of Human Behavior*, 2nd ed., New York: Basic Books, 1967.

57. Ruesch, Jurgen, and Gregory Bateson, *Communication, the Social Matrix of Psychiatry*. New York: Norton, 1951, 1968.

58. Schroder, Harold M., Michael J. Driver, and Siegfried Streufert, *Human Information Processing*. New York: Holt, Rinehart and Winston, 1967.

59. Shannon, Claude E., and Warren Weaver, *The Mathematical Theory of Communication*. Urbana: University of Illinois Press, 1949.

60. Simon, Herbert A., "The Architecture of Complexity," *Proceedings of the American Philosophical Society*, Vol. 106, No. 6, 1962.

61. Thayer, Lee, *Communication and Communication Systems*. Homewood, Ill.: Irwin, 1968.

62. Thayer, Lee, "Communication and Organization Theory," in *Human Communication Theory*, ed. by Frank E. X. Dance. New York: Holt, Rinehart and Winston, 1967.

63. Thayer, Lee, "Communication: Sine Qua Non of the Behavioral Sciences," in *Vistas in Science*, ed. by D. L. Arm. Albuquerque: University of New Mexico Press, 1968.

64. Thayer, Lee, "Communication Systems," in *The Relevance of General Systems Theory*, ed. by E. Laszlo. New York: Braziller, 1972.

65. Thayer, Lee, "On Communication and Change," *Systematics*, Vol. 6, No. 3, 1968.

66. Thayer, Lee, "On Human Communication and Social Development," a paper presented at the first World Conference on Social Communication for Development, Mexico City, March, 1970.

67. Thompson, John W., "Mental Science, Meteorology, and General System Theory," *General Systems*, Vol. 5, 1960.

68. Vickers, Geoffrey, "A Classification of Systems," *General Systems*, Vol. 15, 1970.

69. Vickers, Geoffrey, "Control, Stability and Choice," *General Systems*, Vol. 2, 1957.

70. Vickers, Geoffrey, "Is Adaptability Enough?," *Behavioral Science*, Vol. 4, 1959.

71. Vickers, Geoffrey, *Value Systems and Social Process*. New York: Basic Books, 1968.

72. Watzlawick, Paul, Janet H. Beavin, and Don D. Jackson, *Pragmatics of Human Communication*. New York: Norton, 1967.

73. Wiener, N., *Cybernetics*. New York: Wiley, 1948.

74. Wiener, N., "Cybernetics and Society," in *The Human Dialogue*, ed. by Floyd W. Matson and Ashley Montagu. New York: Free Press, 1967.

75. Wiener, N., *The Human Use of Human Beings*. New York: Avon, 1950.

76. Wilson, Donna, "Forms of Hierarchy," *General Systems*, Vol. 14, 1969.

77. Wisdom, J. O., "The Hypothesis of Cybernetics," *The British Journal for the Philosophy of Sciences*, Vol. 2, 1951.

78. Young, O. R., "The Impact of General Systems on Political Science," *General Systems*, Vol. 8, 1963.

79. Young, O. R., "A Survey of General Systems Theory," *General Systems*, Vol. 8, 1963.

6

Neurophysiology

JOSÉ M.R. DELGADO

I N Plato's works, Socrates is presented as a kind of intellectual midwife who extracted from the person he questioned knowledge that already existed. According to the doctrine of recollection, learning is only the remembering of knowledge possessed in a former life. In the *Phaedo*, the second argument for the survival of the soul is that knowledge is recollection, and therefore the soul must have existed before birth.

Aristotle rejected the theory of inborn ideas, and proposed the metaphorical tabula rasa, which was subsequently accepted in the seventeenth and eighteenth centuries by empirical physiologists including Locke and Helvétius. The newborn mind was considered a blank tablet on which experience would write messages, and the dissimilarities between individuals were attributed solely to differences in education.

The Aristotelian principle, *"Nihil est in intellectu quod no prius suent in sensu,"* repeated among others by Leonardo da Vinci, expressed the still prevalent idea that "nothing is in the intellect which was not first in the senses." Some authors, including Epicurus and the sensualists, stressed to the limit the importance of sensory inputs, proposing that the intellect is only *what* is in our senses.

WHEN AND HOW THE MIND IS FORMED

Between the extremes of considering the mind either sophisticated or naïve at birth, contemporary opinion holds that both genetic and experiential components are essential, although their functions and relative importance remain controversial. According to several child psychiatrists, heredity and experience are equipotent.[40; 52] Piaget has already emphasized that while the human brain is an almost entirely hereditary regulatory organ, it has practically "no hereditary programming of these regulations, quite unlike the case of so many instincts in birds or fishes. . . ." [45] Intelligence combines two cognitive systems: experience and endogenous regulations. The latter system is a source of intellectual operations. By prolonging the feedbacks and correcting the mistakes, it transforms them into instruments of precognition.

The genetic determination of mental functions has been supported by Rainer, who believes that the fertilized ovum contains "the primordia of what we later call mind," and that "the newborn infant is already as much of an individual 'mentally' as he is physiognomically." [47] According to the evolutionary theories of William James:

> the new forms of being that make their appearance are really nothing more than results of the redistribution of the original and unchanging materials . . . the evolution of the brains, if understood, would be simply the account of how the atoms came to be so caught and jammed. In this story no new *natures*, no factors not present at the beginning, are introduced at any later stage. [26]

In agreement with these ideas, Sherrington writes:

> Mind as attaching to any unicellular life would seem to me unrecognizable to observation; but I would not feel that permits me to affirm it is not there. Indeed, I would think that since mind appears in the developing soma, that amounts to showing that it is potential in the ovum (and sperm) from which the soma sprang. The appearance of recognizable mind in the soma would then be not a creation *de nova* but a development of mind from unrecognizable into recognizable. [49]

Prenatal Factors in the Development of the Mind

The importance of the prenatal period as a determinant of future behavior crystallized in the concept of "ontogenetic zero," [21] has been accepted by most child psychologists. [7] At the moment of fertilization, the life of a unique individual is initiated (at birth, a child is already nine months old); and some experts have suggested that its beginning should be traced back through evolution of the parental reproductive cells, or even through previous generations.

These theories have the merit of stressing the role of genetics in the formation of the mind, but they give the false impression that genetic factors alone are able to create a mind, or that in some mysterious way, a minute, undeveloped mind already exists in the cells. At the core of this discussion is the meaning of "potentiality," which is a convenient concept provided that we understand its limitations. If we say "a block of marble is potentially a piece of sculpture," we mean that marble is an element which can be shaped into a symbolic pattern with chisels and hammers and with appropriate skills. We may say that all shapes and artistic creations exist potentially in the marble, but the reality is that the piece of stone per se lacks the essential elements to become a work of art in the absence of a sculptor. It would be incorrect to think that tools or skills are hidden within the block of marble, or that if we waited long enough, a statue would emerge spontaneously from the block. This type of incorrect reasoning has been called the "error of potentiality." [30] It has infiltrated the field of embryology and has influenced analyses of the origin and evolution of mental functions by assuming that at a certain stage of development properties exist which are present only at a later stage, and which depend on a series of essential conditions neither present in, nor determined by, the stage under consideration.

If we say that the mind is in the sperm, we can also say that each man has one million children, that a newborn baby will be the inventor of spaceships, or that a worm may evolve into a monkey. These statements may be potentially valid, but their fulfillment is contingent upon a constellation of factors which are not present in the original material. A man, in spite of his genes and his potentials, cannot create a single child without the collaboration of a woman; and a baby will not invent rockets unless he is exposed to a highly sophisticated level of physics. We believe that worms have evolved into more complex forms of life, and that potentially, they may produce dinosaurs, supermen, or inhabitants of the moon; but before we allow our imaginations to wander among the limitless possibilities of nature, it is preferable to identify the factors responsible for the observed reality among an infinite number of theoretical potentials.

According to early theories of preformism, the germinal cell—the ovum—held a miniature organism with microscopic eyes, arms, legs, and other parts of the body, which eventually would grow. The ovaries of Eve had potentially the bodies—and minds—of all mankind. Through scientific embryology it became evident that the germinal cell did not contain a compressed homunculus, but only a plan which required the interaction of other elements in order to develop into a human being.

A relatively small group of organization centers (the genes), with the collaboration of molecules supplied from the outside (the mother), produce another series of organizers (enzymes, hormones, and other active substances) which will arrange patterns of molecules for the construction of cells, tissues, and organs and will also produce a new series of organizers to direct the interaction of these new elements. The organizers are not completely stereotyped in performance, but are influenced by their medium. A particular gene may have different phenotypic effects in different environments, and "genes control the 'reaction norm' of the organism to the environmental conditions." [8] Blood vessels, muscles, and the various organs are differentiated; neurons appear, their interconnections are established, and the brain evolves. Chromosomes have neither heart nor brain —only a set of architectonic plans which under suitable conditions will evolve into a complete organism. These plans are unfulfilled for millions of sexual cells and for countless embryos that are casualties in spontaneous abortions. The possibilities of evolution are far from accomplished realities.

If we accept these ideas, we may also state that the fecundated germinal cell does not talk, understand, or think, and that the resulting embryo has no mental functions before the medullary plate rolls up to form the neural tube. When can we detect the first signs of a functioning mind? How are they correlated with the anatomical development of the central nervous system? The study of these questions may be simplified if we first examine the initial signs of a functioning brain, as revealed by behavioral expression in lower animals. Motor neurons are already growing out to establish neural contacts with muscles before they develop. The order of growth is a "progressive individualism within a totally integrated matrix, and not a progressive integration of primarily individuated units." [10] Motions, therefore, are basically a part of a total pattern, and their relative individualization is only a secondary acquisition. Some efferent motor pathways appear before any afferent fiber enters the cerebrum. Initially, the cerebral association system develops toward the motor system, and the peripheral sensory fibers grow toward the receptor field. Significant conclusions from these facts are that "the individual acts on its environment before it reacts to its environment," [9] that efferent nerves must be stimulated by products of the organism's metabolism, and that "behavior in response to such stimulation is spontaneous in the sense that it is the expression of the intrinsic dynamics of the organism as a whole." [12] Total behavior is not made up of reflexes; rather, "the mechanism of the total pattern is an essential component of the performance of the part, that is, the reflex," and behavior therefore "cannot be fully expressed in terms of S-R (Stimulus-Response)." [12] It is significant that, in man, vestibular connections develop before vestibular sense organs, because this reveals that "the cerebral growth determines the attitude of the individual to its environment before that individual is able to receive any sensory impression of its environment. Hence, the initiative is within the organism." [11]

Some of these findings have been confirmed in the toadfish and the cunner. [54] On the first day that the cunner larva swim around freely, they do not respond to external stimuli. Thus, under natural conditions, this species moves about without an effective exteroceptive mechanism, evidently propelled by a mechanism of motility activated from within. The afferent sensory system grows gradually until it finally captures the primitive motor system. The conclusion is that behavior has two components: "endogenous activity, the fundamental motility conditioned by the inner physiological adjustments of the organism; and exogenous activity, the oriented activity by which endogenous activity is so modified as to render response to external stimuli possible." [15]

This information emphasizes the importance of genetic determination and indicates that some mechanisms for behavioral performance are organized in the absence of environmental inputs. It is generally accepted that development of the nervous system is basic for the onset and elaboration of mammalian behavior, but it is not clear whether any factor can be singled out as decisive. Without synaptic conduction, impulses obviously cannot be transmitted: Thus the functional maturity of synapsis must be essential. [56; 49; 36; 24] Objections have been raised about the acceptance of synaptic permeability as the main reason for onset of behavior, [32] and other factors may be equally important. Activity of peripheral nerve fibers is considered essential for the differentiation and specificity of behavioral performance, [16; 17] and the anatomical development of neurofibrillae may be specifically related to the onset of behavior. [29] These and other studies have provided important information, but its interpretation has often been biased by methodological distortions.

It is a common error in behavioral embryology, and in science generally, to try to simplify the observed phenomena and to reduce causality to a single factor, excluding all other variables. This is the *fallacy of the single cause,* [27] or failure to understand that a biological phenomena is always the product of a complex situation, not of a single determinant. With this pitfall in mind, we must face the task of identifying the several elements essential for the development of any given phenomenon—and both conduction and synaptic mechanisms are certainly basic for the onset of behavior.

Myelin is a substance with insulating properties, covering the nerves. Its appearance in neuronal sheaths has often been associated with the onset and differentiation of behavior by neuroanatomists. A correlation perhaps exists for some specific behavior patterns in the cat and the opossum, [31; 53] but most authors today agree that the myelogenetic law cannot be generalized. In the newborn rat, myelination does not take place for several days, although the fetus starts moving many days before birth, and some discrete reflexes and inhibitory activity in higher centers can be observed in a rat fetus nineteen days after conception. [2] Myelination, therefore, cannot be interpreted as necessary for the conduction of impulses or for functional insulation.

Differences in anatomical and behavioral evolution certainly exist between mammals and lower life forms. In the guinea pig, for example, limbs are well formed in the embryo before the appearance of the first behavioral response, while in the salamander, motor behavior is initiated before morphological differentiation of the limbs. Evidently, embryologic studies of man cannot be as extensive and as well controlled as those of amphibia, but valuable information on this subject already exists.[7] Inside the uterus, the human embryo has a comfortable and sheltered life, without facing responsibilities or making choices. Cells multiply automatically, and organs take shape while the growing fetus floats weightless in the silent night of amniotic fluid. Food and oxygen are provided, and wastes are removed continuously and effortlessly by the maternal placenta. As the fetus grows, many organs perform something like a dress rehearsal before their functions are really required. This is usually referred to as the principle of anticipatory morphological maturation. The heart starts to beat when there is no blood to pump; the gastrointestinal tract shows peristaltic movements and begins to secrete juices in the absence of food; the eyelids open and close in the eternal darkness of the uterus; the arms and legs move, giving the mother the indescribable joy of feeling a new life inside herself; even breathing movements appear several weeks before birth, when there is no air to breathe.[1]

Some extensive information about human fetal behavior has been obtained from pregnant women by indirect methods, while other findings were obtained directly from fetuses removed surgically for medical reasions.[25; 39; 44] The first movement observed in a 4-millimeter-long, three-week-old fetus is the heartbeat, which has intrinsic determinants because it starts before the organ has received any nervous connections. The neural elements needed for a reflex act can be demonstrated in the spinal cord at the second month of embryonic life, and at that time, cutaneous stimulation may induce motor responses. A fourteen-week fetus shows most of the responses which can be observed in the neonate, with the exception of vocalization, the tonic grasping reflex, and respiration. With fetal growth, spontaneous motility increases inside the mother's womb, and it is well known that responses from the fetus may be elicited by tapping the mother's abdominal wall.

Sensory Perception of the Developing Fetus

Sensory perception in the fetus has been investigated in detail by several scientists.[55; 57] Cutaneous reception is well developed long before birth, and mechanical or thermal stimulation of the skin elicits motor activity appropriately related to the stimulated area. The existence of pain perception is doubtful. Proprioceptors of the muscles (the spindles) develop at the fourth month of fetal life, and the labyrinth is evident even earlier. Both organs are active during fetal life; they are capable of postural adjustments and may be partially responsible for fetal motility in the uterus.

The possibility of fetal perception of gastrointestinal movements, hunger, thirst, suffocation, and other types of organic experience, has been debated, and it is generally accepted that internal stimuli may activate skeletal musculature. Distinction of sweet from other tastes, and of unpleasant odors such as asafetida, have been demonstrated in premature babies, showing that these receptor mechanisms are already developed. It is doubtful, however, that with the nose and mouth immersed in amniotic fluid, the fetus could have gustatory or olfactory experiences before birth.

The auditory apparatus is well developed at birth, but the general consensus is that the infant is deaf until the liquid of the fetal middle ear is drained through the Eustachian tube by breathing, crying, and perhaps yawning. Loud noises, however, might be perceived, and some cases of presumed fetal hearing have been reported. [18]

The optic apparatus is sufficiently developed in the newborn infant to permit perception of light and darkness, but the optic nerve is not yet fully developed, and its evolution continues after birth and is probably influenced by sensory perception. [46] It is highly improbable that the fetus has any visual experience during its uterine life.

In summary, it is unlikely that before the moment of birth the baby has had any significant visual, auditory, olfactory, or gustatory experience, and it is probable that it has received only a very limited amount of tactile, organic, and proprioceptive information. The newborn has an elaborated system of reflexes; and coughing, sneezing, sucking, swallowing, grasping, and other actions may be evoked by the appropriate sensory stimulation. In an experimental study of seventeen behavioral responses, their intercorrelations proved to be zero, indicating that "there is no mental integration in the newborn child." [19] This integration usually takes place during the first postnatal month.

Whether or not the fetus is capable of conscious experience was a classic philosophical and psychological problem debated at length with a flourish of words and speculations, but with little factual support. [13; 28; 37; 43] It is difficult to understand the basis for this controversy, since there is no evidence that the fetus has visual, auditory, olfactory, or gustatory stimulation. In the absence of the main sensory faculties, the possibility of fetal awareness is therefore reduced to a limited input of organic sensations of proprioception and touch. Whether or not these phenomena can by themselves create consciousness is mainly a question of definition and arbitrary agreement, but it may be stated that they cannot produce manifestations comparable to those of consciousness in children or adults, which are mainly based on visual and auditory perception and experience. The mystery is perhaps insoluble, due to the impossibility of establishing verbal communication with the newborn.

Anticipatory morphological maturation is present in various mechanisms which remain quiescent in the fetus, ready to perform with physiological efficiency as soon as they are needed. Their necessary links are established before birth and are triggered by appropriate stimulation. These functions, which include oral suction, respiration, kidney secretion, and gastrointestinal activity, are able to act several weeks before an expected delivery, in case the baby is born prematurely.

INFORMATION PROCESSING AND THE MIND

No comparable provisions exist for mental functions. The newborn brain is not capable of speech, symbolic understanding, or of directing skillful motility. It has no ideas, words, or concepts, no tools for communication, no significant sensory experience, no culture. The newborn baby never smiles. He is unable to comprehend the loving phrases of his mother or to be aware of the environment. We must conclude that there are no detectable signs of mental activity at birth, and *that human beings are born without minds.* This statement may seem startling, but it should not be rejected. Potentiality should not be confused with reality. A project is not an accomplished fact, especially when essential elements are lacking in the original design. Naturally, a baby lacks experience, but by recognizing this fact, we are accepting the essentiality of extracerebral elements which originate in the outside world and are independent of both the organism and its genetic endowment. As Cantril and Livingston [6] have said, organisms are in a constant transaction, in a process of becoming, constantly changing into something different from what they were before. Early in life, an infant is attracted to sources of comfort and repelled by sources of distress. These experiences lead to the intelligent recognition of objects and persons associated with positive or negative reinforcement, and they will determine selective patterns of behavioral response. "It is at this point, we think, that 'mind' is born." [6]

The concept of the mindless newborn brain is useful because it clarifies our search for the origin of the mind. If this origin depended on genetic endowment, then mental functions should appear in the absence of other external elements (as respiratory functions do). If genetic determination alone is not sufficient, then we must investigate the source and characteristics of the extracerebral elements responsible for the appearance of the mind as the baby matures.

Sensory Dependence of the Adult Mind

Even if reception of sensory information is accepted as totally essential for the onset and development of mental functions, it is more or less explicitly assumed that an adult has a well-established mental capacity which functions with relative independence from the environment. Individuality, initiative, and free will are expressed in the ability to accept or reject ideas and select behavioral responses. A man can isolate himself, meditate, and explore the depths of his own thoughts. To a great extent, education, especially in Occidental cultures, is based on the belief that individual personality is a self-contained and relatively independent entity with its own destiny, well differentiated from its surroundings and able to function by itself even when isolated from earth and traveling in an orbiting capsule.

A more detailed analysis of reality, however, shows that cerebral activity is essentially dependent on sensory inputs from the environment, not only at birth, but also throughout life. Normal mental functions cannot be preserved in the absence of a stream of information coming from the outside world. The mature brain, with all its wealth of past experience and acquired skills, is not capable of maintaining the thinking process, or even normal awareness and reactivity, in a vacuum of sensory deprivation: *The individual mind is not self-sufficient.*

Support for this statement derives from neurophysiological and psychological experimentation. In mammals, the central organization of motor activity is localized in special regions of the cerebral cortex where muscles and ideokinetic formulas are represented. The motor pathways descend through the spinal cord and emerge through the central roots to form plexus and motor nerves. As should be expected, experimental destruction of the ventral roots in animals or pathological damage of these in man produces complete motor paralysis, because the cerebral impulses cannot reach the muscle target. Considering the input side, we know that all sensory information from the periphery, including proprioceptive impulses from the muscles, is carried by the dorsal roots of the spinal cord. As anticipated, destruction of all dorsal roots produces a loss of sensation, but, in addition, there is a paralysis of the musculature as pronounced as when the motor roots are interrupted. These experiments show that in the absence of sensory information, motor activity is totally disrupted. The brain and motor pathways are not sufficient in themselves; and for proper motor behavior, sensory inputs are absolutely necessary.

The studies of Sprague and others [5] of the cat confirmed the importance of incoming information for normal functioning of the brain. These scientists destroyed the lateral portion of the upper midbrain, including the main sensory pathways, and they observed that, in addition to the expected, marked sensory deficit, the cats exhibited a lack of affect, aggression, and pleasurable responses, and did not solicit petting. The animals remained mute, expressionless, and showed minimal autonomic responses; but in spite of this passivity, they showed hyperexploratory activity with incessant stereotyped wandering, sniffing, and searching, as if hallucinating.

> Without a patterned afferent input to the forebrain via the lemnisci, the remaining portions of the central nervous system . . . seem incapable of elaborating a large part of the animal's repertoire of adaptive behavior. [50]

Psychological data also confirm the essential importance of continuous reception of inputs. Experiments on sensory deprivation in animals and man have shown that maintenance of normal mental activity is difficult or impossible when sensory information is reduced and, moreover, that monotonous sensation is aversive. Animals and humans require novelty and continual and varied stimulation from their surroundings.

MAN'S NEED FOR CHANGING ENVIRONMENT

Perception of the environment has positive reinforcing properties. When monkeys were confined in a cage, they would press levers and perform other instrumental responses for the reward of opening a little window and looking at the outside world. Curiosity derives from expectancy of novel sensory stimulation and motivates exploratory behavior in both animals and man, while boredom has negative reinforcing properties and is related to the absence of novel sensory inputs. [3; 22] To be entertained means to be provided with new and changing sensations, mainly visual and auditory. Primitive man probably derived pleasure from looking at the changing beauty of nature, which retains its fascination to the present day. Civilization has provided the technical means for a far greater choice of inputs, and a major portion of our time, effort, mental activity, and economic resources are now devoted to entertainment through books, theaters, radio, television, museums, and other cultural media.

Symbolically, we may speak about "psychic energy" as the level of intracerebral activity which could perhaps be identified in neurophysiological terms by electrical and chemical processes located at specific neuronal fields. This psychic energy may be considered a main determinant of the quantity of intellectual and behavioral manifestations. While this energy obviously depends on cerebral physiology (and indirectly on the health of the whole body), its actual source is extracerebral, because mental activity is not a property of neurons, but is contingent on the received information which activates stored information and past experiences, creating emotions and ideas.

To be alone with our own mind is not enough. Even if all past experiences are included, the exclusion of new perceptions creates serious functional difficulties. This has been shown, for instance, in the studies by Hebb and his group [4] in which college students were asked to lie comfortably on beds in soundproof, lighted cubicles, wearing translucent goggles to minimize optic sensation and gloves with cardboard cuffs to limit tactual perception. The purpose of this isolation experiment was not to cut out all sensory stimulation, but only to remove patterns and symbolic information. Most of the subjects expected to spend their idle time alone, reviewing their studies, planning term papers, or organizing ideas for lectures. The surprising result—for the investigators as well as for the participants—was that the students "were unable to think clearly about anything for any length of time, and their thought process seemed to be affected in other ways." After several hours of isolation, many of them began to see images, such as "a rock shaded by a tree," "a procession of squirrels," or "prehistoric animals walking about in a jungle." Initially, the subjects were surprised and amused, but after a while their hallucinations became disturbing and vivid enough to interfere with sleep. The students had little control over these phenomena, which, in some cases, included acoustic as well as optic perceptions, such as people talking, a music box playing, or a choir singing in full stereophonic sound. Some subjects reported sensations of movement or touch, or feelings of "otherness," or that another body was lying beside them on the bed. Isolation also tended to increase the belief in supernatural phenomena, and several of the students reported that for a few days after their isolation experiment, they were afraid that they were going to see ghosts. The conclusion was that "a changing sensory environment seems essential for human beings. Without it, the brain ceases to function in an adequate way, and abnormalities of behavior develop." [23]

In patients with long-term hospital confinements in beds or in iron lungs or body casts, psychoticlike symptoms including anxiety, delusions, and hallucinations have appeared which did not respond to standard medical or psychiatric treatment, but were easily alleviated by social contact or by sensory stimulation from a radio or television. [33]

In our century, the classic punishment of solitary confinement has been combined with sleep deprivation and used in psychological warfare. Exhaustion and decreased sensory inputs are known to cause mental disturbances and reduce defense mechanisms, and they have been effectively manipulated during brainwashing or "thought-reform" procedures to indoctrinate prisoners. [35; 57]

The literature on sensory deprivation is voluminous [48] and shows conclusively that the cerebral cortex requires a stream of stimulation for the preservation of behavioral and mental normality. We should realize, therefore, that our cerebral and mental functions rely on the umbilical cord of sensory inputs and become disrupted if isolated from the environment. This fact has been recognized by philosophers, and is reflected in the words of Ortega y Gasset who wrote: "Man has no nature; what he has is a history. . . . I am I and my circumstance." [41] The recognition of environmental inputs as a part of personal identity is one of the important contributions of Ortega y Gasset. This idea is presented in *Meditations on Quixote*, [42] when one of the characters states that "circumstantial reality forms the other half of my person. . . . reabsorption of circumstances is the specific destiny of man." A similar thought is expressed in Tennyson's poem "Ulysses," when Ulysses says, "I am a part of all that I have met."

Ortega y Gasset's position is important to philosophical thinking, but we should probably go further and question the existence of that half of personal identity thought not to originate in the environment. If we could erase all individual history, all circumstances and experiences, would there be anything left of our personality? The brain would remain, and neuronal nets would perhaps continue their spiking activity; but devoid of history —of past experiences and knowledge—there could be no mental activity, and the mind would, in fact, be an Aristotelian tabula rasa. Let us remember with Dobzhansky that "genes determine not 'characters' or 'traits' but reactions or response." [14] Our frame of reference and the building blocks of our personality are the materials received from the outside. The role of cerebral mechanisms, which to a great extent are also determined by previous experience, is to receive, bias, combine, and store the received information, but *not to create it*. Originality is the discovery of novel associations between previously received information. We must realize that the anatomical structure of man's brain has not evolved perceptibly in the past several millenniums; what has changed is the amount of information received by the brain and the training to deal with it. The major differences between a caveman and a modern scientist are not genetic but environmental and cultural.

For centuries, philosophical tradition has accepted the existence of the "I," soul, or ego. This more or less metaphysical entity is relatively independent of the environment (and perhaps even of the genes), and is the essence that endows individual man with his unique personal identity and characteristics. Later this essence may be threatened or disallowed by the social medium.

The concept of this "I" is so strong that it has permeated the thinking of authors as original and revolutionary as Marcuse. In *One Dimensional Man,* he distinguishes between true and false needs, declaring:

> False are those who are superimposed upon the individual by particular social interest in his repression. . . . Most of the prevailing needs to relax, to have fun, to behave and consume in accordance with the advertisements, to love and hate what others love and hate, belong to the category of false needs . . . which are determined by external forces over which the individual has no control. . . . The only needs that have an unqualified claim for satisfaction are the vital ones—nourishment, clothing, lodging. [38]

According to Marcuse, inner freedom "designates the private space in which man may become and remain 'himself.' . . . Today the private space has been invaded and whittled down by technological reality."

The basic questions are obviously, Who is this "himself," and What is the origin of his structural elements? Is there any way to provide the experience which will form a baby's mind except by means of the "external powers" of parents, teachers, and culture over which the baby has no control? Are we then going to classify a child's needs as false because they were inculcated? Where is the inner man?

Marcuse's pleas for "intellectual freedom" and his criticism of "material and intellectual needs that perpetuate obsolete forms of the struggle for existence" are certainly valid, but a state of unqualified liberty cannot be supposed to exist for the infant, who is totally dependent physically and psychologically on his surroundings. Freedom must be taught and created.

The mutual dependence of the individual and the "psychic environment" or "noosphere" has been elaborated by Teilhard de Chardin, who wrote that the Universal and Personal "grow in the same direction and culminate simultaneously in each other," the "Hyper-Personal" consciousness at the "Omega point." [51] While it is true that each of us personally receives, interprets, and feels the world around us, why should our individual half be opposed by the noospheric half? Teilhard de Chardin, like Ortega y Gasset and most other philosophers, accepts the existence of the quasi-mystical, inviolable self, an entity somehow identified with the individual mind, ego, or personality, related to the environment, but with a relatively independent existence.

Recent neurophysiological and psychological studies discussed here reveal that this is not the case. The origin of memories, emotional reactivity, motor skills, words, ideas, and behavioral patterns which constitute our personal self can be traced to the environment outside of the individual. Each person is a transitory composite of materials borrowed from the environment, and his mind is the intracerebral elaboration of extracerebral information. The "personal half" is a regrouping of elements of the environment. For the final result, which is manifested as individual reactivity and behavioral responses, the building blocks from culture are more decisive than the individual substratum within which the regrouping is performed.

It is impressive that this is actually the philosophy, as described by Levi-Strauss, [34] of the Bororo Indians, a very primitive tribe living by the Vermelho River in the Amazon jungles of Brazil. For the Bororo, a man is not an individual, but a part of a sociological universe. Their villages exist "for all eternity," forming part of the physical universe along with other animate beings, celestial bodies, and meteorological phenomena. Human shape is transitory, midway between that of the fish and the arara. Human life is merely a department of culture. Death is both natural and anticultural, and whenever a native dies, damage is inflicted not only on his relatives, but on society as a whole. Nature is blamed, and Nature must pay the debt; therefore, a collective hunt is organized to kill some sizable animal, if possible a jaguar, in order to bring home its skin, teeth, and nails, which will constitute the dead man's *mori*, his everlasting personal value.

The conclusion that human beings are part of culture does not deny the fact that individuals have individual reactions and that their brains are unique combinations of elements, but simply points to the source and quality of the factors of personal identity. The cerebral mechanisms which allow us to receive, interpret, feel, and react, as well as the extracerebral sources of stimuli, can and should be investigated experimentally. Then we shall gain a new awareness of the structure of the individual and his relations with the surrounding noosphere.

REFERENCES AND SUGGESTED READINGS

1. Ahfeld, J. F., "Beiträge zur Lehre vom Uebergange der instrauterinen Athmung zur extrauterinen," in *Beiträge zur Physiologie, Festschrift zu Carl Ludwig, zu seinem 20. Geburtstage gewidmet von seinen Schülern.* Leipzig: Vogel, 1890.
2. Angulo Y. Gonzalez, A. W., "Is Myelinogeny an Absolute Index of Behavioral Capability?" *Journal of Comparative Neurology*, Vol. 48, 1929.
3. Berlyne, D. E., *Conflict, Arousal, and Curiosity.* New York: McGraw-Hill, 1960.
4. Bexton, W. H., W. Heron, and T. H. Scott, "Effects of Decreased Variation in the Sensory Environment," *Canadian Journal of Psychology*, Vol. 8, 1954.
5. Canestrini, S., "Uber das Sinnesleben des Neugeborenen," *Monographien aus dem Gesamtgebiete der Neurologie und Psychiatrie*, No. 5, Berlin: Springer, 1913.
6. Cantril, Hadley, and W. K. Livingston, "The Concept of Transaction in Psychology and Neurology," *Journal of Individual Psychology*, Vol. 19, 1963.
7. Carmichael, L., "The Onset and Early Development of Behavior," in *Manual of Child Psychology*, 3rd. ed., ed. by L. Carmichael. New York: Wiley, 1960, pp. 60–185.
8. Caspari, E., "Genetic Basis of Behavior," in *Behavior and Evolution*, ed. by A. Role and G. G. Simpson. New Haven, Conn.: Yale University Press, 1958, pp. 103–127.
9. Coghill, G. E., "Correlated Anatomical and Physiological Studies of the Growth of the Nervous System and Amphibia: The Mechanism of Association of Amblystoma Punctatum," *Journal of Comparative Neurology*, Vol. 51, 1930.
10. Coghill, G. E., "The Mechanism of Integration in Amblystoma Punctatum," *Journal of Comparative Neurology*, Vol. 41, 1926.
11. Coghill, G. E., "The Structural Basis of the Integration of Behavior," *Proceedings of the National Academy of Sciences*, Vol. 16, 1930.
12. Coghill, G. E., "Correlaries of the Anatomical and Physiological Study of Amblystoma from the Age of Earliest Movement to Swimming," *Journal of Comparative Neurology*, Vol. 53, 1931.
13. Cole, L. C., "Can The World Be Saved?" *BioScience*, Vol. 18, 1968.
14. Dobzhansky, T., "Genetics, Society and Evolution," *Bulletin of the New York Academy of Medicine*, Vol. 38, 1862.

15. Dunbar, F., *Emotions and Bodily Changes. A Survey of Literature on Psychosomatic Interrelationships 1910–1953*, 4th ed. New York: Columbia University Press, 1954.
16. Erlanger, J. E., and H. S. Gasser, *Electrical Signs of Nervous Activity*. Philadelphia: University of Pennsylvania Press, 1937.
17. Forbes, A., "The Interpretation of Spinal Reflexes in Terms of Present Knowledge of Nerve Conduction," *Physiology Revue*, Vol. 3, 1922.
18. Forbes, H. S., and H. B. Forbes, "Fetal Sense Reaction: Hearing," *Journal of Comparative Psychology*, Vol. 7, 1927.
19. Furfey, P. H., M. A. Bonham, and M. K. Sargent, "The Mental Organization of the Newborn," *Child Development*, Vol. 1, 1930.
20. Genzmer, A., *Untersuchungen über die Sinneswahrnehmungen des Neugeborenen Menschen*, dissertation, 1873. Halle: Niemeyer, 1882.
21. Gesell, A. L., *Infancy and Human Growth*. New York: Macmillan, 1928.
22. Harlow, H. F., M. K. Harlow, and D. R. Meyer, "Learning Motivated by a Manipulation Drive," *Journal of Experimental Psychology*, Vol. 40, 1950.
23. Heron, W., "The Pathology of Boredom," *Scientific American*, Vol. 196, 1957.
24. Herrick, C. H., *Neurological Foundations of Animal Behavior*. New York: Hafner, 1962.
25. Hooker, D., "Fetal Behavior," *Association for Research in Nervous and Mental Disease Research Publications*, Vol. 19, 1939.
26. James, W., *Principles of Psychology*, Vols. I and II. New York: Dover, 1950.
27. Jennings, H. S., *The Biological Basis of Human Nature*. New York: Norton, 1930.
28. Kussmaul, A., *Untersuchungen über das Seelenleben des Neugeborenen Menschen*, Leipzig, 1859.
29. Lane, H. H., "The Correlation Between Structure and Function in the Development of the Special Senses of the White Rat," *University of Oklahoma Bulletin*, N.S. No. 140, 1917.
30. Lange, F. A., *History of Materialism*. New York: Harcourt, Brace, 1925.
31. Langworthy, O. R., "A Correlated Study of the Development of Reflex Activity in Fetal and Young Kittens and the Myelinization of Tracts in the Nervous System," *Contributions to Embryology*, Carnegie Institute, Washington, 20, No. 114, 1929.
32. Lashley, K. S., "Studies of Cerebral Function in Learning: VI. The Theory That Synaptic Resistance is Reduced by the Passage of the Nerve Impulse," *Psychology Revue*, Vol. 31, 1924.
33. Leiderman, P. H., J. H. Mendelson, D. Wexler, and P. Solomon, "Sensory Deprivation: Clinical Aspects," *Archives of Internal Medicine*, Vol. 101, 1958.
34. Levi-Strauss, C., *A World of the Wane*, trans. by J. Russell, London: Hutchinson, 1961.
35. Lifton, R. J., *Thought Reform and the Psychology of Totalism: A Study of "Brainwashing" in China*. New York: Norton, 1961.
36. Lillie, R. S., *Protoplasmic Action and Nervous System*, 2nd ed. Chicago: University of Chicago Press, 1932.
37. Locke, J., *Essays Concerning Human Understanding*. Cambridge, Mass.: Harvard University Press, 1931.
38. Marcuse, Herbert, *One Dimensional Man*. Boston: Beacon Press, 1964.
39. Minkowski, M., "Sur Les Mouvements, Les Réflexes, et Les Réactions Musculaieres du Foetus Humain de 2 à 5 Mois et Leur Rélations Avec le Système Nerveux Foetal," *Revue of Embryology*, Vol. 37, 1921.

40. Mittleman, B., "Motility in Infants, Children, and Adults: Patterning and Psychodynamics," *Psychoanalytical Study of the Child,* Vol. 9, 1954.
41. Ortega y Gasset, José, *History as a System.* New York: Norton, 1961.
42. Ortega y Gasset, José, *Meditations on Quixote,* trans. by E. Rugg and D. Marin, with notes and introduction by J. Marias. New York: Norton, 1961.
43. Peterson, F., and L. H. Rainey, "The Beginnings of Mind in the Newborn," *Bulletin of Lying-in Hospital,* New York, Vol. 7, 1910.
44. Pflüger, E., "Die Lebensfähigkeit des menschlichen Foetus," *Pflüger Archiv für die gesamte Physiologie,* Vol. 14, 1877.
45. Piaget,.Jean, *The Origins of Intelligence in Children,* trans. by Margaret Cook. New York: International Universities, 1952.
46. Pratt, K. C., A. K. Nelson, and K. H. Sun, "The Behavior of the Newborn Infant," *Ohio State University Studies, Contributions in Psychology,* No. 19, 1930.
47. Rainer, J. D., "The Concept of Mind in the Framework of Genetics," in *Theories of the Mind,* ed. by J. M. Scher. New York: Free Press, 1962, pp. 65–79.
48. Schultz, D. P., *Sensory Restriction, Effects on Behavior.* New York: Academic Press, 1965.
49. Sherrington, C. S., *The Integrative Action of the Nervous System.* New York: Cambridge University Press, 2nd ed., 1947.
50. Sprague, J. M., W. W. Chambers, and E. Stellar, "Attentive, Affective, and Adaptive Behavior in the Cat," *Science,* Vol. 133, 1961.
51. Teilhard de Chardin, P., *The Phenomenon of Man.* New York: Harper & Row, 1959.
52. Thomas, A., and S. Chess, "An Approach to the Study of Sources of Individual Differences in Child Behavior," *Journal of Clinical Experimental Psychopathology,* Vol. 19, 1957.
53. Tilney, F., and L. Casamajor, "Myelinogeny as Applied to the Study of Behavior," *Archives of Neurological Psychiatry,* Vol. 12, 1924.
54. Tracy, H. C., "The Development of Motility and Behavior Reactions in the Toadfish (Opsanus Tau)," *Journal of Comparative Neurology,* Vol. 40, 1926.
55. Weiss, A. P., "The Measurement of Infant Behavior," *Psychology Revue,* Vol. 36, 1929.
56. Weiss, P., "Self-differentiation of the Basic Patterns of Coordination," *Comparative Psychology Monographs,* Vol. 17, 1941.
57. West, L. J., "Psychiatry, 'Brainwashing,' and the American Character," *American Journal of Psychiatry,* Vol. 120, 1964.

7

Symbolic Interaction

HERBERT BLUMER

SYMBOLIC INTERACTIONISM

Symbolic interactionism rests, in the last analysis, on three simple premises. The first premise is that human beings act toward things on the basis of the meanings that the things have for them. Such things include everything that the human being may note in his world—physical objects, such as trees or chairs; other human beings, such as a mother or a store clerk; categories of human beings, such as friends or enemies; institutions, such as a school or a government; guiding ideals, such as individual independence or honesty; activities of others, such as their commands or requests; and such situations as an individual encounters in his daily life. The second premise is that the meaning of such things is derived from, or arises out of, the social interaction that one has with one's fellows. The third premise is that these meanings are handled in, and modified through, an interpretative process used by the person in dealing with the things he encounters. I wish to discuss briefly each of these three fundamental premises.

It would seem that few scholars would see anything wrong with the first premise—that human beings act toward things on the basis of the meanings which these things have for them. Yet, oddly enough, this simple view is ignored or played down in practically all of the thought and work in contemporary social science and psychological science. Meaning is either taken for granted and thus pushed aside as unimportant or it is regarded as a mere neutral link between the factors responsible for human behavior

135

and this behavior as the product of such factors. We can see this clearly in the predominant posture of psychological and social science today. Common to both of these fields is the tendency to treat human behavior as the product of various factors that play upon human beings; concern is with the behavior and with the factors regarded as producing them. Thus, psychologists turn to such factors as stimuli, attitudes, conscious or unconscious motives, various kinds of psychological inputs, perception and cognition, and various features of personal organization to account for given forms or instances of human conduct. In a similar fashion sociologists rely on such factors as social position, status demands, social roles, cultural prescriptions, norms and values, social pressures, and group affiliation to provide such explanations. In both such typical psychological and sociological explanations the meanings of things for the human beings who are acting are either bypassed or swallowed up in the factors used to account for their behavior. If one declares that the given kinds of behavior are the result of the particular factors regarded as producing them, there is no need to concern oneself with the meaning of the things toward which human beings act; one merely identifies the initiating factors and the resulting behavior. Or one may, if pressed, seek to accommodate the element of meaning by lodging it in the initiating factors or by regarding it as a neutral link intervening between the initiating factors and the behavior they are alleged to produce. In the first of these latter cases the meaning disappears by being merged into the initiating or causative factors; in the second case meaning becomes a mere transmission link that can be ignored in favor of the initiating factors.

The position of symbolic interactionism, in contrast, is that the meanings that things have for human beings are central in their own right. To ignore the meaning of the things toward which people act is seen as falsifying the behavior under study. To bypass the meaning in favor of factors alleged to produce the behavior is seen as a grievous neglect of the role of meaning in the formation of behavior.

The simple premise that human beings act toward things on the basis of the meaning of such things is much too simple in itself to differentiate symbolic interactionism—there are several other approaches that share this premise. A major line of difference between them and symbolic interactionism is set by the second premise, which refers to the source of meaning. There are two well-known traditional ways of accounting for the origin of meaning. One of them is to regard meaning as being intrinsic, as being a natural part of the objective makeup of the thing. Thus, a chair is clearly a chair in itself, a cow a cow, a cloud a cloud, a rebellion a rebellion, and so forth. Being inherent, meaning needs merely to be disengaged by observing the objective thing that has the meaning. Since the meaning emanates, so to speak, from the thing, there is no process involved in its formation; all that is necessary is to recognize it. It should be immediately apparent that this view reflects the traditional position of "realism" in philosophy—a position that is widely held and deeply entrenched in the social and psychological sciences. The other major traditional view regards "meaning" as a psychical accretion brought to the thing by the person for whom the thing has meaning. This psychical accretion is treated as being an expression of constituent elements of the person's psyche, mind, or psychological organization. The constituent elements are such things as sensations, feelings, ideas, memories, motives, and attitudes. The meaning of a thing is but the expression of the given psychological elements that are brought into play in connection with the perception of the thing; thus one seeks to explain the meaning of a thing by isolating the particular psychological elements that produce the meaning. One sees this in the somewhat ancient and classical psychological practice of analyzing the meaning of an object by identifying the sensations that enter into perception of that object; or in the contemporary practice of tracing the meaning of a thing, such as let us say prostitution, to the attitude of the person who views it. This lodging of the meaning of things in psychological elements limits the processes of the formation of meaning to whatever processes are involved in arousing and bringing together the given psychological elements that produce the meaning. Such processes are psychological in nature, and include perception, cognition, repression, transfer of feelings, and association of ideas.

Symbolic interactionism views meaning as having a different source than those held by the two dominant views just considered. It does not regard meaning as emanating from the intrinsic makeup of the thing that has meaning, nor does it see meaning as arising through a coalescence of psychological elements in the person. Instead, it sees meaning as arising in the process of interaction between people. The meaning of a thing for a person grows out of the ways in which other persons act toward the person with regard to the thing. Their actions operate to define the thing for the person. Thus, symbolic interactionism sees meanings as social products, as creations that are formed in and through the defining activities of people as they interact. This point of view gives symbolic interactionism a very distinctive position, with profound implications that will be discussed later.

The third premise mentioned above further differentiates symbolic interactionism. While the meaning of things is formed in the context of social interaction and is derived by the person from that interaction, it is a mistake to think that the use of meaning by a person is but an application of the meaning so derived. This mistake seriously mars the work of many scholars who otherwise follow the symbolic-interactionist approach. They fail to see that the use of meanings by a person in his action involves an interpretative process. In this respect they are similar to the adherents of the two dominant views spoken of above—to those who lodge meaning in the objective makeup of the thing that has it and those who regard it as an expression of psychological elements. All three are alike in viewing the use of meaning by the human being in his action as being no more than an arousing and application of already established meanings. As a result, all three fail to see that the use of meanings by the actor occurs through a *process of interpretation.* This process has two distinct steps. First, the actor indicates to himself the things toward which he is acting; he has to point out to himself the things that have meaning. The making of such indications is an internalized social process in that the actor is interacting with himself. This interaction with himself is something other than an interplay of psychological elements; it is an instance of the person engaging in a process of communication with himself. Second, by virtue of this process of communicating with himself, interpretation becomes a matter of handling meanings. The actor selects, checks, suspends, regroups, and transforms the meanings in the light of the situation in which he is placed and the direction of his action. Accordingly, interpretation should not be regarded as a mere automatic application of established meanings, but as a formative process in which meanings are used and revised as instruments for the guidance and formation of action. It is necessary to see that meanings play their part in action through a process of self-interaction.

It is not my purpose to discuss at this point the merits of the three views that lodge meaning respectively in the thing, in the psyche, and in social action, nor to elaborate on the contention that meanings are handled flexibly by the actor in the course of forming his action. Instead, I wish merely to note that by being based on these three premises, symbolic interaction is necessarily led to develop an analytical scheme of human society and human conduct that is quite distinctive. It is this scheme that I now propose to outline.

Symbolic interactionism is grounded on a number of basic ideas, or "root images," as I prefer to call them. These root images refer to and depict the nature of the following matters: human groups or societies, social interaction, objects, the human being as an actor, human action, and the interconnection of the lines of action. Taken together, these root images represent the way in which symbolic interactionism views human society and conduct. They constitute the framework of study and analysis. Let me describe briefly each of these root images.

NATURE OF HUMAN SOCIETY

Human groups are seen as consisting of human beings who are engaging in action. The action consists of the multitudinous activities that the individuals perform in their life as they encounter one another and as they deal with the succession of situations confronting them. The individuals may act singly, they may act collectively, and they may act as representatives of some organization or group. The activities belong to the acting individuals and are carried on by them always with regard to the situations in which they have to act. The import of this simple and essentially redundant characterization is that fundamentally human groups or society *exists in action* and must be seen in terms of action. This picture of human society as action must be the starting point (and the point of return) for any scheme that purports to treat and analyze human society empirically. Conceptual schemes that depict society in some other fashion can only be derivations from the complex of ongoing activity that constitutes group life. This is true of the two dominant conceptions of society in contemporary sociology—that of culture and that of social structure. Culture as a conception, whether defined as custom, tradition, norm, value, rules, or the like, is clearly derived from what people do. Similarly, social structure in any of its aspects, as represented by such terms as social position, status, role, authority, and prestige, refers to relationships derived from how people act toward one another. The life of any human society consists necessarily of an ongoing process of fitting together the activities of its members. It is this complex of ongoing activity that establishes and portrays structure or organization. A cardinal principle of symbolic interactionism is that any empirically oriented scheme of human society, however derived, must respect the fact that in the first and last instances human society consists of people engaging in action. To be empirically valid the scheme must be consistent with the nature of the social action of human beings.

Nature of Social Interaction

Group life necessarily presupposes interaction between the group members; or, put otherwise, a society consists of individuals interacting with one another. The activities of the members occur predominantly in response to one another or in relation to one another. Even though this is recognized almost universally in definitions of human society, social interaction is usually taken for granted and treated as having little, if any, significance in its own right. This is evident in typical sociological and psychological schemes—they treat social interaction as merely a medium through which the determinants of behavior pass to produce the behavior. Thus, the typical sociological scheme ascribes behavior to such factors as status position, cultural prescriptions, norms, values, sanctions, role demands, and social-system requirements; explanation in terms of such factors suffices without paying attention to the social interaction that their play necessarily presupposes. Similarly, in the typical psychological scheme such factors as motives, attitudes, hidden complexes, elements of psychological organization, and psychological processes are used to account for behavior, without any need of considering social interaction. One jumps from such causative factors to the behavior they are supposed to produce. Social interaction becomes a mere forum through which sociological or psychological determinants move to bring about given forms of human behavior. I may add that this ignoring of social interaction is not corrected by speaking of an interaction of societal elements (as when a sociologist speaks of an interaction of social roles or an interaction between the components of a social system) or an interaction of psychological elements (as when a psychologist speaks of an interaction between the attitudes held by different people). Social interaction is an interaction between actors and not between factors imputed to them.

Symbolic interactionism does not merely give a ceremonious nod to social interaction. It recognizes social interaction as being of vital importance in its own right. This importance lies in the fact that social interaction is a process that forms human conduct instead of being merely a means or a setting for the expression or release of human conduct. Put simply, human beings in interacting with one another have to take account of what the other is doing or is about to do; they are forced to direct their own conduct or handle their situations in terms of what they take into account. Thus, the activities of others enter as positive factors in the formation of their own conduct; in the face of the actions of others one may abandon an intention or purpose, revise it, check or suspend it, intensify it, or replace it. The actions of others enter to set what one plans to do, may oppose or prevent such plans, may require a revision of such plans, and may demand a very different set of such plans. One has to fit one's own line of activity in some manner to the actions of others. The actions of others have to be taken into account and cannot be regarded as merely an arena for the expression of what one is disposed to do or sets out to do.

We are indebted to George Herbert Mead for the most penetrating analysis of social interaction—an analysis that squares with the realistic account just given. Mead identifies two forms or levels of social interaction in human society. He refers to them respectively as "the conversation of gestures" and "the use of significant symbols"; I shall term them respectively "nonsymbolic interaction" and "symbolic interaction." Nonsymbolic interaction takes place when one responds directly to the action of another without interpreting that action; symbolic interaction involves interpretation of the action. Nonsymbolic interaction is most readily apparent in reflex responses, as in the case of a boxer who automatically raises his arm to parry a blow. However, if the boxer were reflectively to identify the forthcoming blow from his opponent as a feint designed to trap him, he would be engaging in symbolic interaction. In this case, he would endeavor to ascertain the meaning of the blow—that is, what the blow signifies as to his opponent's plan. In their association human beings engage plentifully in nonsymbolic interaction as they respond immediately and unreflectively to each other's bodily movements, expressions, and tones of voice, but their characteristic mode of interaction is on the symbolic level, as they seek to understand the meaning of one another's action.

Mead's analysis of symbolic interaction is highly important. He sees it as a presentation of gestures and a response to the meaning of those gestures. A gesture is any part or aspect of an ongoing action that signifies the larger act of which it is a part—for example, the shaking of a fist as an indication of a possible attack, or the declaration of war by a nation as an indication of a posture and line of action of that nation. Such things as requests, orders, commands, cues, and declarations are gestures that convey to the person who recognizes them an idea of the intention and plan of forthcoming action of the individual who presents them. The person who responds organizes his response on the basis of what the gestures mean to him; the person who presents the gestures advances them as indications or signs of what he is planning to do, as well as of what he wants the respondent to do or understand. Thus, the gesture has meaning both for the person who makes it and for the person to whom it is directed. When the gesture has the same meaning for both, the two parties understand each other. From this brief account it can be seen that the meaning of the gesture flows out along three lines (Mead's triadic nature of meaning): It signifies what the person to whom it is directed is to do; it signifies what the person who is making the gesture plans to do; and it signifies the joint action that is to arise by the articulation of the acts of both. Thus, for illustration, a robber's command to his victim to put up his hands is (1) an indication of what the victim is to do; (2) an indication of what the robber plans to do, that is, relieve the victim of his money; and (3) an indication of the joint act being formed, in this case a holdup. If there is confusion or misunderstanding along any one of these three lines of meaning, communication is ineffective, interaction is impeded, and the formation of joint action is blocked.

One additional feature should be added to round out Mead's analysis of symbolic interaction, namely, that the parties to such interaction must necessarily take each other's roles. To indicate to another what he is to do, one has to make the indication from the standpoint of that other; to order the victim to put up his hands the robber has to see this response in terms of the victim making it. Correspondingly, the victim has to see the command from the standpoint of the robber who gives the command; he has to grasp the intention and forthcoming action of the robber. Such mutual role taking is the *sine qua non* of communication and effective symbolic interaction.

The central place and importance of symbolic interaction in human group life and conduct should be apparent. A human society or group consists of people in association. Such association exists necessarily in the form of people acting toward one another and thus engaging in social interaction. Such interaction in human society is characteristically and predominantly on the symbolic level; as individuals acting individually, collectively, or as agents of some organization encounter one another they are necessarily required to take account of the actions of one another as they form their own action. They do this by a dual process of indicating to others how to act and of interpreting the indications made by others. Human group life is a vast process of such defining to others what to do and of interpreting their definitions: through this process people come to fit their activities to one another and to form their own individual conduct. Both such joint activity and individual conduct are formed *in* and *through* this ongoing process; they are not mere expressions or products of what people bring to their interaction or of conditions that are antecedent to their interaction. The failure to accommodate to this vital point constitutes the fundamental deficiency of schemes that seek to account for human society in terms of social organization or psychological factors, or of any combination of the two. By virtue of symbolic interaction, human group life is necessarily a formative process and not a mere arena for the expression of preexisting factors.

Nature of Objects

The position of symbolic interactionism is that the "worlds" that exist for human beings and for their groups are composed of "objects" and that these objects are the product of symbolic interaction. An object is anything that can be indicated, anything that is pointed to or referred to—a cloud, a book, a legislature, a banker, a religious doctrine, a ghost, and so forth. For purposes of convenience one can classify objects in three categories: (1) physical objects, such as chairs, trees, or bicycles; (2) social objects, such as students, priests, a president, a mother, or a friend; and (3) abstract objects, such as moral principles, philosophical doctrines, or ideas such as justice, exploitation, or compassion. I repeat that an object is anything that can be indicated or referred to. The nature of an object —of any and every object—consists of the meaning that it has for the person for whom it is an object. This meaning sets the way in which he sees the object, the way in which he is prepared to act toward it, and the way in which he is ready to talk about it. An object may have a different meaning for different individuals: A tree will be a different object to a botanist, a lumberman, a poet, and a home gardener; the President of the United States can be a very different object to a devoted member of his political party than to a member of the opposition; the members of an ethnic group may be seen as a different kind of object by members of other groups. The meaning of objects for a person arises fundamentally out of the way they are defined to him by others with whom he interacts. Thus, we come to learn through the indications of others that a chair is a chair, that doctors are a certain kind of professional, that the United States Constitution is a given kind of legal document, and so forth. Out of a process of mutual indications, common objects emerge—objects that have the same meaning for a given set of people and are seen in the same manner by them.

Several noteworthy consequences follow from the foregoing discussion of objects. First, it gives us a different picture of the environment or milieu of human beings. From their standpoint the environment consists *only* of the objects that the given human beings recognize and know. The nature of this environment is set by the meaning that the objects composing it have for those human beings. Individuals, also groups, occupying or living in the same spatial location may have, accordingly, very different environments; as we say, people may be living side by side yet be living in different worlds. Indeed, the term *world* is more suitable than the word *environment* to designate the setting, the surroundings, and the texture of things that confront them. It is the world of their objects with which people have to deal and toward which they develop their actions. It follows that in order to understand the action of people it is necessary to identify their world of objects—an important point that will be elaborated later.

Second, objects (in the sense of their meaning) must be seen as social creations—as being formed in and arising out of the process of definition and interpretation as this process takes place in the interaction of people. The meaning of anything and everything has to be formed, learned, and transmitted through a process of indication—a process that is necessarily a social process. Human group life on the level of symbolic interaction is a vast process in which people are forming, sustaining, and transforming the objects of their world as they come to give meaning to objects. Objects have no fixed status except as their meaning is sustained through indications and definitions that people make of the objects. Nothing is more apparent than that objects in all categories can undergo change in their meaning. A star in the sky is a very different object to a modern astrophysicist than it was to a sheepherder of biblical times; marriage was a different object to later Romans than to earlier Romans; the president of a nation who fails to act successfully through critical times may become a very different object to the citizens of his land. In short, from the standpoint of symbolic interactionism human group life is a process in which objects are being created, affirmed, transformed, and cast aside. The life and action of people necessarily change in line with the changes taking place in their world of objects.

THE HUMAN BEING AS AN ACTING ORGANISM

Symbolic interactionism recognizes that human beings must have a makeup that fits the nature of social interaction. The human being is seen not only as an organism that responds to others on the nonsymbolic level but as one that makes indications to others and interprets their indications. He can do this, as Mead has shown so emphatically, only by virtue of possessing a "self." Nothing esoteric is meant by this expression. It means merely that a human being can be an object of his own action. Thus, he can recognize himself, for instance, as being a man, young in age, a student, in debt, trying to become a doctor, coming from an undistinguished family, and so forth. In all such instances he is an object to himself; and he acts toward himself and guides himself in his actions toward others on the basis of the kind of object he is to himself. This notion of oneself as an object fits into the earlier discussion of objects. Like other objects, the self-object emerges from the process of social interaction in which other people are defining a person to himself. Mead has traced the way in which this occurs in his discussion of role taking. He points out that in order to become an object to himself a person has to see himself from the outside. One can do this only by placing himself in the position of others and viewing himself or acting toward himself from that position. The roles the person takes range from that of discrete individuals (the "play stage"), through that of discrete organized groups (the "game stage") to that of the abstract community (the "generalized other"). In taking such roles the person is in a position to address or approach himself—as in the case of a young girl who in "playing mother" talks to herself as her mother would do, or in the case of a young priest who sees himself through the eyes of the priesthood. We form our objects of ourselves through such a process of role taking. It follows that we see ourselves through the way in which others see or define us—or, more precisely, we see ourselves by taking one of the three types of roles of others that have been mentioned. That one forms an object of himself through the ways in which others define one to himself is recognized fairly well in the literature today, so despite the great significance of this point, I shall not comment on it further.

There is an even more important matter that stems from the fact that the human being has a self, namely that this enables him to interact with himself. This interaction is not in the form of interaction between two or more parts of a psychological system, as between needs, or between emotions, or between ideas, or between the id and the ego in the Freudian scheme. Instead, the interaction is social—a form of communication, with the person addressing himself as a person and responding thereto. We can clearly recognize such interaction in ourselves as each of us notes that he is angry with himself, or that he has to spur himself on in his tasks, or that he reminds himself to do this or that, or that he is talking to himself in working out some plan of action. As such instances suggest, self-interaction exists fundamentally as a process of making indications to oneself. This process is in play continuously during one's waking life, as one notes and considers one or another matter, or observes this or that happening. Indeed, for the human being to be conscious or aware of anything is equivalent to his indicating the thing to himself—he is identifying it as a given kind of object and considering its relevance or importance to his line of action. One's waking life consists of a series of such indications that the person is making to himself, indications that he uses to direct his action.

We have, then, a picture of the human being as an organism that interacts with itself through a social process of making indications to itself. This is a radically different view of the human being from that which dominates contemporary social and psychological science. The dominant prevailing view sees the human being as a complex organism whose behavior is a response to factors playing on the organization of the organism. Schools of thought in the social and psychological sciences differ enormously in which of such factors they regard as significant, as is shown in such a diverse array as stimuli, organic drives, need-dispositions, conscious motives, unconscious motives, emotions, attitudes, ideas, cultural prescriptions, norms, values, status demands, social roles, reference-group affiliations, and institutional pressures. Schools of thought differ also in how they view the organization of the human being, whether as a kind of biological organization, a kind of psychological organization, or a kind of imported societal organization incorporated from the social structure of one's group. Nevertheless, these schools of thought are alike in seeing the human being as a responding organism, with its behavior being a product of the factors playing on its organization or an expression of the interplay of parts of its organization. Under this widely shared view the human being is "social" only in the sense either of being a member of social species, or of responding to others (social stimuli), or of having incorporated within it the organization of his group.

The view of the human being held in symbolic interactionism is fundamentally different. The human being is seen as "social" in a much more profound sense—in the sense of an organism that engages in social interaction with itself by making indications to itself and responding to such indications. By virtue of engaging in self-interaction the human being stands in a markedly different relation to his environment than is presupposed by the widespread conventional view described above. Instead of being regarded as merely an organism that responds to the play of factors on or through it, the human being is seen as an organism that has to deal with what it notes. It meets what it so notes by engaging in a process of self-indication in which it makes an object of what it notes, gives it a meaning, and uses the meaning as the basis for directing its action. Its behavior with regard to what it notes is not a response called forth by the presentation of what it notes but instead is an action that arises out of the interpretation made through the process of self-indication. In this sense, the human being who is engaging in self-interaction is not a mere responding organism but an acting organism—an organism that has to mold a line of action on the basis of what it takes into account instead of merely releasing a response to the play of some factor on its organization.

Nature of Human Action

The capacity of the human being to make indications to himself gives a distinctive character to human action. It means that the human individual confronts a world that he must interpret in order to act instead of an environment to which he responds because of his organization. He has to cope with the situations in which he is called on to act, ascertaining the meaning of the actions of others and mapping out his own line of action in the light of such interpretation. He has to construct and guide his action instead of merely releasing it in response to factors playing on him or operating through him. He may do a miserable job in constructing his action, but he has to construct it.

This view of the human being directing his action by making indications to himself stands sharply in contrast to the view of human action that dominates current psychological and social science. This dominant view, as already stated, ascribes human action to an initiating factor or a combination of such factors as motives, attitudes, need-dispositions, unconscious complexes, stimuli configurations, status demands, role requirements, and situational demands. To link the action to one or more of such initiating agents is regarded as fulfilling the scientific task. Yet, such an approach ignores the process of self-interaction through which the individual handles his world and constructs his action. The door is closed to the vital process of interpretation in which the individual notes and assesses what is presented to him and through which he maps out lines of overt behavior prior to their execution.

Fundamentally, action on the part of a human being consists of taking account of various things that he notes and forging a line of conduct on the basis of how he interprets them. The things taken into account cover such matters as his wishes and wants, his objectives, the available means for their achievement, the actions and anticipated actions of others, his image of himself, and the likely result of a given line of action. His conduct is formed and guided through such a process of indication and interpretation. In this process, given lines of action may be started or stopped, they may be abandoned or postponed, they may be confined to mere planning or to an inner life of reverie, or if initiated, they may be transformed. My purpose is not to analyze this process but to call attention to its presence and operation in the formation of human action. We must recognize that the activity of human beings consists of meeting a flow of situations in which they have to act and that their action is built on the basis of what they note, how they assess and interpret what they note, and what kind of projected lines of action they map out. This process is not caught by ascribing action to some kind of factor (for example, motives, need-dispositions, role requirements, social expectations, or social rules) that is thought to initiate the action and propel it to its conclusion; such a factor, or some expression of it, is a matter the human actor takes into account in mapping his line of action. The initiating factor does not embrace or explain how it and other matters are taken into account in the situation that calls for action. One has to get inside of the defining process of the actor in order to understand his action.

This view of human action applies equally well to joint or collective action in which numbers of individuals are implicated. Joint or collective action constitutes the domain of sociological concern, as exemplified in the behavior of groups, institutions, organizations, and social classes. Such instances of societal behavior, whatever they may be, consist of individuals fitting their lines of action to one another. It is both proper and possible to view and study such behavior in its joint or collective character instead of in its individual components. Such joint behavior does not lose its character of being constructed through an interpretative process in meeting the situations in which the collectivity is called on to act. Whether the collectivity be an army engaged in a campaign, a corporation seeking to expand its operations, or a nation trying to correct an unfavorable balance of trade, it needs to construct its action through an interpretation of what is happening in its area of operation. The interpretative process takes place by participants making indications to one another, not merely each to himself. Joint or collective action is an outcome of such a process of interpretative interaction.

Interlinkage of Action

As stated earlier, human group life consists of, and exists in, the fitting of lines of action to one another by the members of the group. Such articulation of lines of action gives rise to and constitutes "joint action"—a societal organization of conduct of different acts by diverse participants. A joint action, while made up of diverse component acts, is different from any one of them and from their mere aggregation. The joint action has a distinctive character in its own right, a character that lies in the articulation or linkage as apart from what may be articulated or linked. Thus, the joint action may be identified as such and may be spoken of and handled without having to break it down into the separate acts that comprise it. This is what we do when we speak of such things as marriage, a trading transaction, war, a parliamentary discussion, or a church service. Similarly, we can speak of the collectivity that engages in joint action without having to identify the individual members of that collectivity, as we do in speaking of a family, a business corporation, a church, a university, or a nation. It is evident that the domain of the social scientist is constituted precisely by the study of joint action and of the collectivities that engage in joint action.

In dealing with collectivities and with joint action, one can easily be trapped in an erroneous position by failing to recognize that the joint action of the collectivity is an interlinkage of the separate acts of the participants. This failure leads one to overlook the fact that a joint action always has to undergo a process of formation; even though it may be a well-established and repetitive form of social action, each instance of it has to be formed anew. Further, this career of formation through which it comes into being necessarily takes place through the dual process of designation and interpretation that was discussed above. The participants still have to guide their respective acts for forming and using meanings.

With these remarks as a background I wish to make three observations on the implications of the interlinkage that constitutes joint action. I wish to consider first those instances of joint action that are repetitive and stable. The preponderant portion of social action in a human society, particularly in a settled society, exists in the form of recurrent patterns of joint action. In most situations in which people act toward one another they have in advance a firm understanding of how to act and of how other people will act. They share common and preestablished meanings of what is expected in the action of the participants, and each participant is able to guide his own behavior accordingly. Instances of repetitive and preestablished forms of joint action are so frequent that it is easy to understand why scholars have viewed them as the essence or natural form of human group life. Such a view is especially apparent in the concepts of "culture" and "social order" that are so dominant in social-science literature. Most sociological schemes rest on the belief that a human society exists in the form of an established order of living, with that order resolvable into adherence to sets of rules, norms, values, and sanctions that specify to people how they are to act in their different situations.

Several comments are in order with regard to this neat scheme. First, it is just not true that the full expanse of life in a human society, in any human society, is but an expression of preestablished forms of joint action. New situations are constantly arising within the scope of group life that are problematic and for which existing rules are inadequate. I have never heard of any society that was free of problems nor any society in which members did not have to engage in discussion to work out ways of action. Such areas of unprescribed conduct are just as indigenous and recurrent in human group life as are those areas covered by preestablished and faithfully followed prescriptions of joint action. Second, we have to recognize that even in the case of preestablished and repetitive joint action each instance of such joint action has to be formed anew. The participants still have to build up their lines of action and fit them to one another through the dual process of designation and interpretation. They do this in the case of repetitive joint action, of course, by using the same recurrent and constant meanings. If we recognize this, we are forced to realize that the play and fate of meanings are what is important, not the joint action in its established form. Repetitive and stable joint action is just as much a result of an interpretative process as is a new form of joint action that is being developed for the first time. This is not an idle or pedantic point; the meanings that underlie established and recurrent joint action are themselves subject to pressure as well as to reinforcement, to incipient dissatisfaction as well as to indifference; they may be challenged as well as affirmed, allowed to slip along without concern as well as subjected to infusions of new vigor. Behind the facade of the objectively perceived joint action the set of meanings that sustains that joint action has a life that the social scientists can ill afford to ignore. A gratuitous acceptance of the concepts of norms, values, social rules, and the like should not blind the social scientist to the fact that any one of them is subtended by a process of social interaction—a process that is necessary not only for their change but equally for their retention in a fixed form. It is the social process in group life that creates and upholds the rules, not the rules that create and uphold group life.

The second observation on the interlinkage that constitutes joint action refers to the extended connection of actions that make up much of human group life. We are familiar with these large, complex networks of action involving an interlinkage and interdependency of diverse actions of diverse people—as in the division of labor extending from the growing of grain by the farmer to an eventual sale of bread in a store, or in the elaborate chain extending from the arrest of a suspect to his eventual release from a penitentiary. These networks with their regularized participation of diverse people by diverse action at diverse points yield a picture of institutions that have been appropriately a major concern of sociologists. They also give substance to the idea that human group life has the character of a system. In seeing such a large complex of diversified activities, all hanging together in a regularized operation, and in seeing the complementary organization of participants in well-knit interdependent relationships, it is easy to understand why so many scholars view such networks or institutions as self-operating entities, following their own dynamics and not requiring that attention be given to the participants within the network. Most of the sociological analysis of institutions and social organization adhere to this view. Such adherence, in my judgment, is a serious mistake. One should recognize what is true, namely, that the diverse array of participants occupying different points in the network engage in their actions at those points on the basis of using given sets of meanings. A network or an institution does not function automatically because of some inner dynamics or system requirements; it functions because people at different points do something, and what they do is a result of how they define the situation in which they are called on to act. A limited appreciation of this point is reflected today in some of the work on decision making, but on the whole, the point is grossly ignored. It is necessary to recognize that the sets of meanings that lead participants to act as they do at their stationed points in the network have their own setting in a localized process of social interaction—and that these meanings are formed, sustained, weakened, strengthened, or transformed, as the case may be, through a socially defining process. Both the functioning and the fate of institutions are set by this process of interpretation as it takes place among the diverse sets of participants.

A third important observation needs to be made, namely, that any instance of joint action, whether newly formed or long established, has necessarily arisen out of a background of previous actions of the participants. A new kind of joint action never comes into existence apart from such a background. The participants involved in the formation of the new joint action always bring to that formation the world of objects, the sets of meanings, and the schemes of interpretation that they already possess. Thus, the new form of joint action always emerges out of and is connected with a context of previous joint action. It cannot be understood apart from that context; one has to bring into one's consideration this linkage with preceding forms of joint action. One is on treacherous and empirically invalid ground if he thinks that any given form of joint action can be sliced off from its historical linkage, as if its makeup and character arose out of the air through spontaneous generation instead of growing out of what went before. One cannot understand the new form without incorporating knowledge of this continuity into one's analysis of the new form. Joint action not only represents a horizontal linkage, so to speak, of the activities of the participants, but also a vertical linkage with previous joint action.

Summary Remarks

The general perspective of symbolic interactionism should be clear from our brief sketch of its root images. This approach sees a human society as people engaged in living. Such living is a process of ongoing activity in which participants are developing lines of action in the multitudinous situations they encounter. They are caught up in a vast process of interaction in which they have to fit their developing actions to one another. This process of interaction consists in making indications to others of what to do and in interpreting the indications made by others. They live in worlds of objects and are guided in their orientation and action by the meaning of these objects. Their objects, including objects of themselves, are formed, sustained, weakened, and transformed in their interaction with one another. This general process should be seen, of course, in the differentiated character which it necessarily has by virtue of the fact that people cluster in different groups, belong to different associations, and occupy different positions. They accordingly approach each other differently, live in different worlds, and guide themselves by different sets of meanings. Nevertheless, whether one is dealing with a family, a boys' gang, an industrial corporation, or a political party, one must see the activities of the collectivity as being formed through a process of designation and interpretation.

SUGGESTED READINGS

1. Blumer, Herbert, "Attitudes and the Social Act," *Social Problems,* Vol. 3, October, 1955.
2. Blumer, Herbert, "Society as Symbolic Interaction," in *Human Behavior and Social Processes,* ed. by Arnold Rose. Boston: Houghton Mifflin, 1962.
3. Blumer, Herbert, "Sociological Implications of the Thought of George Herbert Mead," *American Journal of Sociology,* Vol. 71, March, 1966.
4. Blumer, Herbert, *Symbolic Interactionism: Perspective and Method.* Englewood Cliffs, N.J.: Prentice-Hall, 1969.
5. Bonner, Hubert, *Social Psychology.* New York: American Book, 1953.
6. Cooley, Charles H., *Human Nature and Social Order.* New York: Scribner, 1902.
7. Coutu, Walter, *Emergent Human Behavior: A Symbolic Field Interpretation.* New York: Knopf, 1949.
8. Dewey, John, "Communication, Individual and Society," in *Symbolic Interaction,* ed. by J. G. Manis and B. N. Meltzer. Boston: Allyn and Bacon, 1967.
9. Dewey, John, *Experience and Nature.* New York: Dover, 1958.
10. Dewey, John, *Human Nature and Conduct.* New York: Holt, Rinehart and Winston, 1950.
11. Faris, Robert E. L., *Social Psychology.* New York: Ronald Press, 1952.
12. Farberman, Harvey A., and Gregory Stone, *Social Psychology Through Symbolic Interaction.* Waltham, Mass.: Ginn-Blaisdell, 1970.

13. Gerth, Hans, and C. Wright Mills, *Character and Social Structure*. New York: Harcourt, Brace, 1953.
14. Goffman, Erving, *Behavior in Public Places*. New York: Free Press, 1963.
15. Goffman, Erving, *Encounters*. Indianapolis: Bobbs-Merrill, 1961.
16. Goffman, Erving, *Interaction Ritual*. Garden City, N.Y.: Doubleday, 1967.
17. Goffman, Erving, "The Nature of Deference and Demeanor," *American Anthropologist*, Vol. 58, June, 1956.
18. Goffman, Erving, *The Presentation of Self in Everyday Life*. Garden City, N.Y.: Doubleday, 1959.
19. Goffman, Erving, *Stigma*. Englewood Cliffs, N.J.: Prentice-Hall, 1963.
20. Goffman, Erving, *Strategic Interaction*. Philadelphia: University of Pennsylvania Press, 1969.
21. Homans, George C., "Social Behavior as Exchange," *American Journal of Sociology*, May, 1958.
22. House, Floyd Nelson, *The Development of Sociology*. New York: McGraw-Hill, 1936.
23. Karpf, Fay Berger, *American Social Psychology*. New York: McGraw-Hill, 1932.
24. Krueger, E. T., and Walter C. Reckless, *Social Psychology*. London: Longmans, 1930.
25. Kuhn, Manford H., "Major Trends in Symbolic Interaction in the Past Twenty-Five Years," *The Sociological Quarterly*, Vol. 5, Winter, 1964.
26. Kuhn, Manford H., "The Reference Group Considered," *The Sociological Quarterly*, Vol. 5, Winter, 1964.
27. Lindesmith, Alfred R., and Anselm L. Strauss, eds., *Readings in Social Psychology*. New York: Holt, Rinehart and Winston, 1962.
28. Manis, Jerome G., and Bernard N. Meltzer, *Symbolic Interaction: A Reader in Social Psychology*. Boston: Allyn and Bacon, 1967.
29. Martindale, Don, *The Nature and Types of Sociological Theory*. Boston: Houghton Mifflin, 1960.
30. Mead, George Herbert, *Mind, Self and Society*, ed. by Charles W. Morris. Chicago: University of Chicago Press, 1934.
31. Mead, George Herbert, *The Philosophy of the Act*, ed. by Charles W. Morris. Chicago: University of Chicago Press, 1938.
32. Rose, Arnold M., ed., *Human Behavior and Social Processes*. Boston: Houghton Mifflin, 1962.
33. Secord, Paul F., and Carl W. Backman, *Social Psychology*. New York: McGraw-Hill, 1964.
34. Shibutani, Tamotsu, *Human Behavior and Collective Behavior: Papers in Honor of Herbert Blumer*. Englewood Cliffs, N.J.: Prentice-Hall, 1970.
35. Shibutani, Tamotsu, *Society and Personality: An Interactionist's Approach to Social Psychology*. Englewood Cliffs, N.J.: Prentice-Hall, 1961.
36. Stone, Gregory, "Appearance and Self," *Human Behavior and Social Processes*, ed. by Arnold M. Rose. Boston: Houghton Mifflin, 1962.
37. Stone, Gregory, and Edward Gross, "Embarrassment and the Analysis of Role Requirements," *American Journal of Sociology*, Vol. 70, July, 1964.
38. Strauss, Anselm, and Barney G. Glaser, "Awareness Contexts and Social Interaction," *American Sociological Review*, Vol. 29, October, 1964.
39. Strauss, Anselm, ed., *George Herbert Mead: On Social Psychology*. Chicago: University of Chicago Press, 1964.

40. Stryker, Sheldon, "Symbolic Interaction as an Approach to Family Research," *Marriage and Family Living*, Vol. 21, May, 1959.
41. Turner, Ralph H., "Role-Taking: Process Versus Conformity," in *Human Behavior and Social Process*, ed. by Arnold M. Rose. Boston: Houghton Mifflin, 1962.
42. Turner, Ralph H., "The Self-Conception in Social Interaction," in *The Self in Social Interaction*, ed. by Chard Gordon and K. J. Gergen. New York: Wiley, 1968.

8

Sociology of Knowledge

PETER L. BERGER

SOCIETY is a dialectic phenomenon in that it is a human product, and nothing but a human product, that yet continuously acts back upon its producer. Society is a product of man. It has no other being except that which is bestowed upon it by human activity and consciousness. There can be no social reality apart from man. Yet it may also be stated that man is a product of society. Every individual biography is an episode within the history of society, which both precedes and survives it. Society was there before the individual was born and it will be there after he has died. What is more, it is within society, and as a result of social processes, that the individual becomes a person, that he attains and holds onto an identity, and that he carries out the various projects that constitute his life. Man cannot exist apart from society. The two statements, that society is the product of man and that man is the product of society, are not contradictory. They rather reflect the inherently dialectic character of the societal phenomenon. Only if this character is recognized will society be understood in terms that are adequate to its empirical realtiy. [1]

The fundamental dialectic process of society consists of three moments, or steps. These are externalization, objectivation, and internalization. Only if these three moments are understood together can an empirically adequate view of society be maintained. Externalization is the ongoing outpouring of human beings into the world, both in the physical and the mental activity of men. Objectivation is the attainment, by the products of this activity (again both physical and mental), of a reality that confronts its original producers as a facticity external to and other than themselves.

155

Internalization is the reappropriation by men of this same reality, transforming it once again from structures of the objective world into structures of the subjective consciousness. It is through externalization that society is a human product. It is through objectivation that society becomes a reality *sui generis*. It is through internalization that man is a product of society.[2]

Externalization is an anthropological necessity. Man, as we know him empirically, cannot be conceived of apart from the continuous outpouring of himself into the world in which he finds himself. A human being cannot be understood as somehow resting within itself, in some closed sphere of interiority, and *then* setting out to express itself in the surrounding world. A human being is externalizing in its essence and from the beginning.[3] This anthropological root fact is very probably grounded in the biological constitution of man.[4] *Homo sapiens* occupies a peculiar position in the animal kingdom. This peculiarity manifests itself in man's relationship both to his own body and to the world. Unlike the other higher mammals, who are born with an essentially completed organism, man is curiously "unfinished" at birth.[5] Essential steps in the process of "finishing" man's development, which have already taken place in the fetal period for the other higher mammals, occur in the first year after birth, in the case of man. That is, the biological process of "becoming man" occurs at a time when the human infant is in interaction with an extra-organismic environment, which includes both the physical and the human world of the infant. There is thus a biological foundation to the process of "becoming man" in the sense of developing personality and appropriating culture. The latter developments are not somehow superimposed as alien mutations upon the biological development of man, but they are grounded in it.

The "unfinished" character of the human organism at birth is closely related to the relatively unspecialized character of its instinctual structure. The nonhuman animal enters the world with highly specialized and firmly directed drives. As a result, it lives in a world that is more or less completely determined by its instinctual structure. This world is closed in terms of its possibilities, programmed, as it were, by the animal's own constitution. Consequently, each animal lives in an environment that is specific to its particular species. There is a mouse-world, a dog-world, a horse-world, and so forth. By contrast, man's instinctual structure at birth is both underspecialized and undirected toward a species-specific environment. There is no man-world in the above sense. Man's world is imperfectly programmed by his own constitution. It is an open world. That is, it is a world that must be fashioned by man's own activity. Compared with the other higher mammals, man thus has a double relationship to the world. Like the other mammals, man is *in* a world that antedates his appearance. But unlike the other mammals, this world is not simply given, prefabricated for him. Man must *make* a world for himself. The world-building activity of man, therefore, is not a biologically extraneous phenomenon, but the direct consequence of man's biological constitution.

The condition of the human organism in the world is thus characterized by a built-in instability. Man does not have a given relationship to the world. He must ongoingly establish a relationship with it. The same instability marks man's relationship to his own body.[6] In a curious way, man is "out of balance" with himself. He cannot rest within himself, but must continuously come to terms with himself by expressing himself in activity. Human existence is an ongoing "balancing act" between man and his body, man and his world. One may put this differently by saying that man is constantly in the process of "catching up with himself." It is in this process that man produces a world. Only in such a world produced by himself can he locate himself and realize his life. But the same process that builds his world also "finishes" his own being. In other words, man not only produces a world, but he also produces himself. More precisely, he produces himself in a world.

In the process of world-building, man, by his own activity, specializes his drives and provides stability for himself. Biologically deprived of a man-world, he constructs a human world. This world, of course, is culture. Its fundamental purpose is to provide the firm structures for human life that are lacking biologically. It follows that these humanly produced structures can never have the stability that marks the structures of the animal world. Culture, although it becomes for man a "second nature," remains something quite different from nature precisely because it is the product of man's own activity. Culture must be continuously produced and reproduced by man. Its structures are, therefore, inherently precarious and predestined to change. The cultural imperative of stability and the inherent character of culture as *un*stable together posit the fundamental problem of man's world-building activity. Its far-reaching implications will occupy us in considerable detail a little further on. For the moment, suffice it to say that, while it is necessary that worlds be built, it is quite difficult to keep them going.

Culture consists of the totality of man's products.[7] Some of these are material, others are not. Man produces tools of every conceivable kind, by means of which he modifies his physical environment and bends nature to his will. Man also produces language and, on its foundation and by means of it, a towering edifice of symbols that permeate every aspect of his life. There is good reason for thinking that the production of non-material culture has always gone hand in hand with man's activity of physically modifying his environment.[8] Be this as it may, society is, of course, nothing but part and parcel of nonmaterial culture. Society is that aspect of the latter that structures man's ongoing relations with his fellow-men.[9] As but an element of culture, society fully shares in the latter's character as a human product. Society is constituted and maintained by acting human beings. It has no being, no reality, apart from this activity. Its patterns, always relative in time and space, are not given in nature, nor can they be deduced in any specific manner from the "nature of man." If one wants to use such a term as designating more than certain biological constants, one can only say that it is the "nature of man" to produce a world. What appears at any particular historical moment as "human nature" is itself a product of man's world-building activity.[10]

However, while society appears as but an aspect of culture, it occupies a privileged position among man's cultural formations. This is due to yet another basic anthropological fact, namely the essential sociality of man.[11] *Homo sapiens* is the social animal. This means very much more than the surface fact that man always lives in collectivities and, indeed, loses his humanity when he is thrust into isolation from other men. Much more importantly, the world-building activity of man is always and inevitably a collective enterprise. While it may be possible, perhaps for heuristic purposes, to analyze man's relationship to his world in purely individual terms, the empirical reality of human world-building is always a social one. Men *together* shape tools, invent languages, adhere to values, devise institutions, and so on. Not only is the individual's participation in a culture contingent upon a social process (namely, the process called socialization), but his continuing cultural existence depends upon the maintenance of specfiic social arrangements. Society, therefore, is not only an outcome of culture, but a necessary condition of the latter. Society structures, distributes, and coordinates the world-building activities of men. And only in society can the products of those activities persist over time.

The understanding of society as rooted in man's externalization, that is, as a product of human activity, is particularly important in view of the fact that society appears to common sense as something quite different, as independent of human activity and as sharing in the inert givenness of nature. We shall turn in a moment to the process of objectivation that makes this appearance possible. Suffice it to say here that one of the most important gains of a sociological perspective is its reiterated reduction of the hypostatized entities that make up society in the imagination of the man in the street to the human activity of which these entities are products and without which they have no status in reality. The "stuff" out of which society and all its formations are made is human meanings externalized in human activity. The great societal hypostases (such as "the family," "the economy," "the state," and so forth) are over again reduced by sociological analysis to the human activity that is their only underlying substance. For this reason it is very unhelpful if the sociologist, except for heuristic purposes, deals with such social phenomena as if they were, in actual fact, hypostases independent of the human enterprise that originally produced them and keeps on producing them. There is nothing wrong, in itself, with the sociologists speaking of institutions, structures, functions, patterns, and so on. The harm comes only when he thinks of these, like the man in the street, as entities existing in and of themselves, detached from human activity and production. One of the merits of the concept of externalization as applied to society, is the prevention of this sort of static, hypostatizing thinking. Another way of putting this is to say that sociological understanding ought always to be humanizing, that is, ought to refer back the imposing configurations of social structure to the living human beings who have created them.[12]

Society, then, is a product of man, rooted in the phenomenon of externalization, which in turn is grounded in the very biological constitution of man. As soon as one speaks of externalized products, however, one is implying that the latter attain a degree of distinctiveness as against their producer. This transformation of man's products into a world that not only derives from man, but that comes to confront him as a facticity outside of himself, is intended in the concept of objectivation. The humanly produced world becomes something "out there." It consists of objects, both material and nonmaterial, that are capable of resisting the desires of their producer. Once produced, this world cannot simply be wished away. Although all culture originates and is rooted in the subjective consciousness of human beings, once formed it cannot be reabsorbed into consciousness at will. It stands outside the subjectivity of the individual as, indeed, a world. In other words, the humanly produced world attains the character of objective reality.

This acquired objectivity of man's cultural products pertains both to the material and the nonmaterial ones. It can readily be understood in the case of the former. Man manufactures a tool and by that action enriches the totality of physical objects present in the world. Once produced, the tool has a being of its own that cannot be readily changed by those who employ it. Indeed, the tool (say, an agricultural implement) may even enforce the logic of its being upon its users, sometimes in a way that may not be particularly agreeable to them. For instance, a plow, though obviously a human product, is an external object not only in the sense that its users may fall over it and hurt themselves as a result, just as they may by falling over a rock or a stump or any other natural object. More interestingly, the plow may compel its users to arrange their agricultural activity, and perhaps also other aspects of their lives, in a way that conforms to *its* own logic and that may have been neither intended nor foreseen by those who originally devised it. The same objectivity, however, characterizes the nonmaterial element of culture as well. Man invents a language and then finds that both his speaking and his thinking are dominated by its grammar. Man produces values and discovers that he feels guilt when he contravenes them. Man concocts institutions, which come to confront him as powerfully controlling and even menacing constellations of the external world. The relationship between man and culture is thus aptly illustrated by the tale of the sorcerer's apprentice. The mighty buckets, magically called out of nothingness by human *fiat,* are set in motion. From that point on, they go about drawing water in accordance with an inherent logic of their own being that, at the very least, is less than completely controlled by their creator. It is possible, as happens in that story, that man may find an additional magic that will bring back under his control the vast forces he has unleashed upon reality. This power, though, is not identical with the one that first set these forces in motion. And, of course, it can also happen that man drowns in the floods that he himself has produced.

If culture is credited with the status of objectivity, there is a double meaning to this appellation. Culture is objective in that is confronts man as an assemblage of objects in the real world existing outside his own consciousness. Culture is *there.* But culture is also objective in that it may be experienced and apprehended, as it were, in company. Culture is *there for everybody.* This means that the objects of culture (again, both the material and nonmaterial ones) may be shared with others. This distinguishes them sharply from any constructions of the subjective consciousness of the solitary individual. This is obvious when one compares a tool that belongs to the technology of a particular culture with some utensil, however interesting, that forms part of a dream. The objectivity of culture as shared facticity, though, is even more important to understand with reference to its nonmaterial constituents. The individual may dream up any number of, say, institutional arrangements that might well be more interesting, perhaps even more functional, than the institutions actually recognized in his culture. As long as these sociological dreams, so to speak, are confined to the individual's own consciousness and are not recognized by others as at least empirical possibilities, they will exist only as shadowlike phantasmata. By contrast, the institutions of the individual's society, however much he may dislike them, will be *real.* In other words, the cultural world is not only collectively produced, but it remains real by virtue of collective recognition. To be in culture means to share in a particular world of objectivities with others. [13]

The same conditions, of course, apply to that segment of cultures we call society. It is not enough, therefore, to say that society is rooted in human activity. One must also say that society is *objectivated* human activity. That is, society is a product of human activity that has attained the status of objective reality. The social formations are experienced by man as elements of an objective world. Society confronts man as external, subjectively opaque and coercive facticity.[14] Indeed, society is commonly apprehended by man as virtually equivalent to the physical universe in its objective presence—a "second nature," indeed. Society is experienced as given "out there," extraneous to subjective consciousness and not controllable by the latter. The representations of solitary fantasy offer relatively little resistance to the individual's volition. The representations of society are immensely more resistant. The individual can dream of different societies and imagine himself in various contexts. Unless he exists in solipsistic madness, he will know the difference between these fantasies and the *reality* of his actual life in society, which prescribes a commonly recognized context for him and imposes it upon him regardless of his wishes. Since society is encountered by the individual as a reality external to himself, it may often happen that its workings remain opaque to his understanding. He cannot discover the meaning of a social phenomenon by introspection. He must, for this purpose, go outside himself and engage in the basically same kind of empirical inquiry that is necessary if he is to understand anything located outside his own mind. Above all, society manifests itself by its coercive power. The final test of its objective reality is its capacity to impose itself upon the reluctance of individuals. Society directs, sanctions, controls, and punishes individual conduct. In its most powerful apotheoses, society may even destroy the individual.

The coercive objectivity of society can, of course, be seen most readily in its procedures of social control, that is, in those procedures that are specifically designed to "bring back into line" recalcitrant individuals or groups. Political and legal institutions may serve as obvious illustrations of this. It is important to understand, however, that the same coercive objectivity characterizes society *as a whole* and is present in *all* social institutions, including those institutions that were founded on consensus. This (most emphatically) does *not* mean that all societies are variations of tyranny. It *does* mean that no human construction can be accurately called a social phenomenon unless it has achieved that measure of objectivity that compels the individual to recognize it as real. In other words, the fundamental coerciveness of society lies not in its machineries of social control, but in its power to constitute and to impose itself as reality. The paradigmatic case of this is language. Hardly anyone, however far removed from sociological thinking, is likely to deny that language is a human product. Any particular language is the result of a long history of human inventiveness, imagination and even caprice. While man's vocal organs impose certain physiological limitations on his liguistic fancy, there are no laws of nature that can be called upon to explain the development of, say, the English language. Nor does the latter have any status in the nature of things other than its status as a human production. The English language originated in specific human events, was developed throughout its history by human activity, and it exists only insofar and as long as human beings continue to use and understand it. Nevertheless, the English language presents itself to the individual as an objective reality, which he must recognize as such or suffer the consequences. Its rules are objectively given. They must be learned by the individual, whether as his first or as a foreign language, and he cannot change them at will. There are objective standards for correct and incorrect English, and although there may be differences of opinion about minor details, the existence of such standards is a precondition for the use of the language in the first place. There are, of course, penalties for offending against these standards, from failing in school to social embarrassment in later life, but the objective reality of the English language is not primarily constituted by these penalties. Rather, the English language is real objectively by virtue of the simple fact that it is *there,* a ready-made and collectively recognized universe of discourse within which individuals may understand each other and themselves.[15]

Society, as objective reality, provides a world for man to inhabit. This world encompasses the biography of the individual, which unfolds as a series of events *within* that world. Indeed, the individual's own biography is objectively real only insofar as it may be comprehended within the significant structures of the social world. To be sure, the individual may have any number of highly subjective self-interpretations, which will strike others as bizarre or as downright incomprehensible. Whatever these self-interpretations may be, there will remain the objective interpretation of the individual's biography that locates the latter in a collectively recognized frame of reference. The objective facts of this biography may be minimally ascertained by consulting the relevant personal documents. Name, legal descent, citizenship, civil status, occupation—these are but some of the "official" interpretations of individual existence, objectively valid not only by force of law but by the fundamental reality-bestowing potency of society. What is more, the individual himself, unless again he encloses himself in a solipsistic world of withdrawal from the common reality, will seek to validate his self-interpretations by comparing them with the objectively available coordinates of his biography. In other words, the individual's own life appears as objectively real, to himself as well as to others, only as it is located within a social world that itself has the character of objective reality.[16]

The objectivity of society extends to all its constituent elements. Institutions, roles, and identities exist as objectively real phenomena in the social world, though they and this world are at the same time nothing but human productions. For example, the family as the institutionalization of human sexuality in a particular society is experienced and apprehended as an objective reality. The institution is *there,* external and coercive, imposing its predefined patterns upon the individual in this particular area of his life. The same objectivity belongs to the roles that the individual is expected to play in the institutional context in question, even if it should happen that he does not particularly enjoy the performance. The roles of, for instance, husband, father, or uncle are objectively defined and available as models for individual conduct. By playing these roles, the individual comes to represent the institutional objectivities in a way that is apprehended, by himself and by others, as detached from the "mere" accidents of his individual existence.[17] He can "put on" the role, as a cultural object, in a manner analogous to the "putting on" of a physical object of clothing or adornment. He can further retain a consciousness of himself as distinct from the role, which then relates to what he apprehends as his "real self" as mask to actor. Thus he can even say that he does not like to perform this or that detail of the role, but must do so against his will—because the objective description of the role so dictates. Furthermore, society not only contains an objectively available assemblage of institutions and roles, but a repertoire of identities endowed with the same status of objective reality. Society assigns to the individual not only a set of roles but a designated identity. In other words, the individual is not only expected to perform as husband, father, or uncle, but to *be* a husband, a father, or an uncle—and, even more basically, to *be* a man, in terms of whatever "being" this implies in the society in question. Thus, in the final resort, the objectivation of human activity means that man becomes capable of objectivating a part of himself within his own consciousness, confronting himself within himself in figures that are generally available as objective elements of the social world. For example, the individual *qua* "real self" can carry on an internal conversation with himself *qua* archbishop. Actually, it is only by means of such internal dialogue with the objectivations of oneself that socialization is possible in the first place.[18]

The world of social objectivations, produced by externalizing consciousness, confronts consciousness as an external facticity. It is apprehended as such. This apprehension, however, cannot as yet be described as internalization, any more than can the apprehension of the world of nature. Internalization is rather the reabsorption into consciousness of the objectivated world in such a way that the structures of this world come to determine the subjective structures of consciousness itself. That is, society now functions as the formative agency for individual consciousness. Insofar as internalization has taken place, the individual now apprehends various elements of the objectivated world as phenomena internal to his consciousness at the same time as he apprehends them as phenomena of external reality.

Every society that continues in time faces the problem of transmitting its objectivated meanings from one generation to the next. This problem is attacked by means of the processes of socialization, that is, the processes by which a new generation is taught to live in accordance with the institutional programs of the society. Socialization can, of course, be described psychologically as a learning process. The new generation is initiated into the meanings of the culture, learns to participate in its established tasks and to accept the roles as well as the identities that make up its social structure. Socialization, however, has a crucial dimension that is not adequately grasped by speaking of a learning process. The individual not only learns the objectivated meanings but identifies with and is shaped by them. He draws them into himself and makes them *his* meanings. He becomes not only one who possesses these meanings, but one who represents and expresses them.

The success of socialization depends upon the establishment of symmetry between the objective world of society and the subjective world of the individual. If one imagines a totally socialized individual, each meaning objectively available in the social world would have its analogous meaning given subjectively within his own consciousness. Such total socialization is empirically nonexistent and theoretically impossible, if only by reason of the biological variability of individuals. However, there are degrees of success in socialization. Highly successful socialization establishes a high degree of objective/subjective symmetry, while failures of socialization lead to various degrees of asymmetry. If socialization is not successful in internalizing at least the most important meaning of a given society, the latter becomes difficult to maintain as a viable enterprise. Specifically, such a society would not be in a position to establish a tradition that would ensure its persistence in time.

Man's world-building activity is always a collective enterprise. Man's internal appropriation of a world must also take place in a collectivity. It has by now become a social-scientific platitude to say that it is impossible to become or to be human, in any empirically recognizable form that goes beyond biological observations, except in society. This becomes less of a platitude if one adds that the internalization of a world is dependent on society in the same way, because one is thereby saying that man is incapable of conceiving of his experience in a comprehensively meaningful way unless such a conception is transmitted to him by means of social processes. The processes that internalize the socially objectivated world are *the same* processes that internalize the socially assigned identities. The individual is socialized *to be* a designated person and to *inhabit* a designated world. Subjective identity and subjective reality are produced in the same dialectic (here, in the etymologically literal sense) between the individual and those significant others who are in charge of his socialization.[19] It is possible to sum up the dialectic formation of identity by saying that the individual becomes that which he is addressed as by others. One may add that the individual appropriates the world in conversation with others and, furthermore, that both identity and world remain real to himself only as long as he can continue the conversation.

The last point is very important, for it implies that socialization can never be completed, that it must be an ongoing process throughout the lifetime of the individual. This is the subjective side of the already remarked-upon precariousness of all humanly constructed worlds. The difficulty of keeping a world going expresses itself psychologically in the difficulty of keeping this world subjectively plausible. The world is built up in the consciousness of the individual by conversation with significant others (such as parents, teachers, "peers"). The world is maintained as subjective reality by the same sort of conversation, be it with the same or with new significant others (such as spouses, friends, or other associates). If such conversation is disrupted (the spouse dies, the friends disappear, or one comes to leave one's original social milieu), the world begins to totter, to lose its subjective plausibility. In other words, the subjective reality of the world hangs on the thin thread of conversation. The reason why most of us are unaware of this precariousness most of the time is grounded in the continuity of our conversation with significant others. The maintenance of such continuity is one of the most important imperatives of social order.

Internalization, then, implies that the objective facticity of the social world becomes a subjective facticity as well. The individual encounters the institutions as *data* of the objective world outside himself, but they are now *data* of his own consciousness as well. The institutional programs set up by society are subjectively real as attitudes, motives, and life projects. The reality of the institutions is appropriated by the individual along with his roles and his identity. For example, the individual appropriates as reality the particular kinship arrangements of his society. Ipso facto, he takes on the roles assigned to him in this context and apprehends his own identity in terms of these roles. Thus, he not only plays the role of uncle, but he *is* an uncle. Nor, if socialization has been fairly successful, does he wish to be anything else. His attitudes toward others and his motives for specific actions are endemically avuncular. If he lives in a society which has established unclehood as a centrally significant institution (not ours, to be sure, but most matrilineal societies), he will conceive of his whole biography (past, present, *and* future) in terms of his career *as* an uncle. Indeed, he may even sacrifice himself for his nephews and derive consolation from the thought that his own life will continue in them. The socially objectivated world is still apprehended as external facticity. Uncles, sisters, nephews exist in objective reality, comparable in facticity to the species of animals or rocks. But this objective world is also apprehended now as subjective meaningfulness. Its initial opaqueness (say, to the child, who must learn the lore of unclehood) has been converted to an internal translucency. The indiivdual may now look within himself and, in the depths of his subjective being, may "discover himself" as an uncle. At this point, always assuming a degree of successful socialization, introspection becomes a viable method for the discovery of institutional meanings.[20]

The process of internalization must always be understood as but one moment of the larger dialectic process that also includes the moments of externalization and objectivation. If this is not done, there emerges a picture of mechanistic determinism, in which the individual is produced by society as cause produces effect in nature. Such a picture distorts the societal phenomenon. Not only is internalization part of the latter's larger dialectic, but the socialization of the individual also occurs in a dialectic manner.[21] The individual is not molded as a passive, inert thing. Rather, he is formed in the course of a protracted conversation (a dialectic, in the literal sense of the word) in which he is a *participant.* That is, the social world (with its appropriate institutions, roles, and identities) is not passively absorbed by the individual, but actively *appropriated* by him. Furthermore, once the individual is formed as a person, with an objectively and subjectively recognizable identity, he must continue to participate in the conversation that sustains him as a person in his ongoing biography. That is, the individual continues to be a *coproducer* of the social world, and thus of himself. No matter how small his power to change the social definitions of reality may be, he must at least continue to assent to those that form him as a person. Even if he should deny this coproduction (say, as a positivistic sociologist or psychologist), he remains a coproducer of his world all the same—and, indeed, his denial of this enters into the dialectic as a formative factor both of his world and of himself. The relationship of the individual to language may, once more, be taken as paradigmatic of the dialectic of socialization. Language confronts the individual as an objective facticity. He subjectively appropriates it by engaging in linguistic interaction with others. In the course of this interaction, however, he inevitably modifies the language, even if (say, as a formalistic grammarian) he should deny the validity of these modifications. Furthermore, his continuing participation in the language is part of the human activity that is the only ontological base for the language in question. The language exists because he, along with others, continues to employ it. In other words, both with regard to language and to the socially objectivated world as a whole, it may be said that the individual keeps "talking back" to the world that formed him and thereby continues to maintain the latter as reality.

It may now be understandable, if the proposition is made, that the socially constructed world is, above all, an ordering of experience. A meaningful order, or nomos, is imposed upon the discrete experiences and meanings of individuals.[22] To say that society is a world-building enterprise is to say that it is ordering, or nomizing, activity. The presuppositition for this is given, as has been indicated before, in the biological constitution of *Homo sapiens*. Man, biologically denied the ordering mechanisms with which other animals are endowed, is compelled to impose his own order upon experience. Man's sociality presupposes the collective character of this ordering activity. The ordering of experience is endemic to any kind of social interaction. Every social action implies that individual meaning is directed toward others and ongoing social interaction implies that the several meanings of the actors are integrated into an order of common meaning.[23] It would be wrong to assume that this nomizing consequence of social interaction must, from the beginning, produce a nomos that embraces *all* the discrete experiences and meanings of the participant individuals. If one can imagine a society in its first origins (something, of course, that is empirically unavailable), one may assume that the range of the common nomos expands as social interaction comes to include ever broader areas of common meaning. It makes no sense to imagine that this nomos will ever include the totality of individual meanings. Just as there can be no totally socialized individual, so there will always be individual meanings that remain outside of or marginal to the common nomos. Indeed, the marginal experiences of the individual are of considerable importance for an understanding of social existence. All the same, there is an inherent logic that impels every nomos to expand into wider areas of meaning. If the ordering activity of society never attains to totality, it may yet be described as totalizing.[24]

The social world constitutes a nomos both objectively and subjectively. The objective nomos is given in the process of objectivation as such. The fact of language, even if taken by itself, can readily be seen as the imposition of order upon experience. Language nomizes by imposing differentiation and structure upon the ongoing flux of experience. As an item of experience is named, it is ipso facto, taken out of this flux and given stability *as* the entity so named. Language further provides a fundamental order of relationships by the addition of syntax and grammar to vocabulary. It is impossible to use language without participating in its order. Every empirical language may be said to constitute a nomos in the making, or, with equal validity, as the historical consequence of the nomizing activity of generations of men. The original nomizing act is to say that an item is *this,* and thus *not that.* As this original incorporation of the item into an order that includes other items is followed by sharper linguistic designations (the item is male and not female, singular and not plural, a noun and not a verb, and so forth), the nomizing act intends a comprehensive order of *all* items that may be linguistically objectivated, that is, intends a totalizing nomos.

On the foundation of language, and by means of it, is built up the cognitive and normative edifice that passes for "knowledge" in a society. In what it "knows," every society imposes a common order of interpretation upon experience that becomes "objective knowledge" by means of the process of objectivation discussed before. Only a relatively small part of this edifice is constituted by theories of one kind or another, though theoretical "knowledge" is particularly important because it usually contains the body of "official" interpretations of reality. Most socially objectivated "knowledge" is pretheoretical. It consists of interpretative schemas, moral maxims, and collections of traditional wisdom that the man in the street frequently shares with the theoreticians. Societies vary in the degree of differentiation in their bodies of "knowledge." Whatever these variations, every society provides for its members an objectively available body of "knowledge." To participate in the society is to share its "knowledge," that is, to coinhabit its nomos.

The objective nomos is internalized in the course of socialization. It is thus appropriated by the individual to become his own subjective ordering of experience. It is by virtue of this appropriation that the individual can come to "make sense" of his own biography. The discrepant elements of his past life are ordered in terms of what he "knows objectively" about his own and others' condition. His ongoing experience is integrated into the same order, though the latter may have to be modified to allow for this integration. The future attains a meaningful shape by virtue of the same order being projected into it. In other words, to live in the social world is to live an ordered and meaningful life. Society is the guardian of order and meaning not only objectively, in its institutional structures, but subjectively as well, in its structuring of individual consciousness.

It is for this reason that radical separation from the social world, or anomy, constitutes such a powerful threat to the individual.[25] It is not only that the individual loses emotionally satisfying ties in such cases. He loses his orientation in experience. In extreme cases, he loses his sense of reality and identity. He becomes anomic in the sense of becoming worldless. Just as an individual's nomos is constructed and sustained in conversation with significant others, so is the individual plunged toward anomy when such conversation is radically interrupted. The circumstances of such nomic disruption may, of course, vary. They might involve large collective forces, such as the loss of status of the entire social group to which the individual belongs. They might be more narrowly biographical, such as the loss of significant others by death, divorce, or physical separation. It is thus possible to speak of collective as well as of individual states of anomy. In both cases, the fundamental order in terms of which the individual can "make sense" of his life and recognize his own identity will be in the process of disintegration. Not only will the individual then begin to lose his moral bearings, with disastrous psychological consequences, but he will become uncertain about his cognitive bearings as well. The world begins to shake at the very instant that its sustaining conversation begins to falter.

The socially established nomos may thus be understood, perhaps in its most important aspect, as a shield against terror. Put differently, the most important function of society is nomization. The anthropological presupposition for this is a human craving for meaning that appears to have the force of instinct. Men are congenitally compelled to impose a meaningful order upon reality. This order, however, presupposes the social enterprise of ordering world-construction. To be separated from society exposes the individual to a multiplicity of dangers with which he is unable to cope by himself, in the extreme case to the danger of imminent extinction. Separation from society also inflicts unbearable psychological tensions upon the individual, tensions that are grounded in the root anthropological fact of sociality. The ultimate danger of such separation, however, is the danger of meaninglessness. This danger is the nightmare *par excellence,* in which the individual is submerged in a world of disorder, senselessness, and madness. Reality and identity are malignantly transformed into meaningless figures of horror. To be in society is to be "sane," precisely in the sense of being shielded from the ultimate "insanity" of such anomic terror. Anomy is unbearable to the point where the individual may seek death in preference to it. Conversely, existence within a nomic world may be sought at the cost of all sorts of sacrifice and suffering—and even at the cost of life itself, if the individual believes that this ultimate sacrifice has nomic significance.[26]

The sheltering quality of social order becomes especially evident if one looks at the marginal situations in the life of the individual, that is, at situations in which he is driven close to or beyond the boundaries of the order that determines his routine, everyday existence.[27] Such marginal situations commonly occur in dreams and fantasy. They may appear on the horizon of consciousness as haunting suspicions that the world may have another aspect than its "normal" one—that is, that the previously accepted definitions of reality may be fragile or even fraudulent.[28] Such suspicions extend to the identity of both self and others, positing the possibility of shattering metamorphoses. When these suspicions invade the central areas of consciousness, they take on, of course, the constellations that modern psychiatry would call neurotic or psychotic. Whatever the epistemological status of these constellations (usually decided upon much too sanguinely by psychiatry, precisely because it is firmly rooted in the everyday, "official," social definitions of reality), their profound terror for the individual lies in the threat they constitute to his previously operative nomos. The marginal situation *par excellence,* however, is death.[29] Witnessing the death of others (notably, of course, of significant others) and anticipating his own death, the individual is strongly propelled to question the ad hoc cognitive and normative operating procedures of his "normal" life in society. Death presents society with a formidable problem not only because of its obvious threat to the continuity of human relationships, but because it threatens the basic assumptions of order on which society rests.

In other words, the marginal situations of human existence reveal the innate precariousness of all social worlds. Every socially defined reality remains threatened by lurking "irrealities." Every socially constructed nomos must face the constant possibility of its collapse into anomy. Seen in the perspective of society, every nomos is an area of meaning carved out of a vast mass of meaninglessness, a small clearing of lucidity in a formless, dark, always ominous jungle. Seen in the perspective of the individual, every nomos represents the bright "dayside" of life, tenuously held onto against the sinister shadows of the "night." In both perspectives, every nomos is an edifice erected in the face of the potent and alien forces of chaos. This chaos must be kept at bay at all cost. To ensure this, every society develops procedures that assist its members to remain "reality-oriented" (that is, to remain within the reality as "officially" defined) and to "return to reality" (that is, to return from the marginal spheres of "irreality" to the socially established nomos). The individual is provided by society with various methods to stave off the nightmare world of anomy and to stay within the safe boundaries of the established nomos.

The social world intends, as far as possible, to be taken for granted.[30] Socialization achieves success to the degree that this taken-for-granted quality is internalized. It is not enough that the individual look upon the key meanings of the social order as useful, desirable, or right. It is much better (better, that is, in terms of social stability) if he looks upon them as inevitable, as part and parcel of the universal "nature of things." If that can be achieved, the individual who strays seriously from the socially defined programs can be considered not only a fool or a knave, but a madman. Subjectively, then, serious deviance provokes not only moral guilt but the terror of madness. For example, the sexual program of a society is taken for granted not simply as a utilitarian or morally correct arrangement, but as an inevitable expression of "human nature." The so-called "homosexual panic" may serve as an excellent illustration of the terror unleashed by the denial of the program. This is not to deny that this terror is also fed by practical apprehensions and qualms of conscience, but its fundamental motorics is the terror of being thrust into an outer darkness that separates one from the "normal" order of men. In other words, institutional programs are endowed with an ontological status to the point where to deny them is to deny being itself—the being of the universal order of things and, consequently, one's own being in this order.

Whenever the socially established nomos attains the quality of being taken for granted, there occurs a merging of its meanings with what are considered to be the fundamental meanings inherent in the universe. Nomos and cosmos appear to be coextensive. In archaic societies, nomos appears as a microcosmic reflection, the world of men as expressing meanings inherent in the universe as such. In contemporary society, this archaic cosmization of the social world is likely to take the form of "scientific" propositions about the nature of men rather than the nature of the universe.[31] Whatever the historical variations, the tendency is for the meanings of the humanly constructed order to be projected into the universe as such.[32]

Human existence is essentially and inevitably externalizing activity. In the course of externalization, men pour out meaning into reality. Every human society is an edifice of externalized and objectivated meanings, always intending a meaningful totality. Every society is engaged in the never completed enterprise of building a humanly meaningful world.

NOTES

1. We would contend that this dialectic understanding of man and society as mutual products makes possible a theoretical synthesis of the Weberian and Durkheimian approaches to sociology without losing the fundamental intention of either (such a loss having occurred, in our opinion, in the Parsonian synthesis). Weber's understanding of social reality as ongoingly constituted by human signification and Durkheim's of the same as having the character of *choseité* as against the individual are *both* correct. They intend, respectively, the subjective foundation and the objective facticity of the societal phenomenon, ipso facto pointing toward the dialectic relationship of subjectivity and its objects. By the same token, the two understandings are only correct *together*. A quasi-Weberian emphasis on subjectivity *only* leads to an idealistic distortion of the societal phenomenon. A quasi-Durkheimian emphasis on objectivity *only* leads to sociological reification, the more disastrous distortion toward which much of contemporary American sociology has tended. It should be stressed that we are not implying here that such a dialectic synthesis would have been agreeable to these two authors themselves. Our interest is systematic rather than exegetical, an interest that permits an eclectic attitude toward previous theoretical constructions. When we say, then, that the latter "intend" such a synthesis, we mean this in the sense of intrinsic theoretical logic rather than of the historical intentions of these authors.

2. The terms "externalization" and "objectivation" are derived from Hegel (*Entaeusserung* and *Versachlichung*), are understood here essentially as they were applied to collective phenomena by Marx. The term "internalization" is understood as commonly used in American social psychology. The theoretical foundation of the latter is above all the work of George Herbert Mead, for which *cf.* his *Mind, Self and Society.* Chicago: University of Chicago Press, 1934; *George Herbert Mead on Social Psychology,* ed. by Anselm Strauss. Chicago: University of Chicago Press, 1956. The term "reality *sui generis,*" as applied to society, is developed by Durkheim in his *Rules of Sociological Method.* Glencoe, Ill.: Free Press, 1950.

3. The anthropological necessity of externalization was developed by Hegel and Marx. For more contemporary developments of this understanding, in addition to the work of Scheler, *cf.* Helmut Plessner, *Die Stufen des Organischen und der Mensch,* 1928, and Arnold Gehlen, *Der Mensch,* 1940.

4. For the biological foundation of this argument, *cf.* F. J. J. Buytendijk, *Mensch und Tier.* Hamburg: Rowohlt, 1958; Adolf Portmann, *Zoologie und das neue Bild des Menschen.* Hamburg: Rowohlt, 1956. The most important application of these biological perspectives to sociological problems is to be found in the work of Gehlen.

5. This has been succinctly put in the opening sentence of a recent anthropological work written from an essentially Marxian viewpoint: "L'homme naît inachevé." Georges Lapassade. *L'entrée Dans la Vie.* Paris: Editions de Minuit, 1963.

6. Plessner has coined the term "eccentricity" to refer to this innate instability in man's relationship to his own body. *Cf. op. cit.*

7. The use of the term "culture" to refer to the totality of man's products follows the current practice in American cultural anthropology. Sociologists have tended to use the term in a narrower sense as referring only to the so-called symbolic sphere (thus Parsons in his concept of the "cultural system"). While there are good reasons to prefer the narrower sense in other theoretical contexts, we have felt that the broader use is more appropriate in the present argument.

8. The linkage of material and nonmaterial production was developed in Marx's concept of "labor" (which cannot be understood as merely an economic category).

9. There are, of course, different concepts of society in use among sociologists. A discussion of these would serve little purpose in this argument. We have, therefore, used a very simple definition, relating it to the aforementioned concept of culture.

10. The understanding of "human nature" as itself a human product is also derived from Marx. It marks the fundamental split between a dialectic and a nondialectic anthropology. Within sociological thought, these anthropological antipodes are best represented, respectively, by Marx and Pareto. The Freudian anthropology, incidentally, must also be designated as an essentially nondialectic one, a point commonly overlooked in recent attempts at a Freudian-Marxian synthesis.

11. The essential sociality of man was clearly seen by Marx, but it is, of course, endemic to the entire sociological tradition. The work of Mead provides an indispensable social-psychological basis for Marx's anthropological insights.

12. The necessity for sociology to dehypostatize the social objectivations was repeatedly stressed in Weber's methodology. Although it is probably wrong to accuse Durkheim of a hypostatized conception of society (as a number of Marxist critics have done), his method easily lends itself to this distortion, as has been shown particularly in its development by the structural-functionalist school.

13. For a development of the understanding of shared objectivity, *cf.* the previously cited works of Schutz.

14. The discussion of the objectivity of society closely follows Durkheim at this point. *Cf.* especially the previously cited *Rules of Sociological Method.*

15. The understanding of language as paradigmatic for the objectivity of social phenomena is also derived from Durkheim. For a discussion of language in essentially Durkheimian terms, *cf.* A. Meillet, *Linguistique Historique et Linguistique Générale.* Paris: Champion, 1958.

16. For the reality of self-interpretations as location in an objectively real social world, *cf.* the work of Maurice Halbwachs on memory, especially his *Les Cadres Sociaux de la Mémoire.* Paris: Presses Universitaires de France, 1952.

17. The concept of roles as objective representation is arrived at by a combination of Meadian and Durkheimian viewpoints. On the latter, *cf.* here especially Durkheim's *Sociology and Philosophy.* London: Cohen & West, 1953.

18. The concept of internal conversation is derived from Mead. *Cf.* his previously cited *Mind, Self and Society*, pp. 135 ff.

19. The term "significant others" is also derived from Mead. It has, of course, gained general currency in American social psychology.

20. We would contend that this affirmation of introspection as a viable method for the understanding of social reality *after* successful socialization may serve to bridge the apparently contradictory propositions of Durkheim about the subjective opaqueness of social phenomena and of Weber about the possibility of *Verstehen*.

21. The dialectical character of socialization is expressed in Mead's concepts of the "I" and the "me." *Cf. op. cit.*, pp. 173 ff.

22. The term "nomos" is indirectly derived from Durkheim by, as it were, turning around his concept of *anomie*. The latter was first developed in his *Suicide*. Glencoe, Ill.: Free Press, 1951; *cf.* especially pp. 241 ff.

23. The definition of social action in terms of meaning derives from Weber. The implications of this definition in terms of the social "world" were especially developed by Schutz.

24. The term "totalization" is derived from Jean-Paul Sartre. *Cf.* his *Critique de la Raison Dialectique*, Vol. I. Paris: Gallimard, 1960.

25. "Anomy" is an Anglicization of Durkheim's *anomie* favored by several American sociologists, though not by Robert Merton (who sought to integrate the concept within his structural-functionalist theory, retaining the French spelling). We have adopted the Anglicized spelling for stylistic reasons only.

26. This suggests that there are nomic as well as anomic suicides, a point alluded to but not developed by Durkheim in his discussion of "altruistic suicide." *Suicide*, pp. 217 ff.

27. The concept of "marginal situations" (*Grenzsituationen*) derives from Karl Jaspers. *Cf.* especially his *Philosophie*, 1932.

28. The notion of the "other aspect" of reality has been developed by Robert Musil in his great unfinished novel, *Der Mann ohne Eigenschaften*, in which it is a major theme. For a critical discussion, *cf.* Ernst Kaiser and Eithne Wilkins, *Robert Musil*. Stuttgart: Kohlhammer, 1962.

29. The concept of death as the most important marginal situation is derived from Martin Heidegger. *Cf.* especially his *Sein und Zeit* 1929.

30. The concept of the world-taken-for-granted is derived from Schutz. *Cf.* especially his *Collected Papers*, Vol. I, pp. 207 ff.

31. The term "cosmization" is derived from Mircea Eliade. *Cf.* his *Cosmos and History*. New York: Harper, 1959, pp. 10 f.

32. The concept of projection was first deevloped by Ludwig Feuerbach. Both Marx and Nietzsche derived it from the latter. It was the Nietzschean derivation that became important for Freud.